A tour from the city of New-York to Detroit in the Michigan Territory : made between the 2d of May and the 22d of September 1818 ...

William Darby

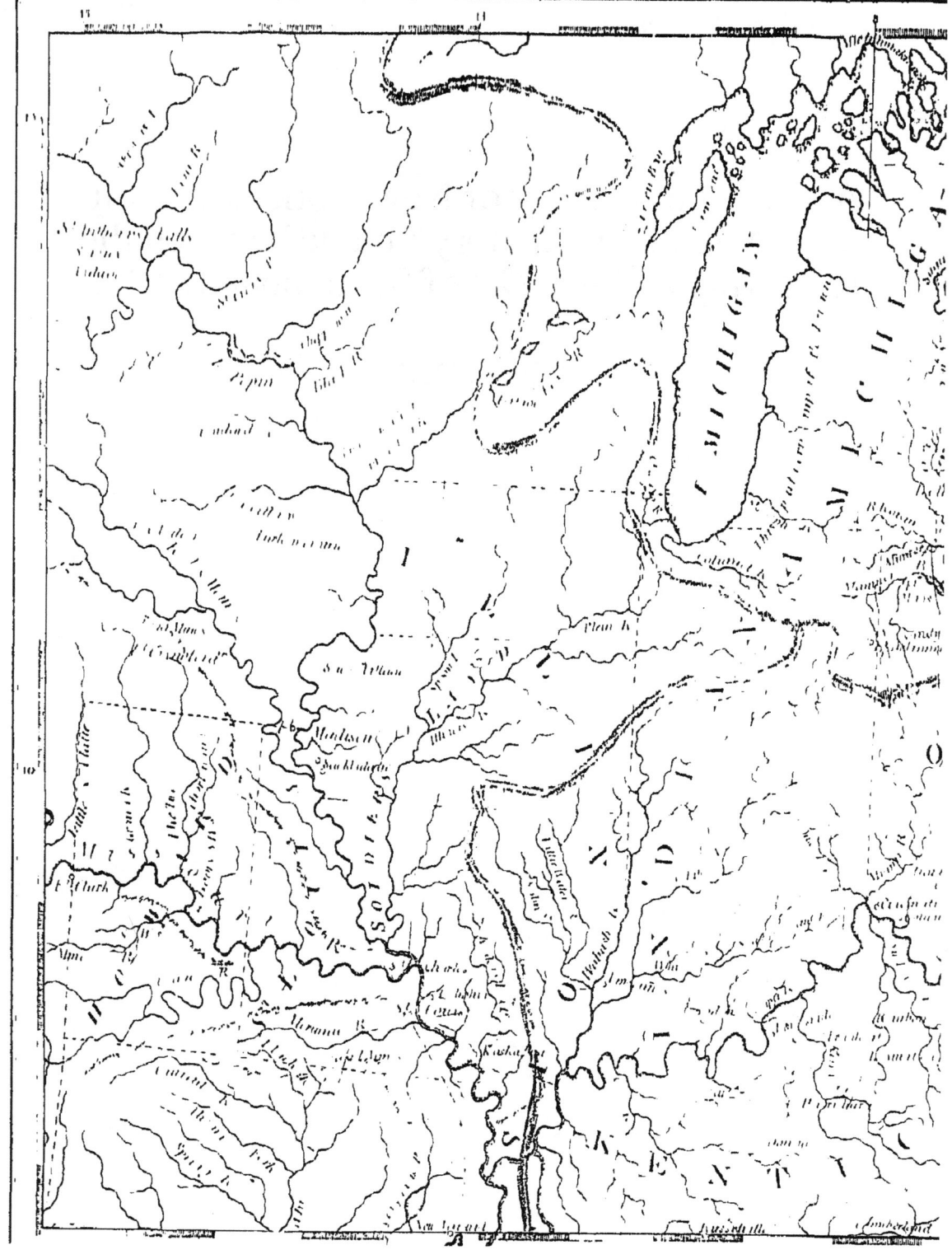

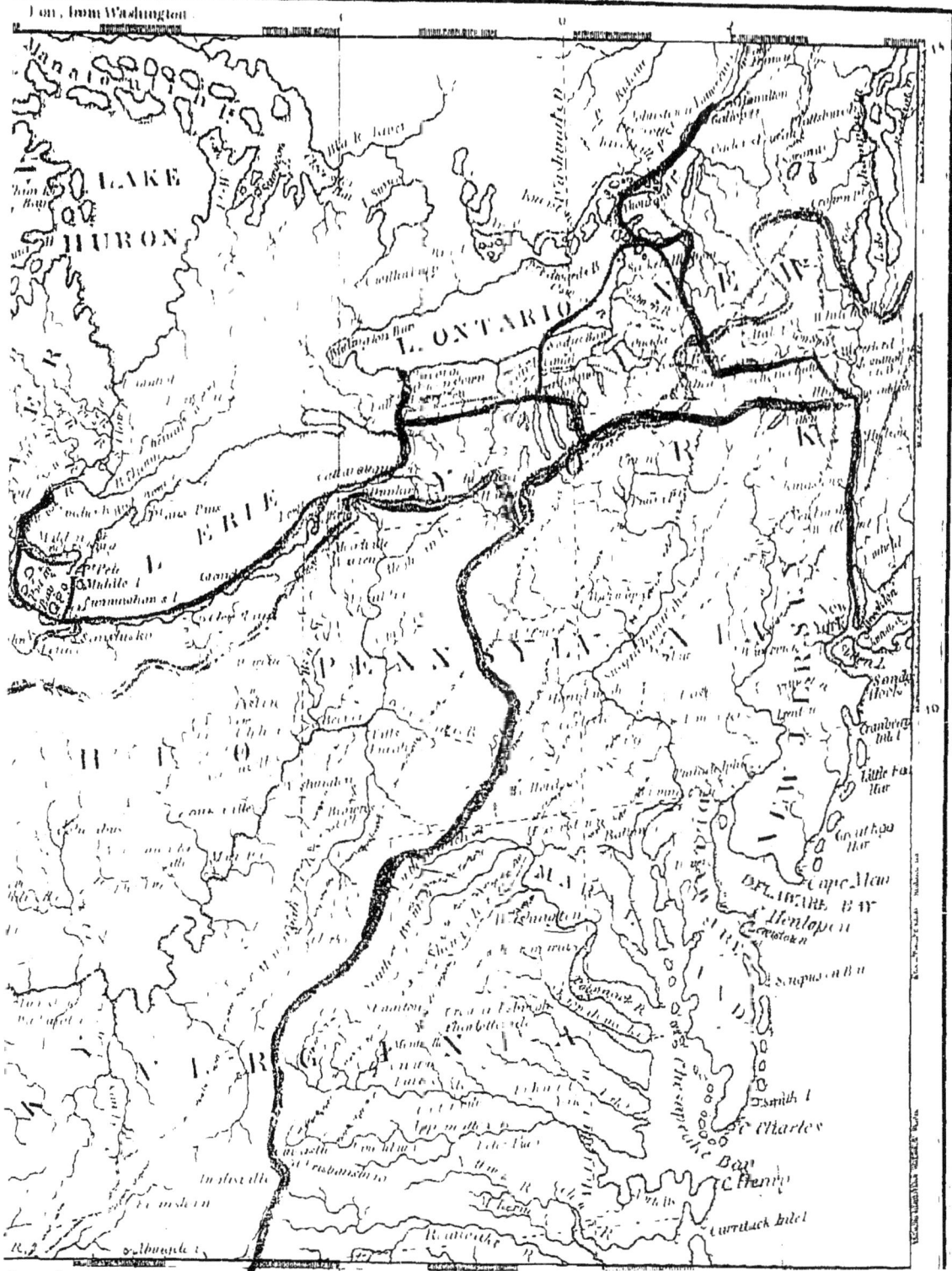

TOUR

FROM THE CITY OF NEW-YORK, TO DETROIT IN THE MICHIGAN TERRITORY.

MADE BETWEEN THE 2d OF MAY AND THE 22d OF SEPTEMBER (?)

The Tour extends from New-York, by Albany, Schenectady, and Utica to Sackett's Harbor, and thence through Lake Ontario, to St. Lawrence river, and down that river to Hamilton village. Thence along the banks of the St. Lawrence, from Hamilton to the Thousand Islands; thence to Sackett's Harbor, by water; from that place by the route of Great Sodus, Geneva, Canandaigua, and Batavia, to Buffalo, and from thence to Black Rock, Fort Erie, the Falls of Niagara, Queenstown, Lewiston, and the memorable fields of Bridgewater and Chippewa, &c. Viewing the interesting pass of Niagara; the author traversed the shore of Lake Erie to the City of Detroit, and visited in the latter range, Dunkirk, Erie, Cleveland, Sandusky, and other places of less note.

The Tour contains notices of what fell under the author's observation concerning the natural history and geography of the region over which his travels extended, with brief remarks upon such remarkable events and characters as have contributed to give interest to different places.

THE TOUR IS ACCOMPANIED WITH A MAP UPON WHICH THE ROUTE WILL BE DESIGNATED, A PARTICULAR MAP OF THE FALLS AND RIVER OF NIAGARA, AND THE ENVIRONS OF THE CITY OF DETROIT.

BY WILLIAM DARBY.

MEMBER OF THE NEW-YORK HISTORICAL SOCIETY
Author of a Map and Statistical Account of Louisiana, and Emigrant's Guide

---

NEW-YORK.

PUBLISHED FOR THE AUTHOR, BY KIRK & MERCEIN,

And sold by Kirk & Mercein, A. T. Goodrich & Co., James Eastburn & Co., W. B. Gilley, Charles Wiley & Co., R. M'Dermut, William Hazard, and Collins & Co. New-York; also by most of the principal Booksellers in the United States.

1819.

SOUTHERN DISTRICT OF NEW YORK, ss.

BE IT REMEMBERED, That on the sixteenth day of January, in the Forty third year of the Independence of the United States of America, A. D. 1819, WILLIAM DARBY, of the said district, hath deposited in this office the Title of a Book, the right whereof he claims as Proprietor, in the words following, to wit:

"A Tour from the City of New York, to Detroit, in the Michigan Territory, made between the 2d of May, and the 2d of September, 1818. The Tour extends from New York, by Albany, Schenectady, and Utica, to Sacket's Harbor, and thence through Lake Ontario, to St. Lawrence river, and down that stream to Hamilton village. Thence along both banks of the St. Lawrence, from Hamilton to the Thousand Islands, thence to Sacket's Harbor by water. From that place by the route of great Sodus, Geneva, Canandaigua, and Batavia, to Buffalo, and from thence to Black Rock, Fort Erie, the Falls of Niagara, Queenstown, Lewiston, and the memorable fields of Bridgewater and Chippewa. After viewing the interesting pass of Niagara, the author traversed the south shore of Lake Erie to the City of Detroit, and visited in the latter range Dunkirk, Erie, Cleveland, Sandusky, and other places of less note. The Tour contains notices of what fell under the author's observation concerning the natural history and geography of the region over which his travels extended, with brief remarks upon such remarkable events and characters as have contributed to give interest to different places. The Tour is accompanied with a Map upon which the route will be designated, a particular Map of the Falls and River of Niagara, and the environs of the City of Detroit. By WILLIAM DARBY, Member of the New York Historical Society. Author of a Map and Statistical Account of Louisiana, and Emigrant's Guide."

In conformity to the Act of the Congress of the United States, entitled, "An Act for the encouragement of learning, by securing the copies of Maps, Charts, and Books, to the Authors and Proprietors of such copies, during the time therein mentioned,"—and also to the Act entitled, "An Act supplementary to an Act entitled an Act for the encouragement of learning, by securing the copies of Maps, Charts, and Books, to the Authors and Proprietors of such copies, during the times therein mentioned, and extending the benefits thereof to the arts of designing, engraving, and etching historical and other prints."

JAMES DILL, Clerk of the Southern District of New York.

The following errors were detected after the above errata were printed.

Page 132, fourteenth line from the top, for "Yates," read Gates.
Page 164, tenth line from the top of the note, for "image," read imagery

PREFACE

"I wrapped myself in my cloak, and lay down on the
laurel, on the bank of the Eurotas. The night was soft
and so serene, and the milky way shed such a light, reflected
by the current of the river, that you might see to read by it.
I fell asleep with my eyes fixed upon the heavens, because the
beautiful constellation of Leda's swan exactly over my head.
I still recollect the pleasure which I formerly received from
thus reposing in the woods of America, and especially from
awaking in the middle of the night. I listened to the whis-
tling of the wind through the wilderness, the bounding of the
does and stags, the roar of a distant cataract; while the
embers of my half extinguished fire, glowed between the foliage of the trees. I loved even to hear the voice of the Iroquois, when he shouted in the recesses of his forests, and when
in the brilliant star-light, amid the silence of nature, I seemed to be proclaiming his unbounded liberty. All this was of
and delight at twenty; because then life suffices, in a manner, for itself, and there is in early youth, a certain restless-
ness and inquietude, which incessantly encourage the creation
of chimeras, roi sibi somnia fingunt; but in mature age, the
mind contracts a relish for more solid pursuits, and loves, in
particular, to dwell on the illustrious examples recorded in
history. Gladly would I again make my couch on the banks
of the Eurotas, or the Jordan, if the heroic shades of the
three hundred Spartans, or the twelve sons of Jacob, would
visit my slumbers; but I would not go again to explore a
gin sod, which the ploughshare has never lacerated. I

the walls of Babylon, or the legions of Pharsalia—grandia ossa; plains whose furrows convey instruction, and where, mortal as I am, I trace the blood, the tears, and the sweat, of human kind."*

I cannot conceive the satisfaction it can give, to a generous and feeling heart to trace the last fragments of a ruined city, or behold reduced to desolation, fields that once waved in golden harvest. To the eye of reason and philosophy, a review may be desirable of the revolutions of human society, in all the various stages from the savage horde to the most refined civilization; but to me, it would yield more pain than gratification, to behold Rome, Athens, or Jerusalem, in dust and ashes. The reminiscence that should recal former greatness, that would raise in imagination from the tomb the Pericles, Euripides, Maccabees, the Scipios or the Cæsars, would excite, rather a tear of bitter regret, than a pleasing sentiment of poetic enthusiasm, on glancing over the ocean of past time. I would rather indulge my fancy in following the future progress, than in surveying the wreck of human happiness; I would rather see one flourishing village rising from the American wilderness, than behold the ruins of Balbec, Palmyra, and Persepolis.

Like Chateaubriand, I have often *reposed in the woods and plains of North America*, in the silence of night, under the glances of the swan of Leda, the gleams of Sirius, or the beams of the pale moon playing amid the leaves of the forest, or exhibiting the fairy picture of the distant prairie. I have thus often in the awful solitude of the cane brake, or the cedar groves, contemplated the rapid march of active industry; I have fancied the rise of towns and villages, the clearing of fields, the creation of rich harvests, of orchards, meadows, and pastures. I have beheld the deep gloom around me dispelled, the majestic but dreary forest disappeared, the savage was turned into civilized man; schools, colleges,

---

* Travels in Greece, Palestine, Egypt, and Barbary, by F. A de Chateaubriand, Shorbell's translation, N. Y p. 109

churches, and legislative halls arose. The river, upon whose banks now grew the tangled vine, and in whose waters the loathsome alligator floated, became covered with barks loaded with the produce of its shores; I heard the songs of joy and gladness; I beheld fair science shed her smiles upon a happy and enlightened people; I beheld the heavenly form of religion, clothed in the simple garb of love and truth, teaching the precepts of present and everlasting peace; I saw liberty and law interposing between the shafts of oppression and the bosom of innocence,—and I saw the stern brow of justice bedewed with a tear over the chastised victim.

Many were the long and tedious hours I have thus beguiled, when no sound interrupted my chain of reflection, except the sighing of the nightly breeze, and I have enjoyed a pleasure greater than man ever felt amongst "*broken columns and disjoined arcades.*" I have seen on an immense surface, these warm anticipations realized. In west Virginia, in west Pennsylvania, in Kentucky, Ohio, Indiana, Illinois, Tennessee, Missouri, Mississippi, Louisiana, and Alabama; in west New-York, Michigan, and in Canada, I have for thirty-five years, been a witness to the change of a wilderness to a cultivated garden. I have roamed in forests, and upon the same ground now stand legislative halls, and temples of religion. New states have risen, and are daily rising upon this once dreary waste. I am willing to leave the man unenvied to his enjoyments, who would prefer the barbaric picture now presented by Greece, Asia Minor, Syria, and Palestine, to the glowing canvass whose tints are daily becoming richer and stronger, upon the rivers and hills of North America. I would rather read the immortal works of Homer, Thucidydes, or Demosthenes, upon the banks of the Ohio or St. Lawrence, than search the deserted tombs of those mighty geniuses, in their now desolate native land. These men have left their bones to oblivion, their works they have bequeathed to the human race. Amid the thousand objects that are constantly before the mental eye, in this new moral creation, none is more wonderful or more alluring than the existence of more than a thousand seminaries of education, where less than thirty years past, stood no mansion of civilized man.

In this as in every other of my works, I have given my naked reflections to the reader. Too much of my life has been spent in actual travelling, to admit the order and polish of a writer who enjoyed more closet leisure; but to relate what I saw, needed not a finished erudition, it demanded a respect for truth and human esteem: a respect, the sense of which I trust never to lose, until I cease to exist amongst mankind.

WILLIAM DARBY

New-York, January 1, 1819.

TO THE READER.

Before perusing this treatise, the reader is respectfully requested to observe and note the following omissions and corrections.

I find on reviewing the sheets, that I have not been sufficiently explicit in my notices of the following places, upon the St. Lawrence river. Hamilton, Ogdensburgh, Prescott, Brockville, and Morristown. I have subjoined the following brief description of these towns.

Hamilton, is a village in St. Lawrence county, in the state of New-York, standing upon the bank of St. Lawrence river, opposite Ogden's island. This village has been recently established; it is thriving, and like all towns upon the St. Lawrence, has a fine effect, from the gentle acclivity of the ground upon which it stands. The soil in this neighborhood is excellent; timber, composed of hemlock, pine, and sugar maple.

Ogdensburgh stands upon the lower point of land, formed by the junction of the Oswegatchie with the St. Lawrence river. the site is high, and like all other parts of the St. Lawrence banks, rises by gradual acclivity from the water. Ogdensburg is the seat of justice in and for St. Lawrence county, and has a prosperous appearance, with a post-office, three or four taverns, eight or ten stores, several mechanics' shops, such as carpenters, hatters, shoemakers, and taylors. The town contains about 80 dwelling-houses, and about 400 inhabitants. The mouth of the Oswegatchie river forms a good harbor for small vessels.

Prescott, in the township of Augusta, county of Grenville, stands upon the Canada shore of St. Lawrence river opposite Ogdensburg. The two towns do not differ much in extent or number of inhabitants. Prescott is the seat of justice for the county in which it is situated, and is a flourishing, commercial village.

Prescott and Ogdensburg, occupy the lowest points of ship navigation from lake Ontario; two steam-boats are in operation between these towns, and Kingston, Sacket's Harbor, and other places in lake Ontario.

Brockville, the seat of justice for the county of Leeds, Upper Canada, stands upon the bank of St. Lawrence, in Elizabeth township, 16 miles above Prescott. The situation of Brockville is pleasing and romantic. The banks on the Canada side, above and below the town, are high, rocky, and precipitous, and the river chequered with islands. The opposite bank of the river, in the state of New-York, is yet a forest. The neighborhood around Brockville is well cultivated and populous, the town is flourishing and commercial.

Morristown is a small village upon the St. Lawrence, in the county of St. Lawrence, about two miles below Brockville. This village has but little to render it remarkable, consisting only of about a dozen houses, with a post-office.

Describing Utica, (see page 55) I omitted to mention its fine bridge over the Mohawk river.

Page 27, third line of the note, for "*this latter circumstance, was, however, no doubt*" read, this latter circumstance was no doubt.

Page 37, 9th line from the top, for "*from the margin dell,*" read from the margin

Page 55, fourth line from the top, for "*city of Utica,*" read, town of Utica

Page 59, line 12th from the top, for "*colonial,*" read, colloquial

Page 61, third line from the top, for "*producing effects,*" read, which produced effects.

Page 72, line 11th from the bottom for "*side land,*" read, land side.

Page 73, lines four and five from the bottom, for "*ten or twelve miles,*" read, two or three miles

Page 91, line 15th from the top, for "*muddings,*" read muddiness

Page 113, I there mention an intention to note the comparative quantity of water in the St Lawrence and the Mississippi rivers, but have omitted that of the latter, the reader will please substitute for ("see appendix, No. 2,") the following words, applied to the Mississippi

"We may imagine a semi-ellipsis, whose longitudinal diameter represents the river's breadth, and whose longest ordinate, its depth, allow 150 feet as the length of the ordinate line, or depth of water at the greatest elevation, and 2,400 feet as the extent of the elliptical diameter or river's breadth, we are confident that those constituent principles will give a very correct result From the application of the above elements, 141,372 cubic feet would be contained within one foot longitudinal section of the river At the rate of one mile an hour, 5,280 feet in length would be discharged every hour, or 746,414,160 cubic feet, of the entire mass"

[*Darby's Louisiana, N. Y. Ed p 56*

Page 161, line 19th from the top, for "G D C, W P." read, G D C, A. T G. and W. P. &c

Page 169, line 7th from the bottom, for October "8*th*, 1814,' read, October 12th, 1812, and bottom line, for "*Real,*" read, Rial

Page 212, line 4th from top, for "*Mr. Isaac Kibbe,*" read, Mr Kibbe Mr Isaac Kibbe is the brother of the gentleman of that name, who keeps a public inn, in the town of Buffalo

A TOUR

FROM NEW-YORK TO DETROIT.

LETTER I.

Albany, May 3d, 1818.

DEAR SIR,

Amid the violence of wind and rain, I arrived in this city at 5 o'clock this afternoon. Though spring has made some advances near New-York, here the face of nature is marked with all the bleakness of winter, except snow. At this season, no scenery can exhibit a more dreary aspect than that of the Hudson; naked rocks or precipices, with a few leafless forest trees, are the only objects that in many places meet the eye of the voyager in passing many miles upon this truly singular river. While the cold damp wind sweeps along the current, the view of the distant farm houses have a solitary and even gloomy appearance.

Perhaps in no equal distance on earth, is the contrast between the smiles of summer and the frowns of winter, so strong as upon the Hudson banks between New-York and Albany. I travelled upon both shores of the Hudson river in the summer of 1816, and visited most places of note on or near its margin.

I had then occasion to make a remark I have since found just; that the arrangements of the Steam-Boats, deprive passengers of the view of much of the richest scenery of this interesting region. The passage of the river, through the Fishkill mountains, is indeed one of the finest landscapes in North America, and yet is seen but by very few of those who traverse through its sublime portals, and who travel expressly for the purpose of beholding nature in her most attractive garb. In the first instance, travelling by a land conveyance and by slow stages, I had the advantage of beholding the various parts rather more in detail, than I could have, had I passed by the ordinary means of the Steam-Boat. As you have imposed upon me the task of relating what I have seen or thought, and as you have had the kindness to express more estimation for the matter than the manner, I will give a detail of my notes, during my first voyage up the Hudson.

I left the city of New-York, on the afternoon of August 20th, 1816; the weather was extremely boisterous for the season; a strong north wind impeded the progress of the Steam-Boat, and as usual, I passed the Highlands in the night, and landed about midnight at Newburg.

The morning of the 21st, repaid amply the fatigue of the evening before, the violence of the wind had subsided, the air was serene and cool; and afforded an excellent opportunity to review with advantage the fine landscapes in this neighborhood.

The seite of Newburg is admirably adapted to produce, from a variety of points, the most striking effect that water, hill, dale, and mountain can give. Rising by rather abrupt acclivity from the water, the houses in the town appear like the steps of a pair of stairs. From a hill to the westward of, and which rises above the village, the entire adjacent country is spread before the eye. The prospect is on all sides extremely picturesque, the fields and farm houses on the east side of the Hudson, are seen lessening into the horizon far into Dutchess county, towards the borders of Connecticut. The Fishkill mountains rising into bold, though not rugged prominences, and covered with trees to their summits. But the passage of the Hudson river, through the Highlands, is far the most pleasing part of this beautiful picture. The smooth surface of the river silently approaching this confined opening, the projecting rocks apparently menacing the flitting vessels beneath, the diversified groups of trees, the distant view of the hills of Putnam county, and the soft white clouds exhibiting their airy forms along the clear blue heaven, forms a landscape that is equalled by few on earth.

It is obvious that the Hudson did not always find its course to the Atlantic Ocean, through the Fishkill mountains. The whole face of the country, north of that pass, evinces an exposure to submersion by water. By either abrasion of a cataract, or disruption by some convulsion of nature, but much more probably the former, the mountain chain has been broken, and the rushing waters found their way to the now New-York Bay.*

During the afternoon of Aug. 21st, I crossed the river from Newburg to Fishkill landing, enjoyed in the traverse, the changing view of the narrows, and after landing, turned and

---

* In Dr. S. L. Mitchel's excellent observations upon the Geology of North America, which are attached to Kirk and Mercein's edition of Cuvier's Theory of the Earth, occur the following observations upon the Fishkill mountains

"They are composed chiefly of granite and kneiss, abounding in loose nodules and solid veins of magnetical iron ore. The width of the chain may be rated at about sixteen miles. The height of the most elevated peaks, have been ascertained barometrically by Capt. Alden Partridge, of the corps of Artillerists and Egineers. According to his observations, Butterhill on the west side of the river, is 1529 feet above tide-water and the new Beacon 1565 feet.

"This thick and solid barrier seems in ancient days, to have impeded the course of the water, and to have raised a lake high enough to cover all the country to Quaker hill and the Taconick mountains on the east, and to the Shawangunk and the Catskill mountains on the west. This lake may be calculated to have extended to the Little Falls of the Mohawk, and to Hadley's Falls on the Hudson."—*Kirk & Mercein's Cuvier, page* 337.

A careful review of the structure of the adjoining country, leaves no reasonable doubt of the correctness of the foregoing conclusions drawn by this able geologist.

beheld the two villages of Newburg and New-Windsor hanging upon the western slope of the opposite shore. I had here again another opportunity of admiring the ever varying scenery of this truly delightful neighborhood. Often as I have beheld with a sensation of real pleasure, the setting of an unclouded sun, never before (or since) did I see that luminary take his nightly leave of man, with more serene majesty, or amid so many objects to heighten the beauty of the scene. Seated upon an elevated bank, in a grove composed of spruce and cedar, I watched the departure of the king of day; the slow and silent advance of darkness, at length shrouded in gloom a picture, whose teints can only be forgotten when my bosom ceases to beat.

Environed by the massy and sublime monuments reared by the hand of nature, and enjoying the softened beauty of such an evening, I could not repress a retrospection upon the march of time; I could not avoid reflecting that an epoch did exist, when the delightful valley in which I then sat was an expanse of water; that the winding and contracting gorge, through which the Hudson now flows, did not exist, or was the scene of another Niagara: I beheld the lake disappear, the roar of the cataract had ceased, the enormous rocky barriers had yielded to the impetuous flood. The river now glides smooth and tranquil, in its passage through this glen, dark and deep. The war of elements have subsided. The mountains have apparently separated, and given the waters free egress to the ocean.

In order to have ample means of reviewing this region, to as much advantage as possible, I hired a man to convey me in a sail boat, from Fishkill landing to West-Point; and on the morning of the 22d, passed the Narrows with a light wind. A slight mist floated over the highest peaks of the mountains, but below the air was clear and pleasant. Approaching the most confined part of the passage, the vast granitic ledges seemed to raise their frowning projections to the clouds, the trees upon their summits appear like shrubs.

In the intervening vales or rather ravines, the fisherman and woodcutter have reared their huts; the curling smoke is seen issuing from cabins embosomed amid these rugged rocks.

West-Point presented its structures perched upon a small cape of level land, but every where surrounded by masses that seemed to mock time itself.

I landed, and rose the winding path-that led to this ever memorable spot;* a place that was the scene of some of

---

* Whilst preparing these sheets for publication, the following elegant lines appeared in the Columbian, from the pen of Dr. Van Gelder, of New-York. I could not deny my readers the pleasure of reading so fine a description of the grandeur, even in ruins, of Fort Putnam.

ON THE RUINS OF FORT PUTNAM, WEST-POINT.

Dreary and lone as the scenes that surround thee,
   Thy battlements rise 'mid the crags of the wild,
Yet dear are thy ruins, for brightly around thee
   'Twas here the first dawn of our Liberty smil'd

But lonely's thy terrace—thy walls are forsaken,
   In ruins around thy proud ramparts are low,
And never again shall thy cannon awaken
   The echo that sleeps in the vallies below.

Silence now reigns thy dark ruins among,
   Where once thrill'd the fife and the war-drum beat loud.
Now the scream of the eaglet slow gliding along,
   Alone sends its note from the mists of the cloud.

But where are the heroes whose home once was here,
   When the legions of Tyranny peopled our shore—
Who here rais'd the standard to Freedom so dear,
   And guarded their home 'mid the battle's fierce roar

They sleep in yon vale—their rude fortress below,
   Where darkly the shade of the cedar is spread,
And hoarse through the valley the mountain-winds blow,
   Where lowly they rest in the sleep of the dead.

The flowers of the forest have brighten'd that spot,
   The wild rose has scatter'd its bloom o'er that ground
Where lonely they lie—now forgetting—forgot—
   Unawak'd by the mountain-storm thundering around.

the most remarkable events of our unequalled revolution. It was here that Arnold's treachery was met by the stern virtue of Washington; it was near this place that Andre expiated his folly with his life, and gained an immortal name by an ignominious death.

West-Point presents but little that can interest the traveller, except it be the noble scenery of its neighborhood, and events of historical reminiscence. The barracks of the officers and cadets, with a few scattering houses belonging to individuals, are all the artificial improvements worth notice at this establishment. The bank is high, and very abrupt from the surface of the water in the river, to the level of the plain upon which the barracks and houses are built.

With considerable fatigue, I scrambled up the mountain to the ruins of Fort Putnam. Silence and delapidation now reign over this once important Fortress. It would be difficult to conceive of a more impregnable position. Seated upon an elevated mass of granite, the Fort occupied almost the entire surface upon which a human foot could be set. A very steep ascent, of more than 500 perpendicular feet, leads from the plain of West-Point to the seite of the Fort, and a deep rock bound valley, separates it from the general mass of the adjacent mountains. A cistern had been hewed out of the solid granite, which was full of water when I visited the spot. Cannon placed upon the walls of this Fort, could rake the entire surface of West-Point; but I could not perceive any serious opposition it could have presented to the passage of ships of war, ascending or descending the Hudson river.

The landscape from the ruined battlements of Fort Putnam, is very interesting. The Fishkill mountains seen from this place, have a much more naked and rude aspect, than from either Newburg or Fishkill landing. Except upon the opposite shore in Putnam county, but very little human culture enlivens the view. West-Point has itself a sol itary appearance, and to the west, nought is seen but woods, and mountains, in their primitive wildness.

If seclusion from the busy haunts of men, can be of any benefit to the students at West Point, they enjoy this advantage in its fullest extent. Isolated upon the confined cape, from which the name of the place is derived, the river on one side and towering mountains on the other, an unbroken silence reigns around this seminary. Looking down from the broken walls of Fort Putnam, Dr. Johnson's Rasselas, came strong to recollection. I could not avoid recalling to imaginary life, the men who once acted on this little but remarkable theatre. I felt a sentiment of awe, amid this now lonely waste, on recalling to mind that here once depended the fate of a new born nation. Even the fallen fragments of stone which once composed part of its buttresses, inspired me with a feeling of respect. Washington, Greene, Putnam, Andre, and Arnold, are no more; their names have now taken their respective stations in history. The opinion of mankind is formed upon the merits of the three former, and the shame of the two latter. It is now as far beyond the reach of calumny, to tarnish the unfading renown of a Washington, a Greene, or a Putnam, as it would be for the human hand to level to common earth the enormous masses of the Fishkill mountains.

With slow steps I descended from the grey remains of this venerable pile, and cast a frequent and repeated retiring look towards its mouldering turrets. The shades of evening were setting in, the darkened sides of the distant mountains, seemed to mark a sympathetic gloom with that which hung over the deserted Fortress. The busy hum of the students in their evening walks, produced an interesting contrast with the repose in which rested the surrounding scenery. Such was the events, and the reflection of my day's visit to West Point.

On the morning of the 23d, I again passed with encreased admiration the Highlands, and returned to Fishkill landing. In the afternoon I went to visit the fine Factory of Mateowan,* owned by Messrs. Schenck's.

The scenery near Mateowan is wild, picturesque, and pleasing. Here I first witnessed the effect, produced upon the smaller streams which flow into the Hudson river, from the high table land from which their sources are derived. Flowing over a surface, elevated many hundred feet above tide water in the Hudson, the tributary waters of that river all enter by cataracts of more or less elevation. Fishkill, (Mateowan) commences its fall some distance above Messrs. Schenck's factory, giving any desirable facility to the application of its volume, in the propulsion of machinery. This characteristic is however, general to almost all streams that fall into the Hudson from either bank, and gives to the inhabitants near the borders of that river, a facility in the construction of labour-saving machinery, possessed on so large a scale in few, if any other parts of the earth.

If it was possible for American industry to contend, in the present order of things, successfully against European monopoly, the banks of the Hudson could become two extended lines of manufacturing establishments; but our native exertions wither in the presence of foreign commerce and perverted taste. Nature is slowly asserting her rights in opposition to absurdly continued custom. If habit had made us familiar with sending our wheat, to be converted into flour in English mills, we would now consider bread made from this native grain and foreign machinery, in the same favourable degree of preference, we now give to muslins made in Europe, from Carolina and Georgia cotton.

---

* Mateowan is the Indian name of Fishkill. No nations, perhaps that ever existed, gave more sonorous names to places, than the native savages of North America. It is much to be regretted that their nomenclature had not been more generally preserved

Above Fishkill the country assumes a hilly and rocky, but not mountainous aspect. The strata are inclined in nearly parallel direction to the Catskill mountains. Some limestone occurs. The general structure of the hills is, however, mica slate. The soil does not exhibit a fertile appearance in general, though Dutchess county has been famed for its productive crops. This character I believe just as respects orchards and meadows. Too much of the land is cleared. A scarcity of timber strikes the eye of the traveller at every step, and the trees which exist have a stinted appearance.*

---

* The following extract demonstrates that improvident waste of timber, and neglect to supply daily consumption, is not confined to Dutchess county. Error, however, gains nothing but notoriety from its extent.

"The Duke of Athol is now enjoying the benefit which provident ancestors sometimes confer upon their heirs. His Grace's estates have been hitherto considered as rather extensive, than productive; but his forests have now attained to such a growth, that, we understand, he will be able to cut timber to the amount of 20,000l. a year, we may say almost in perpetuity, as he has continued the practice of his noble father, and planted millions of trees annually."

In reading the above article, we could not suppress a feeling of regret at the evident contrast presented in the conduct of the Duke of Athol's "provident ancestor," to the improvidence of landholders generally in this country. The decrease of timber for building, fuel, &c is already a great inconvenience, and is every day becoming more serious in the prospects growing out of it. The evil is not so much in the use or consumption of the timber, (although that may be unnecessarily extravagant) but in the utter neglect which appears every where to prevail, of repairing the devastation, by planting new trees, and taking care of the young growth. Observation has convinced us, that in no part of the country is its neglect more apparent, than in the lower parts of Delaware, and the adjacent parts of Maryland. We mention this district of country particularly, because in travelling over it, (we allude especially to the country called the Levels, and on the Bohemia, and Sassafras rivers,) we were struck with its fine appearance, in soil, its fine streams, and its easy access to market. It is probable to this last circumstance that the evil complained of may in some part, be attributed; the high price

In all the extent of settled country within the United States, two epochs have preceded each other in the progress of agriculture. In the first epoch, immense extent of land is cleared of the timber, and the soil rather tortured than cultivated. This lasts until the impoverished fields and ruined forests, oblige the farmers to commence the second epoch. They now come to the point from which they ought to have set out. They now cultivate a more limited extent, but that extent by manure and a careful routine of crops, becomes

of timber at Baltimore having induced the proprietors or tenants to apply the axe with so devastating a hand, that the country is almost bare of timber, and no efforts seem to have been adopted to supply the waste. The consequence of this destructive habit is, that the best land in the peninsula, and as good as any in the country, with all its advantages from fine navigable streams will not sell for more than 15, 20, or 25 dollars per acre, in addition to the inconvenience arising from a deficiency of fuel, and timber for building. It may be said, that the tenures by which real property is held in this country, and its frequent circulation from hand to hand, present an obstacle to any plans of permanent improvement, that farmers do not like to expend money, the profits of which are to be enjoyed by posterity.

We would regret to see such an objection seriously urged, involving as it does a censure upon the freedom of our institutions, which are intimately connected with the proper circulation and equalization of real property. We suggest the subject to the agricultural society of this county, as a proper one for their consideration, if they will encourage the planting of forest trees, and support it with their examples, it will have a good effect. The price of land will be undoubtedly increased, and the interests of agriculture advanced.

There is one fact of which the society must be aware; that in this country and the peninsula generally, it is the custom with farmers to sow or cultivate a much greater quantity of land than they can properly manage; a consequence of which is that a great deal of good land is thrown away; producing about one third or one fourth of what it would if properly manured and attended to. If, therefore, many of our farmers would limit their industry to the cultivation of one half or one third of their usual quantity of land, they would economize their labour greatly, cultivate their lands much better, produce a greater quantity of grain and grass, and the surplus would remain for the propagation of timber."—*Delaware Watchman.*

annually more and more productive. It would no doubt have resulted, from the great labour and expense of clearing land, that farmers would have commenced by making the best use of small enclosures, if agriculture had been understood scientifically. That was not formerly the case any where in the United States, and now only in few places. It is pleasing to see even the germ of a better system. Agriculture is improving, our citizens begin to learn that their fields may be made more profitable, and less expensive.

Dutchess county is about 45 miles long north and south, and twenty-five miles in breadth east and west, from Connecticut line to the Hudson river. This county at present, extends over an area of very nearly 800 square miles. Dutchess was formerly more extensive, the townships south of the Fishkill mountains, Philipstown, Kent, Paterson, Southeast, and Carmel, were in the Legislative session of 1812 erected into a separate county, and named Putnam. By the census of 1810, the entire county of Dutchess, possessed a population of 51,112, but of this amount the now county of Putnam contained 8,182 persons; leaving in Dutchess a nett amount of 42,930. This divided by 800, yields 53,6+ to the square mile, a very thin population; yet the county is perhaps more than two thirds cleared of wood; and if so, allowing the population to be now 60 to the square mile, would average more than seven acres of open land to each individual. I am well convinced this calculation is by no means overrated near the Hudson, or indeed in any part of the county. The great distances between the houses, and the wide sweep of the fields and meadows, give the county a lonely appearance.

Eight miles above Fishkill, Wappinger's creek falls into the Hudson. The latter is a much more considerable stream than the former, but are similar in tumbling over elevated ledges of rock, previous to joining the Hudson.— Where the road passes Wappinger's creek, some mills and other machinery have been erected. The road crosses the creek by a substantial wooden bridge, over nearly the middle of the fall. The volume of water was considerable, even when I passed it, though a long dearth had preceded my journey. The white surge dashing impetuously over the shelving rocks, and amongst the wheels of the different water works, produced a fine effect. This place affords a pleasing variety on this road.

Above Wappinger's creek, the face of the country becomes more uniform, and the soil assumes a less rude aspect than between the creek and the now receding Highlands.

Many points of rising ground, present very extensive and beautiful landscape views. The Highland, Shawangunk, and Catskill mountains, are alternately and often all visible from the same place. The Hudson can sometimes be seen glittering low in the deep vale, through which it flows. Here in many places, appear the vestiges of the ancient lake, which filled the region above the Highlands. Independent of the mountains, the hills which once bounded this sheet of water, are distinctly discernible to the east and west. These hills are about 30 miles separate, the intermediate space was the breadth of the lake, giving it, though on a larger scale, the general characteristic of the yet existing lakes Champlain and George.

Viewing a map of Orange, Ulster and Dutchess counties, a singular fact in the geology of the region they occupy, obtrudes itself to observation. The water courses on the west side of the Hudson, in Orange and Ulster, flow considerably north of east, and enter that river very obliquely. This is the case with the streams of Wallkill, Rondout, and Esopus. In Dutchess, Fishkill, Wappinger's, and other creeks, run south of east, in very nearly parallel courses, but contrary directions to those which enter by the opposite bank.

The elevated table land from which all these streams derive their sources, lies apparently nearly on a general level, and forms a valley, which crosses the Hudson in the direction of the water courses. Are we not justifiable in concluding that this was once the course of the lake discharge? By what process of nature did the Hudson scoop its present channel, so far beneath the bottom of this former inland sea, so far even beneath the level of the ocean, and through a continuous mass of rock? If you can answer this query, if you can explain this phenomenon, you will do me and the world a favor. I am unable to even conjecture the process of this mighty, this unequalled work.

Poughkeepsie, the seat of justice for Dutchess county, stands upon the table land of the Hudson, sixteen miles from Fishkill. I arrived here in the afternoon of the 25th Aug. and on the morning of the 26th, took an extensive ramble over its streets and environs. The town is in the form of a cross, the two principal streets crossing each other nearly at right angles. The houses are scattered, and the intervening spaces planted with trees. A road leads down a long, steep, and in many places very abrupt hill, from Poughkeepsie to the landing, on the Hudson river. This circumstance subjects the inhabitants to great inconvenience. The opposite shore is broken, rocky, barren and desolate. The town contains at present about 2000 inhabitants. The houses have a decent plainness in their exterior, a character they have no doubt received from the moral taste of the inhabitants. I have visited few places, where a more mild, conciliating deportment was observed to the stranger.

Some manufactures are established in Poughkeepsie; the principal of which, is that of Messrs. Booth's woollen cloth manufactory. Some very beautiful and very excellent cloth has been made at this establishment. It is now contending like all similar works in the United States, with high wages, enhanced price of raw material, European competition, and long established public prejudice in favor of foreign productions.

Except the inconsistency of their opinions and conduct, nothing can be more idle, than the expressions you may now hear in every conversation in our country, upon domestic manufactured goods of any kind. "Encourage the framers "of our own products. I prefer to see my neighbors dres-"sed in home made cloth. The day we trust is not far dis-"tant when we can put European nations at defiance. Our "necessities will be supplied at home." A thousand such declamations may be heard in every assembly of people, and in many instances, not one yard of home made clothing could be found upon the whole company.

This is not, however, the only instance, where theory and practice are at variance in the affairs of mankind.

Stepping into a Bookstore in Poughkeepsie, I was led to make a reflection I have often made before. Bookstores afford, particularly in small villages and country places, the best data, from which can be calculated the state of public literary improvement. Booksellers, like other merchants, are regulated in their importations by the taste of their customers.

In large cities, where schools, colleges, and other establishments for the promotion of general instruction, exist on a large scale, almost all kinds of books are found in Bookstores; but in remote country villages few books are offered for sale, except those of daily demand.

After school books, the most common are religious tracts of different kinds, published for the use of the various sects which inhabit the country; these, with a few of the most popular novels, form the mass of the volumes upon the shelves of the village bookseller.

Works on general science are rare, and even treatises upon political economy, (except pamphlets upon daily occurrences, mostly personal) are not often seen beyond the limits of our large commercial cities.

In the United States, the most useful of all human reading, HISTORY, is neglected. The most prominent events of their own country, are known to but comparatively few of our citizens. British history has shared the most attention from our readers, but even that heterogeneous and conflicting subject, they generally but superficially understand. Though it may be doubted whether the reading of history, tends to produce all the beneficial results, usually expected to flow from that species of literature; yet it is in history alone, that the treasured experience of our race is recorded. It is true that lessons of experience, when not taught by physical suffering, are seldom very profoundly remembered, or correctly acted upon. It is also true, that though the impressions made upon our minds by the virtue or crimes, the wisdom or folly of others, are slight and transient, in a ratio of distance from the scenes of our own personal cares; yet salutary impressions are made, and liberal opinions contracted, from reading the events of nations that exist no more, as well as from those which concern the most remote people upon our planet.

August 27th, I left Poughkeepsie early in the morning; a shower in the preceding night had given freshness to the air. Proceeding along the road towards Rhinebeck, I found the country extremely pleasant. A turnpike road has been made from Poughkeepsie 11 miles; the surface of the ground uneven rather than hilly. A few miles from Poughkeepsie the table land becomes more flat, and in some places so much so, as to resemble the bottom of a large river. Rhinebeck stands upon one of those elevated plains, is built in the Dutch taste; all the houses have a comfortable, and a few an elegant exterior: they are interspersed with orchards, meadows, grain fields and gardens. To me, no object is more satisfactory than these scattered villages, where every species of cultivation seem blended. In large cities, the great field and rich mead are banished, to make way for the various objects of luxury and commerce; but in these rural villages, enough remains of rude nature to recal the mind to the ages of primitive simplicity, whilst enough is created by art to gratify the wants of civilized man.

In ascending towards the north from the Highlands, along the elevated plains of the Hudson, as the Fishkill mountains are depressed by recession, those of Catskill rise from approach. The latter chain presents a bold and imposing front from Rhinebeck. Rising in majesty their blue tops, and gradually sloping sides, are peculiarly pleasing to the eye, whilst their pyrimidal form evince a duration, commensurate with time itself. The village of Rhinebeck stands near two miles from the margin of the Hudson, with, as usual, a high rocky intervening bank. From Rhinebeck village the ground falls rapidly. When the river is approached, a wild and picturesque landscape opens; the west bank of the Hudson is rugged and extremely broken; the Catskill mountains rise upon the back ground, and terminate with their rounded cones the distant view. The road from Rhinebeck ferry, winds up the western steeps of the Hudson, amid broken fragments of rock. The eminences are clothed with pine, cedar and oak; every object announces sterility. Nothing is seen, that can give the slightest anticipation of the fertile and beautiful valley of Esopus, into which, a ride of three miles from the Hudson river carries the traveller.

I do not remember to have ever enjoyed a more agreeable surprize, or to have seen a transition more rapid, than in passing from the sterile and shapeless summits of the Hudson hills, to the fine and extended plain, upon which stands the romantic village of Esopus or Kingston. This little, but interesting town, recals to mind some memorable events of the revolutionary war. Its inhabitants were amongst the first and most zealous opposers of British aggression, in the then colony of New-York, and of course marked for vengeance by the officers of the crown, who commanded on the New-York station. In the summer of 1777, while Gen. Burgoyne was penetrating from the north towards Albany, a British squadron ascended the Hudson river from New York, and landed a body of troops near the mouth of the Wallkill, who marched to, and burnt the defenceless village of Kingston.

The inhabitants had but a few moments' information of the approach of their enemy, before their actual arrival. A tumultuous flight ensued, and before quitting the view of their dwellings, the smoke of the fire that devoured them ascended to heaven. The consequence of this act of blind rage, was just what common sense would have expected : a more inveterate opposition to the British government. To feelings of revolutionary enthusiasm, was added personal resentment. Some of the stone walls still remain, to attest the destructive scene. Most of the houses then burned, have long since been repaired or re-built ; but a few stand untouched ; their mouldering remains, force the imagination to retrace the lapse of thirty-nine years, and amid the smoking ruins of their once happy homes, behold the mournful visages of the returning inhabitants, behold them turning an eye of vengeance after the destroyers of their property. An inscription upon the end of the village church, records this deed of barbarism, this day of mourning, the 11th of October, 1777. The hour of vengeance was indeed near, three days after, Burgoyne and his army surrendered prisoners of war at Saratoga. The pride of the spoiler was turned to defeat, mortification and disgrace.

Time and industry have here effaced the ravages of war. Few, if any villages in the United States, present at this moment, an air of more domestic comfort, plenty and ease, than does Kingston. The houses are scattered, and generally built after the old Dutch taste, low, with few windows, and those small. Some more modern dwellings, are exceptions to the common mode, being constructed with an elegance and convenience equal to the houses of any of our country towns.

Kingston stands upon an elevated and extensive plain, between the Rondout and Esopus creeks. Confining the view to the site of the town and adjacent country, the traveller would suppose himself on the alluvion of a river. He is so in fact, the plain is a complete accretion, formed by the ancient state of the country, and by the neighboring streams. The soil is sandy, but extremely fertile and well cultivated; the meadows and orchards are numerous and excellent. I had no means to ascertain with precision, the elevation of the Kingston plain above the level of tide water in the Hudson, but carefully examining the ground, along which the intervening road winds, should be led to believe that the difference of level, must exceed three hundred feet. Though 16 miles distant, the Catskill mountains, from their elevation, seem to be much nearer, and give to Kingston an appearance of lying low, though standing upon ground so much above the surface of Hudson river.

In making the tour of this part of the United States, no traveller ought to pass without visiting Kingston, and every stranger will be pleased with the soft beauty of its scenery, with its retired situation, and with the plain but affable manners of its inhabitants.

August 29th, I left Kingston, and in the evening of the same day arrived in Hudson. It is along this part of the Hudson, that the Catskill mountains can be seen to most advantage. Their august cones seem almost to rise from the river though eight or ten miles distant.*

* The following statement of the heights of mountains on the Hudson river, were calculated by Capt. Partridge, and are deemed correct.

Highlands.

Anthony's Nose,	935 feet,	Sugar Loaf,	866 feet,
Bare Mount,	1350 feet,	Bull Hill,	1484 feet,
Crow's Nest,	1418 feet,	Break Neck,	1187 feet,
Butter Hill,	1529 feet,	Old Beacon,	1471 feet,
New Beacon,	1535 feet,	W. Point Plain,	188 feet.
Fort Putnam,	598 feet,		

Catskill Mountains.

Round Top,	3105 feet,	High Peak,	3019 feet.

Below New-York.

Neversink Heights,	282 feet,
Staten Island,	307 feet,
Hempstead Harbour Hill,	319 feet.

[*Newburg Political Index.*]

Concealed by the peninsula, between the Hudson and Catskill creek, but a small part of the town of Catskill can be seen from the river. As I desired to see all the towns near the margin of the Hudson, I determined to return to Catskill, before ascending to the north of the town of Hudson.

This latter village has a prosperous appearance; its site is the most favorable to connect the adjacent country to the river, of any town on the Hudson, between New-York and Troy. The situation of Hudson is pleasant, rising first by a steep bank of 50 or 60 feet, and thence gradually from the bank. That part of the town which approaches the water, stands upon a peninsula projecting considerably into the river, and affording a very fine view both to the north and south, particularly the former. On the opposite shore stands the village of Athens, in Greene county. The latter town rises like Newburg, though less abrupt from the water edge; every house and the adjacent farms can be seen at one view, from the bank of the Hudson. Athens is small, and no great prospect exists of any augmentation of consequence. The Schoharie turnpike road leaves the Hudson river at Athens, and following the valley of Catskill along its north side, penetrates the interior of New-York, by winding round the Catskill mountains. The Susquehanna turnpike road leaves the Hudson at the town of Catskill, and following the south side of the creek of that name, runs

---

When I passed the same part of the Hudson on my last tour, May 3d, 1818,) the Catskill mountains were covered with snow, apparently almost to their base. This latter circumstance, was however, no doubt a deception in vision, as many of the hills near the Hudson bank, are five or six hundred feet high, and the snow had now disappeared from their summits. The whole country had, however, the dreary marks of winter. Scarce a new born leaf announced the approach of spring. The air was cold, chilly, and moist. The mountains of Berkshire, in Massachusetts, and the Green mountains in Vermont, appeared far on the N. E. horizon, also white with snow.

nearly parallel to the Schoharie road, and like it leads through Greene county, into the central parts of the state. These roads render Hudson a thoroughfare from the New England states, for emigrants passing to the north part of Pennsylvania, and the contiguous part of New-York.

A ridge of land, rocky, precipitous, and generally very barren, follows both banks of the Hudson river, occasionally interrupted. Behind these ridges and parallel to them, lies two broken valleys of more or less width. All the towns upon this singular river, are placed upon the interruptions of these ridges. Hudson is a remarkable example. I have already noticed the peninsula, which forms the port of Hudson. This peninsula is bounded on the north by a bay, terminated by clay bluffs, which are yielding to the action of the water, and on the south extends another bay, which gradually shallows, and ends in a deep morass. South of this swamp rises a very high hill, the north abutment of one of the ridges I have already noticed. Behind the town of Hudson, to the eastward, the ground rises into considerable elevation, overlooking from its summit a vast expanse of country, including the towns of Hudson and Athens; the river for many miles; its variegated shores, and perhaps the best prospect that exists of the Catskill mountains. To point out the charming views included in this elegant picture, would be to describe every hill, dale and slope within its limits. In every direction to which the eye can be turned, a new and elegant landscape opens, and presents its beauties, its character of distinctive attraction, and an outline that renders it a little whole in itself.

It may indeed be considered as peculiar to the Hudson scenery, that almost all the variety that the face of the earth can afford, is often condensed into a compass of very limited extent. Environed by cliffs, crowned with dwarf oak, pine and cedar, the traveller often finds a projecting bank, sometimes rising bold, rude and rocky, at others, swelling above the wave in rounded prominences. Upon such banks, are built many of the finest country seats in the United States: and if a variegated country can give gratification to refined taste, there are few places on earth where summer can be enjoyed with more delight. In passing the Hudson, it is in the highest degree pleasing, to view those edifices amid so many natural contrasts. From the city of New-York this elegant variety greets the voyager, above the highlands it becomes more frequent and striking, and in no extent of the Hudson river, does its peculiar traits arrest attention with more force, than near the town of Hudson. The second day after my arrival in the neighborhood, I traversed the road from Hudson to Columbiaville, near the mouth of Kinderhook. The road follows the dividing ridge between the eastern branch of Kinderhook creek and the Hudson river, and in many places, commands very extensive views of the surrounding country.

At one glance is often seen the majestic Hudson, its ever varied banks, the fleeting sail, apparently mingling with the farm houses, and above and beyond this soft picture of peaceful industry, rises the blue ridges of the distant mountains.

Near the mouth of Kinderhook, commences a very striking change in the physiognomy of the banks of the Hudson; the hills are less abrupt, and the bottoms are now more extensive than farther south. The soil presents no very striking difference from that found in the interval between this place and the Highlands; but the general aspect of the country assumes a new character. Though still broken, the face of the country on both banks, is more uniform than the surface of either Dutchess, Orange, or Greene counties.

Kinderhook Creek is formed from two branches, the Claverack, and the Kinderhook properly so called. The former rises in the township of Hillsdale in Columbia county, and running first east, gradually turns south and south-west, and approaching within three or four miles of that river, finally assumes a northern course, forming in all its course, a semi-ellipse of about thirty miles in length. Kinderhook rises in the township of Berlin, in Rensselaer county, and pursuing a course south or south-east, in very nearly an opposite direction, joins the Claverack about one mile and a half from the Hudson; the united stream unites with that river, after being precipitated over considerable ledges of transition slate. The curious structure of this country appears from the circumstance, that the Jansens or Ancram creek, rising also in Hillsdale, winds round the Claverack, at seven or eight miles distance from the latter stream. The courses of, indeed, nearly all the water courses in this neighbourhood, have a correspondence, approaching the regularity of art: their position must have been determined by some general cause, some operation of nature, common to a considerable extent of country. It preserves, however, so much of the general character of the Hudson banks, as to present a more broken surface near, than at a distance from that river.

Where the road from Hudson to Albany crosses Kinderhook creek, a fine wooden bridge was erected a few years past. Within a few paces below the bridge, on the south side of the creek, the Messrs. Jenkins' of Hudson, have a fine merchant mill, and directly opposite the mill, stands a large cotton factory. During the last war a little village rose around this factory, inhabited by weavers, spinners and other workmen. It is now languishing like other similar establishments, and from like causes.

The creek rolls over different ledges of rock, under and above the bridge, which produces the fall of water necessary to propel the machinery below. The tide flows up to the mill and factory. The adjacent country is hilly, particularly south of the creek. The works lie so low that the traveller is within a few paces before he can perceive their position; and when viewing them from the south bank, cannot but be pleased with the rural features of the place. From the eminence above the mill, can be seen the fine farm and seat of Mr. Robert Livingston, upon the point of land between the mouth of Kinderhook creek and Hudson river, the opposite shores rising gently from the water, and retiring far into the distant landscape, in the township of Coxackie. Turning the view a little more to the south, rises the highest peaks of Catskill mountains, in the township of Windham.

The south side of the little bay, made by Kinderhook creek, is steep and in many places precipitous, clothed with timber and underwood, its scenery is romantic and solitary. I had the good fortune to be kindly and hospitably treated, by Mr. Marks Barker and his family, who reside near this seductive spot. In company with those innocent and friendly people, and the sweet companion of my life and of this journey, I traversed those wilds. Within a few paces of the cultivated farm, or " busy mill," we might have imagined ourselves transported to the abodes of primeval silence ; we could have conceived ourselves carried back to the primitive ages, when cultivation had neither disfigured or adorned the face of the earth. Many of the dells, dark and deep, overshadowed with oaks, pine, cedar and maple, seemed to have never before been visited by human beings ; the turn of a step dispelled this illusion, by disclosing the gay aspect of the garden, orchard, field and meadow. I had before ranged over many of the most uncultivated and unvisited parts of this continent. I had often seen the rapid change, from the savage waste to the highly decorated abode of civilized man, but I do not remember to have been ever before, so strongly impressed with the contrast. The scenes were before me in all their majesty. The whole contour, shading, and parts of one of the most finely blended pictures in nature, was open to view. It was a day I can only forget when I cease to exist. It was enjoyed amid objects that now retain in my mind all their force of recollected interest. And it is a spot that the traveller may again, and again revisit, and never cease to admire.

August 30th, with great reluctance I left Columbiaville ; the name given to the little establishment on Kinderhook, and returned through Hudson and Athens, to Catskill. Like Columbiaville, Catskill stands upon the bay or mouth of a large creek, surrounded, overshadowed and almost concealed by hills. The latter town is apparently flourishing and commercial, having a rich and well cultivated country along Catskill, to support its prosperity. It was with pain I was obliged, from the nature of my private concerns, to forego the pleasure of visiting the vicinity of Catskill town. From the alpine nature of part of this region, from the beauty and variety of aspect it presented to my eye, when seen from the Hudson hills, and from all the descriptions of its features, that I have seen, I am confident I lost much, in not being able to range over its plains and mountains. There is no doubt, but that this is one of the most interesting tracts in the United States, and perhaps the one where the strongest contrasts can be found in the shortest space. All the variety of soil, and formation from primitive granite to the most recent alluvion, can be examined here in less than one day.

A good statistical and geological description of Greene county, would present many of the noblest features of the United States to view. The mouth of Catskill creek lies level with the Atlantic tides, and the most elevated of the Catsbergs in Windham, rises to about 3500 feet. Between these extremes, how immense the variety of vegetable production; perhaps the mineral kingdom would not be less productive, if as accessible to human research.

In this region, the traveller now finds some scenes of sublime interest. "The *round-top*, is found to be elevated
" 3655 feet above the level of the river; the high-peak,
" 3487. These summits are in Windham, Greene county,
" about 20 miles west of *Hudson*, and in full view from that
" city. A turnpike road which crosses this range of moun-
" tains, near these summits, winds up until it reaches the
" astonishing altitude of 2274 feet; and from this spot the

"view is inexpressibly grand."* This is the highest road in the United States, exceeding by far in elevation any of the passes of the Allegany chain, south of this place.

In this alpine region, exists also, one of the most interesting cataracts in North America; not from the mass of water, but from the perpendicular descent of the stream, and peculiar structure of the adjacent country. It is a curiosity but little known beyond the neighborhood where it exists, though within a very short distance of the mountain road I have already noticed. "The high fall of the Katerskill is "about half a mile from this road, near the summit of the "mountain and twelve miles from Catskill. The stream "arises from two small ponds, one quarter of a mile apart, "and runs gently two miles, where it breaks over a rocky "precipice of 310 feet, perpendicular height."† The mountains are inhabited to their summits, enabling travellers, who visit them, to find accommodation in their most elevated valleys.

My time spent in the vicinity of Catskill, was too short to gratify my own curiosity, or to collect extensive information on local subjects. The general outline was all I could examine, and even that imperfectly. I saw enough to excite a regret, I can only eradicate by returning under circumstances, which will enable me to remain long enough to ascend the highest mountain, and range the lowest valley in this diversified tract.

September 4th. I set out from Hudson for Albany. Above the village of Columbiaville, the road follows the valley of the Kinderhook creek. The country in many places level; so much so, as to remind me often of even Louisiana. This recollection was, however, only momentary; high rocky hills appearing to the eastward at short intervals. The flourishing village of Kinderhook, stands upon the alto

* Spafford's Gazetteer, page 9
† Spafford's Gazetteer, page 9

vial banks of the creek of the same name, twelve miles above Hudson. Above Kinderhook village, commences a body of level land, covered in its native state with pine timber. This tract affords a very remarkable instance of the revolutions, to which the price of landed property is subject I was informed on the spot, that about thirty years ago, this pine land was considered of so little value, as to render its possession onerous to the proprietor. Now, some of the most valuable farms in the two counties of Columbia and Rensselaer, are formed upon its surface. To my eye, who had travelled over so many millions of acres of pine land, in the states of Louisiana, Mississippi, and the Alabama territory, the very existence of pine timber in any great bodies, produced ideas of sterility. It is to gypsum that the region I am now speaking of, owes most of its reputation as productive soil. Improved modes of agriculture, and the use of manure, have their share very extensively in producing so beneficial a change. It delighted me the more, to see flourishing farms amid forests of pine, as it convinced my mind, that the pine regions I once considered condemned to irremediable barrenness, may be made highly fruitful. If this conclusion is correct, and I now see its practical demonstration, the possible existence of many millions of human beings is made manifest, that could never exist if pine lands were unimprovable. Considerably more than one half of all that part of the United States, south of lat 35, east of the Mississippi river, and bounded south by the Gulph of Mexico and Florida, is covered with pine. All Florida may be considered a pine country

Approaching Albany, the road from Hudson passes over a very hilly and sandy tract. The plains terminate with the waters of Kinderhook; but pine every where now presents itself as the prevailing tree, and though I had seen the practical possibility of cultivating usefully, land upon which this tree abounds, to even the exclusion of all others, yet so confirmed were my habits of thinking on the subject, that if

gave to the vicinity of Albany an air of barrenness I have since been convinced it does not deserve.

The approach to Albany upon this road, affords one of the finest landscapes on the Hudson. About one and a half miles from the city, the valley of the Hudson opens, presenting Albany, Greenbush, the wide sweeping bottoms of the river, and the adjacent farms, though thirty miles distant the peaks of Windham, and up the Hudson, the elevated country beyond Troy and Lansingburgh. The view of Albany itself, is from this hill extremely advantageous; from the rapid acclivity upon which that city is built, scarce a house is unseen. There is no point in the respective vicinity of either Baltimore, Philadelphia, New-York, or Boston, where those cities can be so completely engrasped at one glance of the eye; the view of Pittsburg from the Monongahela coal hill, is the only position that I have seen, which equals that near Albany. The latter is, however, superior as commanding a much wider field of vision.

Yours,

LETTER II.

Troy, May 5th, 1818.

Dear Sir,

The weather has been uniformly and excessively inclement since my departure from New-York, and in a particular manner since my arrival in Albany. The roads in this neighborhood are scarcely passable. With some danger and difficulty I yesterday came to this town. We have this morning an interval of clear sun-shine, which is cheerful, and has exposed from the front street the snow capped summits of the Catsbergs. The absence indeed of ice and snow, is the only circumstance that even here marked the approach of spring; every object has otherwise, the cold and solitary aspect of winter. The Hudson is excessively swelled by the recent rains, and by the melting ice and snow towards its source.

The banks near this town, at Albany, and for a few miles below that city, indicate the diminished influence of the tide, and the effects produced by mountain streams. Extended alluvial bottoms, and a continued current to the southward, though still checked by the swell below, are changes that obtrude themselves to the immediate notice of the traveller.

This town is the first upon the Hudson, that can be considered as built upon the bottoms of that river. The site is not elevated more than eight or ten feet above the level of high water mark on the river bank, sloping gradually to the water edge. Some of the lower parts are now inundated. The base of the bottom on which the town is placed, is rolled pebble with an alluvial covering; it is about 800 yards wide, from the foot of the hill to the river bank. The hills rise with a very steep acclivity, but without precipices.

I measured a base 255 feet, in Col. Albert Pawlin's garden, upon a very level plain from the extremity of which I took angles of elevation, to standing objects upon the hill in the rear of the city: the calculations founded upon the base and angles gave 254 feet as the height of the hill, at the distance of 5951 feet from the south extremity of the base. The garden, in which this operation was performed, is situated at the lower end of the city, about 100 feet from the margin dell, and not more than two feet above the level of the Hudson river, at the time the admeasurement was made.

Troy is formed by one main street inclining with the inflections of the river, and crossed by others running from the river, to the base of the adjacent hills. Standing at or near the head of tide water, lying so nearly level with the Hudson, and having a well cultivated country above and in its rear, Troy is well situated for a commercial town. In point of wealth, business, population and extent, it is the third town in the state of New-York. Most of the buildings are of brick, and have an elegant and spacious appearance; the inhabitants cannot fall short of seven thousand.

We have often, in conversation, spoke of the Hudson as a long narrow bay, rather than a river. This body of water has indeed but one characteristic, that could ever give it the appellation of a river; that is its great length, when compared with its ordinary width. In every other respect, it exhibits the common features of a bay. I do not remember to have ever read in any author, an attempt to define the real difference between a river and a bay; you will recollect that in our little hydrographical definitions, we considered that body of water a river, whose opposing banks, did actually or very nearly form corresponding curves; and we viewed that body of water a bay, into which, if connected with a sea having tides, those tides flowed, and whose opposite banks did not obey opposing inflections. If these principles of analysis are correct, the Hudson is a bay to the junction of its north branch with the Mohawk. It is to be regretted, that the continuity of the Hudson above Waterford, had not received a distinctive name from the bay or river below. In reality the Mohawk and the upper Hudson, after rolling over considerable falls, both enter the head of a bay. The features of those two latter rivers, except in magnitude, differ but little from the other streams, which have their sources in the higher extremities of the Hudson valley, and which flowing over a comparative table land, approach near, and are then precipitated over elevated ledges of rock, before finding the level of the recumbent bay.

Examining the environs of Troy, Lansingburg, and Waterford, I found Pœsten's-Kill, which enters the Hudson at the lower extremity of the former town, rolling over reiterated cataracts, similar to all the streams I had seen from the Highlands upwards. The Mohawk dashing over the Cahoos falls, and the Hudson over its numerous rapids, all seem influenced in their motion by one common cause.

The view from the hills near Troy is extensive, but the quantity of pine and cedar, give here, as near Albany, a sterile aspect to the neighboring country. I have before observed, that associating ideas of sterility with these evergreens, is in part a mistaken application of data, taken from a distant and in many respects a very different country. Well informed men have observed to me, when speaking of those lands that appeared so barren, that, good husbandry never failed to render them very productive. Your intelligent friend B*****l, of Albany, who has made the experiment upon part of the worst of those lands, confirms in strong language their liability to amelioration. I am fond of dwelling upon, and often recurring to such subjects. It is pleasing to be convinced that a dense and happy population, may be subsisted upon places where once incurable sterility seemed to reign. Adieu.

LETTER III.

Schenectady, May 8th, 1818.

DEAR SIR,

I would have been pleased to have extended my rambles more into the adjacent country, near Albany and Troy, but the incessant rain prevented any comfortable or beneficial excursion. The 6th of May the rain fell in torrents, in the midst of which I returned from Troy to Albany, where I remained until the morning of the 8th, when I set out in the stage for the westward. The rain had ceased in the night, but the roads for about two miles from the city, were so intolerable as to oblige the passengers to leave the stage, in order to enable the horses to drag the vehicle through the deep mud. After attaining the summit level at the western part of Albany, the country is level, the surface a clay mixed with sand; and whether the wretched road that exists there, is the necessary consequence of the nature of the surface or soil, or the effect of a defective police, those most concerned ought to explain. As it was, I was glad to arrive safe over this marsh, and attain the sandy plains farther to the westward.

The distance from Albany to Schenectady is sixteen computed miles; the intermediate country is broken, rolling sandy, and in its natural state extremely barren. The principal timber white pine and red cedar, admixed near the streams with some white oak, black oak, and white birch, with a few stems of red flowering maple. The water courses which cross the road flow north-east towards the Mohawk, and have some fine extensive farms upon their alluvial bottoms. Before reaching Schenectady a high hill gives the traveller a full view of the adjacent country. At the time of the year in which I travelled a few blossoms upon the maples and birch trees, were the only harbingers of approaching spring. The slopes of the Mohawk were clothed with pine and cedar; the leafless branches of the other trees were hid amid the deep green boughs of those hardy sons of the forest. Descending into the vale in which stands the comparatively ancient village of Schenectady, another and more pleasing scene opens. The very flourishing village standing upon the fertile alluvial flats of the Mohawk presents a rich picture of cultivation, contrasting strongly with the sandy hills towards Albany, or the equally arid eminences beyond the Mohawk to the north of Schenectady.

This town, or city, is situated upon the flats at the bottom of the hills, on the south or right side of the Mohawk river; it is more regularly laid out than most of the ancient towns established by the early settlers of New-York, now contains more than 500 houses, and perhaps 3600 inhabitants. Many of the buildings are large, expensive and elegant. This town is well placed to receive the benefits of an extensive commerce with the rich and prosperous settlements which border the Mohawk to its source. The inhabitants seem to have availed themselves of their advantages, the trade of the place appears productive.

Schenectady recals many facts of historical interest. It formed for a long period of time, the frontier town towards the Indian country. In February, 1690, a marauding party of French and Indians surprised the inhabitants before day light in the morning. Aroused from their peaceful beds by the explosion of the fire arms, and the piercing yells of their savage enemies, an indiscriminate slaughter ensued. The mother and the babe, the husband and wife, the brother and sister shared the same fate. A few escaped, who almost naked, through frost and snow carried the distressful tidings to Albany. This was one of the many, and one of the most tragical scenes of savage border warfare, that has occurred with some intervals, around our settlements for upwards of two centuries, and which is far from having terminated. The massacre at Fort Mims, and many others within five years past, are only recent instances of the continuation of this most dreadful of all species of war. The circle is widening, the very nation has ceased to exist, which reduced Schenectady to ashes and buried in its ruins the remains of its murdered citizens, but other hordes of savages have continually presented their ferocious front, and our frontiers have ever been stained with the blood of helpless innocence. Those tribes have apparently receded, but in fact they have been rather extinguished.

The Mohawks,* who once gave law to an immense extent, the centre of which was the present New-York, have also disappeared from the world, and have only now remaining to attest their former existence, the name of the beautiful stream upon which is situated the town of Schenectady. Its current once stained with human gore, now flows gentle, pure and steady, through some of the finest settlements in all America.

Schenectady is the seat of justice for the county of the same name, and as such, contains the usual buildings necessary for courts of justice and prisons. It is also more honourably remarkable, as having within its limits Union College, a respectable literary institution, incorporated in 1791, and took its name from the union of several religious societies in its formation.† It is now in a flourishing situation, having an ample library, philosophical and chymical apparatus, and upwards of 150 students. The annual expense of board and education about $120 per annum. Doubts have been suggested whether a good moral policy would justify the reduction of collegiate education so low. Many reasons more specious than solid, have been adduced, to shew, "*that little learning is a dangerous thing,*" and that man, "*must drink deep, or taste not of the Pierian spring.*" I can never forget your reply, when I once observed, that the time never could arrive when all mankind could be learned. Your expression was, that comparatively, almost any

* The allies, not the enemies of the people of Schenectady.
† Spafford's Gazetteer, page 44.

member of a civilized country was learned, when compared with savages; and the common mode of expression would suppose, that, all men ought to remain savage, or attain the empyrean heights of literary excellence. Some light headed dunces have become pedants by obtaining a few words in the learned languages; as our friend A⸺s, who spouts languages living and dead, without more utility than a parrot would gain by using the same sounds. It cannot now, however, be doubted, but that the human character is ennobled, the human heart softened, and public morals purified, by general instruction. Though slight abuses may arise in some instances from the weakness or depravity of individuals, those abuses deteriorate no more from the value of education, than the ordinary defects of all human institutions do, from any amelioration whatever in the condition of our species.

For my own part, I viewed the buildings composing the three colleges which bear the name of Union in Schenectady, with a similar reverence, with which I had formerly felt when passing Cambridge, Yale, Columbia, Princeton, and Dickinson. Those, and other such edifices, are the true temples of reason.

In the vale of the Mohawk, I considered myself as in a new region. I had now passed the utmost limit of the Atlantic tides. Clinton's Inaugural Discourse, and Dr. Mitchill's notes to Kirk and Mercein's edition of Cuvier's Theory of the Earth, had enflamed my desire to visit the interior of this continent. I also wished to contrast with each other, the two extremities of the United States. My progress from the city of New-York to Albany, and even to Schenectady, as merely introductory to my real tour. Hitherto I had travelled over a region remarkable in itself, but with features of considerable resemblance to the scenes to which you are most familiar, but from hence objects are new, and of a nature very dissimilar, to those over which we have been in the habit of rambling.

You will hear of me again from Utica. Adieu.

LETTER IV.

Utica, May 11th, 1818.

DEAR SIR,

By an unexpected good fortune the weather continued without rain during my journey from Schenectady to this town. The roads were in many places extremely bad, which circumstance had one good effect, it enabled me to keep in advance of the stage, and by travelling on foot, and in some measure at my leisure, procured me a much better view of the country than I could have gained by continuing in the vehicle. I kept my pocket book and pencil in my hand, and made my notes as the objects presented themselves. Rough as these notes are, I have sent you a copy, I can add nothing material by putting them in any other form. You expressed a kind desire to hear from me, and to have as near as possible a picture of my route, and a description of the incidents of my tour, as these incidents transpired. The distances are given from Albany, as it was on leaving that city, that I commenced to note regularly the stages and diversities of the country.

MILES.

16   *From Albany to Schenectady.*

As soon as I had finished breakfast in the latter town, I seized my cane, put your letter in the mail, and preceded the stage over the Mohawk. The road here passes this stream by a fine wooden bridge, said to be the masterpiece of the celebrated bridge builder, Theodore Burr; it is 997 feet in length. The structure was entirely new to me, and could not be satisfactorily given without a diagram. The most facile mode of conveying to you, an idea of the principle upon which this bridge is formed, is by an *oe* placed lengthwise,

MILES.

—16 The decumbent curves resting upon abutments, and the incumbent ones supporting the roof; the whole fabric has the appearance of great strength. The abutments are composed of stone, the superstructure wood; the curved arches are framed out of thick plank.

The road to Ballston leaves that to Utica, at the north extremity of the bridge. The latter road proceeds over the Mohawk flats, a rich and level alluvial bottom, which has much the appearance of having once been the bottom of a lake. These plains are now extremely productive, though environed on the north and south sides by sterile pine hills.

5—21 *Hazeley's tavern.*
8—29 *Groat's tavern.*

Between the two last stages, the country has become extremely variegated and broken. The north bank along which I travelled, was hilly, and often so precipitous, as to leave scarce room for the road to pass: the south side slopes gradually from the river, with numerous farms rising above each other as far as the eye can reach. The soil of the north side appears sandy and sterile, that of the south must be of a greatly superior quality. The prevalent timber on the hills pine, with different kinds of oak and white birch; that on the river bottoms and contiguous banks, white walnut, shell bark hickory, some liriodendron tulipifera and chesnut.

The river is about 250 yards wide, and filled with islands, which follow each other in rapid succession. Sand and rounded pebbles form the superstratum, but schistose limestone appears projecting from the banks in a horizontal position, marking the commencement of a secondary region.

MILES.
1—30 *F. E. Degraff's*
1—31 *G. Hanny's.*

Horizontal or Floetz limestone, becomes more frequent. The opposing banks maintain their relative characters.

1—33 *Village of Amsterdam in Montgomery county.*

This is a romantic village, situated on the slope of the hills, with the Chucktanunda, a large creek foaming over ledges of limestone amongst the buildings, and rushing impetuously down the adjacent declivities towards the Mohawk. The sudden effect of this admixture of houses and cataracts is extremely pleasing and picturesque. The south shore continues to sweep before the eye, in far distant stages of cultivated acclivities.

1—37 *Tripes Hill, opposite the mouth of Scoharie river, or creek.*

This is one of the most singular and difficult passes on the Mohawk river. The hill rises abrupt, is high, sandy, and extremely painful in the ascent. There is no mode to avoid this inconvenience, as the bank of the river is an elevated ledge of rock on the north side. The table land is a sandy plain, and the descent above is also but little less abrupt than the ascent below. From the highest part of the hill, the mouth and valley of the Schoharie is in full view. The bottom of the Mohawk is here extensive, but extremely flat on the south side; the Schoharie is seen meandering over this plain in its course from the hills to the Mohawk river. The bottoms appear extremely fertile, but must be subject to occasional inundation, and from their undeviating level, the crops must suffer great injury when these accidents occur.

MILES
2—39   Conger's tavern.
3—42   Village of Caghnawaga.
1—43   Johnson's creek.
6—49   Connely's tavern.
8—57   Palatine lower village.

Between the two last stages, the road passes generally upon the river bottoms, which are narrow and terminated to the north by steep hills, or perpendicular ledges of secondary rock. The south bank is also broken, rocky and much less cultivated than any equal distance I have yet seen on the Mohawk. The soil black, and no doubt fertile; even that of the hills assumes a more inviting appearance as I have ascended. The timber is now strongly indicative of productive soil; sugar maple is so common as to form the principal article of fuel, this tree never flourishes abundantly, except upon the very best lands; it is here often seen of gigantic size along the bottoms, and often upon the highest and steepest banks visible from the road. Other timber trees, though fewer in number, continue as before noted.

The rock strata is schistose limestone and sand stone, alternately overlaying each other.

4—61   Palatine upper village.

Face of the country continues unchanged, on each side of the river, perpendicular precipices frequent. I remained over night in the latter village, and at the dawn of day, on the morning of the 9th of May, set out on foot in advance of the stage, and walked

6—67   to Palatine church. Slope of the country has now changed to the north or left side of the stream. Sugar maple the prevailing timber, and almost exclusive fuel,

MILES.

7—76 *Mouth of East Canada creek, and village of Oppenheim.*

The village stands near the bank of the Mohawk above the mouth of the creek. Lower or East Canada, is a fine mill stream of about twenty-five miles in length, independent of particular bends, rising in Montgomery county upon the same table land from which flows the Sacondago branch of Hudson river. The two streams interlock, and falling over a number of precipices, pursue their respective courses with great rapidity, until lost in in the larger stream, into which their waters are discharged. It may be here repeated that all the tributary streams of the Hudson, and its branches seem to be peculiarly adapted to the construction of water machinery. East Canada creek forms from its mouth, about twenty miles of the boundary between Montgomery and Herkimer counties.

Oppenheim is a small village, with nothing in its construction or situation worthy particular notice.

—77 *Van Valkenburgh's Inn.*

Since leaving Oppenheim, I travelled over high hills, the slope has now again changed to the south side of the Mohawk, which presents an elegant acclivity rising to considerable elevation, chequered with farms and copses of wood, intermingling in endless variety. A summer excursion over this region must afford the most charming contrasts in nature. It is now pleasing in the undress of nature, with banks of snow still resting upon many of the hill sides.

The timber continues to present similar varieties as before noticed, since leaving Palatine, except that sugar maple, now encroaches still more upon the other species of trees.

MILES.
1—81 *Little Falls.*

This cataract is caused by a chain of granitic mountains of no great elevation, which crosses the Mohawk at this place. The chain is a ramification, or perhaps a continuation of the Catsbergs. Approaching the pass, I was struck with its great resemblance to the passage of the Juniata, through the Warrior mountain below Bedford, in Pennsylvania, except that the scenery of the latter is on a larger scale, and the mountains covered with a less vigorous growth of trees, than those which occasion the Little Falls in the Mohawk. In both, the rivers at the distance below, of half a mile, seem to issue from the base of the mountains, which seen obliquely, conceals the narrow glens through which the waters work their toilsome way.*

---

* The description given by gov. De Witt Clinton, of the Little Falls, will continue to supercede the use of any other. It is indeed a fine specimen of topographical painting, and places the attendant phenomena before the mind's eye. I had Dr Mitchill's notes on Cuvier, into which this description is copied, in my hands when passing this interesting cataract, and amid the wildness of the scene, and in hearing of the roar of the gushing waters, read and felt the truth of this excellent view of one of the great scenes that our country presents to the admiring traveller. Few in this country but who have often read the respective works I have mentioned in my text, and have seen of course, the description of the Little Falls, to which I have alluded. The reader will pardon, however, its insertion from the original work, in a note; some may not have read it, and few who have, will find a second perusal tedious.

" The Little Falls on the Mohawk river, in connexion with the surrounding country, exhibit a very interesting aspect. As you approach the falls the river becomes narrow and deep, and you pass through immense rocks, principally of granite, interpersed with limestone. In various places you observe profound excavations in the rocks made by the agitation of pebbles in the fissures, and in some places the river is not more than twenty yards wide. As you approach the western extremity of the hills, you find them about half a mile distant from summit to summit,

MILLS.

"The scenery near the Little Falls, is wild and striking. As you approach this place, the valley of the river seems to close, the road approaches the pass obliquely, winding along the foot of hills and at least three hundred feet high. The rocks are composed of granite, and many of them are thirty or forty feet thick, and the whole mountain extends at least, half a mile from east to west. You see them piled on each other, like Ossa on Pelion, and in other places, huge fragments scattered about, indicating a violent rupture of the waters through this place, as if they had been formerly dammed up and had formed a passage, and in all directions you behold great rocks exhibiting rotundities, points and cavities as if worn by the violence of the waves, or hurled from their ancient positions.

"The general appearance of the Little Falls indicates the former existence of a great lake above, connected with the Oneida lake, and as the waters forced a passage here and receded, the flats above were formed and composed several thousand acres of the richest land. Rome being the highest point on the lake, the passage of the waters on the east side left it bare, the Oneida lake gradually receded on the west side, and formed the great marsh or swamp, now surrounding the waters on Wood creek. The physiognomy of the country from the commencement of Wood creek to its termination in the Oneida lake, confirms this hypothesis. The westerly and northwesterly winds continually drive the sand of the lake towards the creek, and you can distinctly perceive the alluvion increasing eastward by the accumulation of sand, and the formation of new ground. Near the lake, you observe sand without trees, then to the east a few scattering trees, and as you proceed in that direction, the woods thicken. The whole country from the commencement to the termination of Wood creek, looks like made ground. In digging the canal in Wood creek, pine trees have been found twelve feet deep. An old boatman several years ago, said that he had been fifty years in that employ, and that the Oneida lake had receded half a mile within his memory. William Colbreath, one of the first settlers at Rome, in digging a well, found a large tree at the depth of twelve feet. This great lake, breaking down in the first place, the barriers which opposed the progress of its waters to the east, and then gradually receding to the west, is a subject well deserving of minute investigation."—*Clinton's Introductory Discourse, page* 52.

Since my return to the city of New-York, I had the pleasure of meeting there, with Mr. Isaac Briggs, who is mentioned in this

MIES.

—st covered with enormous sugar maples whose rough boughs hang over the head of the passenger. An elegant white tavern house stands near the entrance into the narrow glen below the cataract. After passing the house a few yards, the road turns suddenly to the right, and scenes of grandeur succeed each other in rapid review. The huge unshapen fragments of granite and other rocks, lie disrupted in an infinity of positions, interspersed and overgrown with sugar maple; elm, hemlock, oak, pine, and other trees. Toiling about half a

corrrespondence as one of the gentlemen employed under the authority of the state of New-York, as an engineer on the grand canal. Mr. Briggs in the execution of his official duty, has measured and levelled the Mohawk river and its banks from Rome to the Little Falls, and who had the goodness to give me the following measurements of the hills adjacent to the Little Falls.

Falls-hill, where the road (on the south side of the Mohawk,) passes it, is 518 feet higher than our level above the falls; 573 feet higher than our level two miles below the falls; 473 feet higher than Rome level; and 323 feet higher than the surface of lake Erie.

This admeasurement shews, that the present level above the Falls is only forty-five feet different from the level of Rome. Of course, if the time ever existed when the water at the Falls was more than forty-five feet above its present level, then did a lake extend to the present Oneida, making the whole one sheet of water. The most incontestible proofs remain upon the rocks, in and near the present fall, that the water once flowed more than fifty feet higher than it does now. What revolutions! what sudden and gradual changes have wrought their effects upon the crust of our planet! what we now see of the surface of our globe is almost composed of water, or of broken fragments torn by violence from their pristine position, at times beyond our records, and in many instances, by means that elude our research.

To pursue the investigation of these changes, is not always an idle application, as in the instance before us, where the examination of the phenomena enables us to form rational opinions upon, how far we can effect beneficial improvements upon the now existent waters in this singular region. A region where rivers appear in many instances in their youth.

MILLS.

—81 mile, you first hear the din and then approach within sight of the foaming surge, tumbling with irresistible violence over its rocky bed. From the foot of the falls, the road winds its tortuous way up the steep ascent, and in about a quarter of a mile, brings the traveller to a beautiful, well built village. Here every feeling of taste meets a rich repast; so many, so variant, and so striking are the objects which the hand of nature and art, have here engrouped in one prospect. The rock in thousands of forms, trees and shrubs rising from their interstices. The white surge of the falling waters; beyond which is seen the smooth surface of the Mohawk, whose placid stream advances slow and silent to the scene of tumult below. Still farther to the south-west, opens the fine expansion of the German flats, chequered with all the decorations of field, orchard, meadow, houses and copses of wood. The clear blue heaven and fleecy clouds form the back ground of this delightful landscape. A landscape the traveller can enjoy from the windows of an excellent inn, which stands in the romantic village which raises its well built houses between the almost perpendicular crags on one side, and the struggling stream on the other. The marks are numerous and manifest of an anterior and much greater elevation of the water than found there at present. Many of the rocks are perforated with round holes, made by the rotation of pebbles in a running stream. Those rocks are often of immense size, and placed where they have lain for countless ages. These imprinted evidences of geological revolution, evince a slow and gradual, not a sudden or violent change. The opposing hills seem as if sawn asunder by the per-

MILES.

—81 petual abrasion of the water. No farther alteration of consequence can take place in future, as the bed of the river is worn down to a level with the bottom of the ancient decumbent lake.

Passing above the falls, the road follows the bank of the river, from which the adjacent hills rise by a very steep ascent. Prominences protrude themselves frequently to the margin of the water, and force the course of the road to rise to considerable elevation, giving reiterated opportunities to enjoy the prospect of the truly rich country, known by the name of the German flats. This region takes it name from the circumstance of the first civilized emigrants being Germans. Upon no part of the United States have the inhabitants suffered more from that murderous border warfare, instigated by whites, and pursued by savages, than did the early settlers on the now smiling German flats. For a long period of time after the settlements made by the French in Canada, and by the English and Dutch upon the Atlantic coast; the Mohawk and Oswego rivers, formed the line of eruptive communication, and blood marked its various points.* The aged yet remember, and recount with a melancholy recollection, many of those tragical scenes. Time has changed the drama, the rage of war has subsided, the savages have perished or dwindled to a wretched remnant. Towns, villages, churches, schools, and farm houses, now adorn this once dreary waste. The cultivated mind may shed a tear upon the horrors of the past, but a tear like rain drops in the beams

---

* Some of the horrors of this long chain of sanguinary events, will be noticed in the sequel of this treatise.

MILES.

—84 of the sun. A review of the present must be delightful to every generous and feeling heart. It is a picture on which is traced, the most interesting revolution in the moral and physical condition of human nature. There is seen the region, where a few years past, roamed the blood stained savage, and where now dwells in peace and plenty the civilized man. Where in times remote, stood an expansive lake, and where now bloom the most luxuriant harvests. Spring had made but little advance, at the time I passed this remarkable place; I amused my fancy in contemplating what it would exhibit when decked in all the gaiety of the vernal season, or when the fields and meadows were clothed in the rich garb of summer. Lost in this pleasing reverie, time past unheaded until my recollection was aroused by finding myself at the mouth of

7—86 *West Canada creek.*

From the projecting hill below this creek, a very comprehensive view is afforded of both the German and Herkimer flats. These expansive bottoms are in fact, the same body of soil, being only divided by the Mohawk river, winding from the hills on its south, to those on its north side. West Canada creek is a stream of considerable magnitude, rising in a very hilly or rather mountainous country which forms the south-west angle of Hamilton county. This elevated tract is the continuation of the same ridge that crosses the Mohawk at, and forms the Little Falls, and which gives rise in the same neighborhood to the two Canadas, and to the Sacondago branch of the Hudson. West Canada, like its namesake, falls impetuously in almost all its course. Its higher branches flow westwardly

MILES.

—56 about twenty miles, unite and enter Herkimer, and bending abruptly south, wind through the latter county twenty more miles, and is then lost in the Mohawk. The spring floods of those short mountain streams, are terrible. A fine wooden bridge formerly crossed West Canada near its mouth, but the freshet of last winter carried it away; the inhabitants are now erecting another, which will be, no doubt, completed in the course of the ensuing summer. I passed the creek in a skiff, and soon found myself in

4—87 *The village of Herkimer.*

This village stands upon an elevated but alluvial plain, composed of rounded pebbles, sand and clay. It occupies the central part of the flats of the same name. The neighboring country is well cultivated, the soil exuberantly fertile, and the improvements exhibit an air of wealth and industry. The Herkimer flats do not appear to be so tamely level as those on the opposite side of the Mohawk. In point of timber, they present one general character; sugar tree, elm, white walnut or butternut, prevails upon the bottoms near the streams; on the hills or elevated slopes are found oak, hemlock, linden, (basswood) sugar maple, elm, ash, and hickory. Of oak, ash, and hickory, several species of each occur.

I remained but a short time in the village of Herkimer, set out, and after passing the small and
6—93 unimportant village of *Schuyler*, found myself about four in the afternoon in

8—101 *Utica.*

The plain of the Herkimer flats continues from that village to Schuyler, where the road rises upon higher but still level land. The slope is here on the north side. Some part of the country is not very well improved. More wood land remains here than I had seen any where else since leaving Schenectady. This character however changes in approaching the city of Utica, whose vicinity exhibits a well cultivated and wealthy neighborhood. The whole country presents marks of not very ancient submersion. The super-stratum is every where sand, loam and rounded pebbles; the materials in various degrees of respective prevalence and commixture; the whole affording in many places a soil of extraordinary fertility.

Utica is approached from the north, in part by a very bad road, and in part by a very good causeway. The latter is about a mile in length, but does not cross the level alluvial flats of the Mohawk. The residue of the road, was, when I passed it, in a wretched condition.

Utica occupies the site of old F. Schuyler, and stands upon the right or south bank of the Mohawk river, in Oneida county, and in north latitude 43° 06.* The site of this town is a gentle ascent, not exceeding two degrees, if so much. The opposite bank of the Mohawk is for about a mile and a half a perfect unbroken plain. The town stands at the lowest depression of the ancient basin. The adjacent country rises so imperceptibly that no elevation of consequence is perceivable from the streets. Few trees are visible except Hemlock and sugar maple. This town has two banks, one a branch of that of Manhattan, in the city of New-York, the other formed by the citizens, and incorporated since 1812. Some very productive manufactories exist in this neighborhood. The commerce of the place appears flourishing; a matter of course, as Utica is a kind of thoroughfare between Albany and the central and western parts of the state of New-York. The grand canal will pass through this town, and add much to its importance as a place of business.

* The latitude I obtained in Utica from that accurate mathematician Isaac Briggs, who also gave me the variation of the magnetic needle there, 4° 19′ W.

Utica contains at this time near 3000 inhabitants, between 4 and 500 houses, with stores, taverns, book stores, and other appendages of a flourishing country town. Here roads diverge in all directions; down the valley of the Mohawk to Schenectady; westward to Auburn, Geneva, Canandaigua, Batavia, and Buffalo; southward towards the valleys of the Delaware and Susquehannah rivers; and northward to Sacket's Harbor.

The day I write is heavy and threatens rain. The stage does not leave this town until to-morrow; I shall however trust the weather and my feet, and set out as usual, with my cane in one hand and my tablets in the other. You will not again hear from me before I reach Sacket's Harbor; in the mean time, though I am daily advancing farther from home, I am not the less sincerely,

Dear Sir,
Your devoted friend.

LETTER V.

Sacket's Harbor, May 12th, 1818.

DEAR SIR,

DRENCHED to the skin, I arrived here yesterday evening, at 10 P. M. Enclosed you have a transcript of my journal from Utica to this town. I was fortunately favored with good weather the greatest part of the way, and only had a heavy rain to close my journey hither.

MILES.
1   *From Utica to cross-roads.*
1—2   *Road to Rome,*
        Leaves that which leads towards Sacket's Harbor; the latter now assumes its north west course.

MILES.

1—3 *Northrop's.*

After leaving Utica and proceeding as far as the cross roads, I had the fortune by carelessness or some other cause to take a wrong road, and wandered to the northward about two miles, but finding my error I with some trouble regained my intended road. I found the country rising more rapidly than I anticipated. A small creek which rises in the high ground north of Utica, and which enters the Mohawk river nearly opposite that town, has cut so deep a ravine in the yielding materials through which it flows, as to be passed with difficulty. I strayed to the east of this creek, and was forced to return to the cross roads to regain my way

Above Northrop's the road ascends in some places gently and others abruptly, along the acclivity of the hills. I frequently turned to enjoy the prospect behind me, which though interrupted by the woods, was exposed at intervals by the farms which have been cleared near the road. As I approached the summit I found the ascent more rapid, and the adjacent land more free from timber, consequently the prospect expanded at every step; and on the extreme brow a large farm exposed to full view the city of Utica, the vicinity, and the valley of the Mohawk to the farthest limit of vision. The eye has a range of more than thirty miles east, south and southwest. Utica, though five miles distant, seemed to lie at my feet. As I stood and gazed upon this noble prospect, I could not avoid exclaiming mentally " that I had seen many " more sublime views, many more grand, but not " one had ever before met my eye, that so com- " pletely answered to my conceptions, of the truly

F

MILES	
1—5	"soft and beautiful in landscape." Certainly I had more than a thousand farms spread before me, many hundreds could be seen at one glance. Those near were seen most distinctly, whilst those more remote gradually diminished in size, and became, from increased distance, less distinct, until, like the vast inclined plane upon which they stood, they were finally lost upon the verge of the distant sky.
	That mind must be void of the least sympathies of human nature, who could behold this fine prospect, without feeling a strong sensation of pleasure. Gratifying indeed must be the reflection upon the sum of domestic peace, plenty, affection, and comfort, enjoyed within its limits.
1—6	*Tavern upon the table land of the hill.*
2—8	*do. upon the bottom northward of the hill.*
1—9	*Carrel's tavern upon nine mile run, flowing southwest into the Mohawk.*
4—13	*Village of Trenton.*

Thus far I proceeded the same evening I left Utica, and found myself very well disposed to rest, after a walk of seventeen miles, including the direct distance, my error and its remedy, in my outset from Utica.

Between Utica and Trenton I found four varieties of soil and timber. Upon the Mohawk flats exist a deep black alluvial loam, with a slight intermixture of pebble. As the different banks rise, pebble becomes more plentiful and decumbent, in relation to the other materials of the soil. The timber upon the alluvial, as also upon the contiguous banks, is composed of hemlock, beech, sugar, maple and elm, with rare examples of other trees. The productive quality of the alluvial soil is very strong, that of the contiguous slopes but little inferior. The latter species of land more spungy and wet than the former, though the contrary would appear from relative position. The general crop in this section of the state of New-York, appears to be maize, wheat, rye, oats, and meadow grass. Fruit trees suitable to the climate, such as apples, pears, plumbs and cherries, appear plentiful. Peach trees cannot here endure the severity of winter cold.

Rising above the alluvion and contiguous banks, appears the second species of soil; this latter variety of land it called in the colonial language of the country *interval land*. This soil is, as I have already observed, more spungy than that of the alluvion, and certainly much less productive. I ought, however, to premise that unusual rains had preceded my visit to this country, and that many places appeared then wet and even inundated, which would not be subject to similar inconvenience in a more moderate season. The water left on the ground by recent rains, could not nevertheless, destroy the means of forming a correct comparative estimate. From a greater slope, every other circumstance equal, the *interval land* ought to be less moist than the alluvion, the contrary is, as I have observed the fact. The varieties of timber upon the interval, does not materially differ from those upon the alluvial land, except black birch (betula nigra) which is more abundant upon the former than upon the latter soil.

Ascending towards the summit of the hills, and before gaining the apex, I found deep ruts made by the wash of the road, the sides of which laid bare projections of secondary mica slate, lying in its original position; forming the the third variety of soil.

Though apparently productive as the interval tract, this slate region must, from its greater elevation, be more subject to early and late frost, than either of the two preceding varieties of land. Farms of great extent are open upon each section. The highest summit of the hill where the road passes is cleared land, and affords to the traveller a convenient opportunity of reviewing the vast expanse around Utica.

Upon the table land above the mica slate, now repose immense bodies of rounded granite and basaltic pebble. The present respective position of these rocks, are so different from that assigned them by geologists, and the difficulty of accounting from any known operation of nature, for the transportation to such distance from their primitive beds, and elevation to such heights of blocks of granite and basalt, often eight or ten feet diameter, that the task of accounting for existent phenomena must be left by me to those better qualified, or more disposed to enter into the disquisition. I can only observe, that the schist or slate demonstrably reposes in its primitive position; whilst the incumbent pebbles, enormous as they are, have evidently been forced into their present state, by the agency of some fluid. Water, as that body now operates in either of its known states of ice or fluidity, could never preserve in motion, consequently transport one of the blocks I have seen to any, even the smallest distance, much less cover an immense surface with those rounded masses, which exhibit all sizes, from a grain of sand to bodies of more than twenty feet diameter. This with many

MILES.
—13 other phenomena I have seen, induces me to believe that an order of things once, and for a great length of time, existed upon this planet, producing effects that remain when their causes have ceased to operate, perhaps forever.

Upon the table land, sugar maple ceases almost entirely, though so very abundant upon the alluvial interval, and even upon the schistose tract. The black birch commences a shrub near the Mohawk river, but when elevated upon the table land, assumes the size and majesty of a forest tree of the first magnitude. Beech on the contrary, a stately tree on the low grounds, dwindles in mounting to a more alpine air, and upon the table land is rare, and of stinted growth. Elm and hemlock forms the mass of the forest upon the table land.

Either from the flatness of the land or from some other cause, the table land is extremely swampy, and of course inconvenient to cultivate; it is here narrow, not exceeding a mile in width.

Upon the northern brow of the hill, a prospect expands of little less dimensions than that seen from its southern slope. The northern landscape is less interesting than the southern at this time, as presenting only a mass of woods with a few openings only, whereas that of the south exhibits an immense surface of cultivated country.

To me this northern view was highly pleasing, as it first laid before me, upon its back ground, part of the basin of the Canadian sea. Descending the declivity, I gazed upon the blue verge before me as if I had felt myself entering into a new world. To me this transition was not illusory. Though upon the same planet, and even upon the same continent, the images I now see around me are so different from those I have been for a long period accustomed to behold, that my sensations would not be much more changed if I was transported to another world in reality.

I found the surface of the slope as I descended, composed of clay, sand, and immense bodies of rounded pebble. The present state of the interior of North America, exhibits phenomena at every step, which demonstrate that water or some other fluid has flowed over the surface of the land for a very great length of time. This fluid has been the agent of modification. Whilst the surface near the Canadian sea continued in a state of submersion, it is very probable that the face of the earth was generally uniform though inclining. When the waters retired, the drain occasioned by rains and springs, were the commencement of our present rivers, which in the long lapse of ages, have been worn down to their present level. Whilst the land continued submersed, fragments of granite, trap, and other rocks, may have been disrupted from their original beds, and gradually forced forward, and whilst in motion rounded by attrition, and finally deposited over more recent formations. As the abrasion of the waters in the new formed rivers deepened their beds, the *debris* of primitive rocks became exposed, and rolled down in vast bodies along the declivities of the hills. This latter process is the only part of the great geological revolution, that continues in operation; the river beds are daily becoming deeper; strata that formerly caused cataracts, are many of them completely cut by the streams, and all are yielding to the force of the ever acting fluid, that passes over their broken ledges.

MILLS.

After reaching the base of the hill, on the side opposite to that of Utica, commences a sandy region, which continues to Trenton. Timber near the latter village, hemlock, beech, sugar maple, elm, ash, and black birch. Though much cleared land appears near the road, I saw but very little winter grain growing in the fields. Demanding of some of the inhabitants the reason, of what appeared to me defective husbandry, I uniformly received in reply, that the early and unseasonable thaws during the winter and spring, destroyed the small grain. How far the opinion of the inhabitants was founded on correct experience, or upon bad farming, I cannot pretend to determine, but am inclined to ascribe the effect to the latter cause. My own opinion is formed from the appearance of the soil and timber, and from the geographical position of the country. Sugar maple is here so abundant, as to form the principal article of fuel used by the inhabitants, and affords them the means of manufacturing a considerable quantity of sugar, an advantage the benefits of which, they have but partially realized. Ever since passing the Little Falls in the Mohawk, I have noticed the constant decrease of every species of oak in the forests; and since passing Utica, I have had still more reason to make this remark. This circumstance is a subject of regret, for many of the most indispensable uses in domestic economy and agriculture, no known tree does effectually answer the purposes of oak. Orchards I perceive are rare, and confined almost exclusively to the apple. Neither the climate or soil can be chargable with this deficiency; it can only be accounted for in unpardonable neglect. The settlements are, in a considera-

MILES.

—13 ble part recent, improvements will follow the increase of population, wealth, and intelligence.*

* The following is from that very valuable citizen Mr. Ray de Chaumont, and was published in the Mercantile Advertiser of the city of New-York, Nov. 14th, 1818. It will be seen that I have the honor to agree in opinion with Mr. Chaumont, as to the true reason why orchards are not more frequent in the north-west part of the state of New-York. I do not remember to have ever seen condensed in so few words, the various inducements to planting and cultivating orchards, as in this short, appropriate, and judicious address.

' Extract from an Address, pronounced before the Agricultural Society of Jefferson county, at their first annual fair, held at Watertown, Sept. 29, 1818—By J. Le Ray de Chaumont, President of the Society.

" To those who have not been sparing enough of their fencing wood, I would recommend the planting of young hemlock to make hedges. I met with such near Philadelphia, on the farm of Judge Peters, one of the most distinguished agriculturalists of the age, whose example alone must have great weight.

" It was for some time doubted by many whether this country would ever become favorable to the growth of fruit trees. It is true, that in many places, the first attempts were rather unsuccessful: but as those of a later date have proved more fortunate, I believe that all are convinced this early failure was owing to some temporary cause. Perhaps it might have been found in the nature of that part of the soil that lay quite at the surface. Generally, to the depth of from 6 to 10 inches, it is a black mould made by the annual decomposition of the leaves of trees and small vegetables. This mould may be too highly charged with vegetable matter to afford nourishment to fruit trees. At any rate, it has been noticed by many, that though orchards have been planted on such land, and totally failed, yet a new attempt upon the same land, after ploughing several years and warming it with animal manure, has been completely successful. Let this be as it may, it is now well ascertained that few countries in the world are more congenial to the growth of the apple, the plumb, many species of the cherry, and most of the smaller fruits, such as the strawberry, raspberry, and currant, which are found to grow luxuriantly, producing in the greatest abundance. It is much to be regretted that so many have neglected this subject, since the results of late experiments must have effectually removed every doubt as to the success of future attempts. The expense of planting an orchard is trivial, compared with its ad-

MILES.

1—17 *Remsen.*
 A village in the right bank of West Canada creek.
2—19 *L. Hough's.*
3—22 *T. M. Sheldons.*
4—23 *Holman's.*
3—26 *Hawley's.*
1—27 *Skinner's.*
4—31 *Boonville upon the head streams of Black river*

vantages, considering it merely as a source of profit. But the comfortable luxury it affords is of itself a sufficient inducement; and I might further add, if necessary, that a man of spirit would draw encouragement from the circumstance, that a good orchard is the ornament of a farm, and gives the stranger a favorable opinion of the wealth, taste, comfort and economy of the owner, while on the contrary, the sight of a farm destitute of these useful improvements, gives him the idea of barrenness and indolence. Those who have neglected the planting of fruit trees would do well to visit some of the flourishing orchards at a small distance from this village. There they would receive a lively reproof for the past, and great encouragement for amending in future. Some will regret that the owners of those fine orchards have not extended their industry to the cultivation of peach trees. Why would they not grow here, when many years ago a number of those fruits arrived to their due maturity in one of the most northern positions in this country, at the old ferry upon the St Lawrence? But I must give place to a judicious observation made by an experienced gardener lately come into this country. We do not let the the roots of our fruit trees have a sufficient share of cold in the winter. Sometimes, before the ground is sufficiently frozen to reach the most nutritive roots of our fruits trees, the snow falls, and communicates genial warmth to the earth, which, accompanied with the melting snow, starts the vegetation too early. Then come the late frosts, which finding the trees too far advanced, give them a check fatal to their production. The remedy offered is to take away in the early part of the winter, the snow which surrounds the more delicate of your fruit trees, the one for instances which produces the peach, so as to let the roots have their share of the cold. Then let the snow be the cover which will foster this protecting cold till a period more desirable for the vegetation of the tree."

MILES.

.—36 *Sugar river,*

One of the main branches of Black river, flowing with great rapidity to the eastward in the main stream. Secondary limestone, with little admixture of shells, and extremely hard, now forms the base of the country. Timber continues as before noted. The country is very hilly and broken. Black river is in every respect a mountain stream; the tributary waters which form it flow on each side from very elevated land, when compared with the bed of the principal river. Hills rising very abruptly range along to the west of the road, and now at near the middle of May, are pouring down floods formed by melting snow, masses of which are frequently visible from the road, reminding the traveller that the chill of winter is not passed.

2—38 *Village of Leyden.*
2—40 *Leyden Post Office.*
6—46 *House's.*
3—49 *Gulf creek,* a large branch of Black river.
2—51 *Martinsburg,* seat of justice, in and for Lewis county. Here I remained over night, and on the morning of May 12th, recommenced my journey.
4—55 *Louville.*
9—64 *Wright's.*
1—65 *Deer river,*

A considerable and extremely rapid branch of Black river. Its banks and bed schistose limestone, a ledge of which forms a beautiful cascade within fifty yards above the road, which passes the stream at this place over a good substantial wooden bridge. The river has worn a deep channel whose banks are nearly perpendicular. Deer river has its source in the same ridge of hills, which produces Salmon river. The very considerable falls which occur in both streams, prove the great ele-

MILES.
—65 vation of their sources. Salmon river rises, partly in Lewis and partly in Oswego county; its general course is, however, in the latter, running west thirty miles, enters Mexico Bay of lake Ontario, twenty-five miles, a little west of south, from Sacket's Harbour. Beside a number of cataracts of lesser note, this short river has in one instance, a fall of upwards of one hundred feet.

1—66 *T. Campbell's.*
3—69 *Champion Village.*
6—75 *Village of Rutland, Tuttle's tavern.*

This village stands upon a bed of schistose limestone, at the foot of a very high and steep hill. The limestone in many places with a very slight covering. Rising the hill above the village, I had the pleasure to behold an extensive prospect backwards over the country towards Utica. Between Rutland and Watertown, Black river has a large bend or sweep to the northeast, and a circumstance worthy of note, is, that both branches of the Oswegatchie have similar and correspondent bends. This adds another to the numerous proofs afforded by the courses of our rivers, that in their original formation, they were influenced in many instances, by causes which operated over extensive tracts of country, and produced a uniformity which strikes forcibly attentive observers, upon our geological phenomena.

6—81 *Watertown.*

A fine newly built village, on the right bank of Black river, in Jefferson county. A very visible change is now apparent in the soil and timber, and surface of the country. From Utica to Deer river, hemlock swamps are frequent, much of the road passes these swamps, on causeways or round logs, producing very tiresome and tedious travelling. These

MILES.

—81 swamps become rare, since passing Deer river, and before reaching Watertown entirely cease. Oak and hickory now intermixes with the other species of timber trees in the composition of the forests. Hemlock has become scarce. The superstratum of the soil, is a black loam, intermixed with rounded pebbles, resting upon a base of stratafied limestone. Fields of small grain are here visible in every direction, and in many places where the stratum of incumbent soil above the limestone, is so scanty as would seem to preclude culture. Good thriving orchards of apple and pear trees also abound.

At Watertown, Black river has worn a channel into the solid limestone of forty or fifty feet in depth. The river is about sixty yards wide, and has by far the most rapid current of any river, great or small, that I have ever seen; it may, indeed, be considered from its source to its mouth as a chain of rapids, interpersed occasionally with placid intervals, which are compensated by falls, of from 10 to 70 feet perpendicular. Black river is, in point of size, the third stream whose entire course is in the state of New-York. The quantity of water in its current at this season, is no doubt, above the medium of its volume, but at all times this stream must discharge a body of water greater than would be expected from its comparative length on our maps.

4—85 *Brownville.*

Leaving Watertown, the road crosses Black river on a fine wooden bridge, and continues to Brownville along the bank of Black river, over a bed of limestone, in many places naked rock without any vegetable earth, trees often standing upon the smooth surface of the stone, and only prevented

MILES.

—85 from falling by extending their roots between the interstices of the rock.

About half a mile below Watertown, the river rushes over a rapid of more than four hundred yards in length. Lined on both banks by precipices of limestone, upon which, the stream impetuous as it is, can make but a very slow impression. Dashing with apparently irresistible force, the rage of the current is repelled by the rough shelving shores. Where the road passes near this cataract, the river is one sheet of foam, presenting a scene of grandeur much superior to what would be commonly expected from the supposed diminutive volume of water.

The village of Brownville is indebted for not only its name, but its existence also, to that distinguished American general, Jacob Brown, who has his family residence within its precincts. The village is built upon the right bank of Black river. A cataract with a perpendicular fall of 15 or 20 feet, opposite the village, has afforded a very eligible site for mills, which has been improved. A substantial wooden bridge has been extended over Black river above the mills. I passed this place in a heavy rain, and had not so good an opportunity of observing its position as I could have desired. From all I could perceive, the village and the adjacent country exhibited marks of prosperity and rapid improvement.

Black river continues below Brownville its ordinary rapidity for about two miles, where it is lost in the head of the former bay de Nivernois, a small part of which forms the well known Sacket's Harbor.

The road after crossing Brownville bridge, winds

MILES.

—55 about three miles down the valley of Black river, then rises upon the flat table land, and continues five miles farther over a bed of schistose limestone, to the village of

8—93 Sacket's Harbor.

At the time I travelled in this quarter, the public stage stopped at Watertown, and travellers were obliged to hire carriages from individuals. My company and myself were able to procure only open waggons; and as disappointment or any other kind of misfortune seldom comes unattended, the moment we set out from Watertown, commenced a heavy and cold rain, which continued to fall in torrents during our journey of twelve miles to Sacket's Harbor, where we arrived chilly, wet and hungry, at a little after 9 P. M. The village affords very good entertainment, and its cheer was never much more welcome than to the cavalcade of which I made a part.

Yours sincerely.

LETTER VI.

Sacket's Harbor, May 12th, 1815.

DEAR SIR,

BROWNVILLE and Sacket's Harbor, but particularly the latter, have gained both in extent and celebrity by the late war with Great Britain. The residence of the land and naval forces of the United States have been, and continue to be of great advantages to the citizens of Sacket's Harbor. This town stands upon the south-west side of the bay, N. lat.

43°, 50'. W. long. 76°. from London, or 1° east of Washington city. The bay and harbor are both well situated for shelter and defence. It is in some measure, land locked by two large, and some smaller islands, standing in the mouth of the bay eight miles distant to the west, from the village. Chaumont bay, is an embranchment of the same sheet of water which forms the harbour below the mouth of Black river. Chaumont bay does not contain as good anchorage, nor does the position of its shores render it so favourable a site, either as a naval, military, or commercial depot as the bay, now known as Sacket's Harbor. The latter is perhaps one of the best situations in the world for ship building. A narrow and low crescent of land extends from the lower extremity of the village, and forms an inner and outer harbour, the latter within two fathoms of the shore has depth of water for the largest ships of the line, that can be formed. The vessels can be framed on nearly a level with the water, and launched with the greatest ease. The depth of water continues to the mouth of Black river, near which another very excellent position exists for the construction of ships, either of war or commerce. In each of those places of ship architecture, now lie the hull of a first rate man of war. One of which, at Sacket's, the NEW-ORLEANS, I have seen. Before seeing this enormous vessel, I had no idea of the immensity of ship building. Under her stern, I really felt a sentiment of awe, when by an upward glance, I received the wide sweeping and towering arch of her swelling sides. I had seen the Franklin on the stocks, near Philadelphia, and had been frequently on board of that vessel after she was launched; I had been on board of the Independence in the harbour of Boston; and had also seen under sail, the British 74, Plantagenet. All of those ships are large according to their rate, but neither gave me an adequate conception of the immensity of a first rate ship of the line, a conception I never formed, until I traversed, from prow to stern, the New-Orleans. Sunk beneath the surface of the water, the hull of a line of battle ship when launched, is concealed, leaving to view her more shewy, but less substantial upper works, but while on the stocks, the vastness of this intended battery is visible.

The naval officers have erected an immense frame building over the New-Orleans. Under the shelter of a close roof, her timbers will rather gain in quality than deteriorate by time. She now stands, in silent, but in terrible preparation. A stair way leads from her prow, to the highest part of her stern, ending in a railed balcony with seats, from which in one comprehensive prospect is included, the town, barracks, harbour and adjacent shores. An ascent to this singular observatory, is amongst the most interesting treats awaiting the traveller to Sacket's. Captain Woolsey, the commodore upon this station, exercises the most laudable politeness towards strangers; his kindness enabled me to enjoy this, which is one of the most gratifying pleasures of my life.

Very excellent stone barracks stand upon the bank of the bay, about 400 yards east of the village. The material is the blue schistose limestone, which forms the base of the whole adjacent neighborhood. The barracks are in the form of three sides of a parallelogram, enclosing the approaches on the side land, the face towards the bay is open.

May 14th. I had the double pleasure of seeing the barracks, and on their parade a review given in honor of gen. Winfield Scott. Gens. Brown, Scott, and their suits were present. The troops made a very respectable appearance, though the weather was unfavorable for their evolutions.

I would have examined more extensively, the vicinity of Sacket's Harbor, but the season was so continually inclement during my stay, that my excursions were necessarily very limited.

Yours with respect and esteem.

LETTER VII.

Hamilton, May 19th, 1818.

DEAR SIR,

I departed from Sacket's Harbor on Saturday last, and reached this neighborhood on Sunday afternoon. The weather during the voyage, and since my arrival, has been very unfavorable for either extensive or accurate observation. I found one circumstance, however, remarkable; the season is much more forward below than above the Thousand Islands. From Sacket's Harbor to the entrance into the St. Lawrence, the shores presented all the desolation of winter; the birch was the only forest tree that indicated approaching spring. This backwardness continued until we passed the Thousand Islands; below which, though advancing northward, an evident change was visible. The sugar tree, willow, birch, and many shrubs and other vegetables, were in considerable advance. The fields on the Canada shore, from the greater exposure to the sun, were more advanced than those opposite, in New-York.

I have now seen, and navigated part of the surface of the two most majestic rivers of North America; and as far as I have observed, no two streams on earth afford features of more marked contrast. Before visiting its banks, I had always considered the St. Lawrence as commencing opposite Kingston; but the current is not perceptible, until within about ten miles above this village. In many places the river, as it is improperly called, is four or five miles wide, and chequered with islands, of infinite variety of shape and size. In fact, it is a continuation of Lake Ontario ten or twelve miles below Ogdensburg, where the true St. Lawrence begins to flow.

On leaving Sacket's Harbor, the adjacent shores of the main, and those of the islands, are low, and composed of what in geognostic language, is called floetz limestone, admixed with animal exuviæ. The border of the lake is uniformly low, not being elevated above the water more than three or four feet; the *debris* thrown up by the action of the lake, are rounded pebbles of limestone, with a very few fragments of some other kind of stone. The timber, sugar tree, pine, linden, elm, oak, (two or three species, though scarce)—birch, and beech; soil extremely fertile. When at some distance from the shore, the high hills near the source of Black river, and between Utica and Oswego, are seen far inland.

This uniformity remains with but little interruption, until the entrance of St. Lawrence; here the islands are many of them thirty or forty feet elevated above the water.— What is called the Thousand Islands, seems to be a granite chain which crosses the river, and divides its bed into a maze, intricate beyond imagination; a scene more savage, rude, and wild, does not perhaps any where exist on earth. The placid and most purely limpid water, reflects the broken rocks, and the few trees and shrubs that rise amid their fractured ruins. No human habitation appears, to enliven for an instant this picture of eternal waste. Passing this region of silent desolation, a fairy scene opens; a scene that to me was the more delightful, because unexpected. Where the Thousand Islands terminate, the river opens first into a kind of bay, and then in two or three miles again contracts; the shore rising on each bank by a gentle acclivity, presents a country I have never before seen equalled, in respect either to soil or situation. The Ohio, beautiful as are its banks, affords in all its extent, nothing comparable to the banks of St. Lawrence, from the Thousand Islands to this place. The Canada side is by far the best cultivated, and as I have already remarked, possesses the advantages of more exposure to the sun. For many miles the margin of this river appears like a well cultivated garden. The

American or U. S. shore, exhibits rapid improvement, and Ogdensburgh and this place are flourishing new villages. I will write you more at large shortly. Adieu for the present.

May 20th, 1818.

AFTER enclosing the within, and returning to our camp, Major Fraser arrived, in the evening. I accompanied him to this village to-day, and finding that my letter was still on hand, I opened it, to convey to you and Mrs. Darby, the latest news of my proceedings. Gen Porter is not yet arrived, but no doubt will in two or three days. The principal surveyor on the side of Great Britain, has not arrived, but is hourly expected. We will, perhaps, commence business on the boundary line, in the ensuing week.

The season continues unpleasant, and though rain does not fall in any great quantities, it is frequent. The river St. Lawrence is about two feet perpendicular above its ordinary level, and slowly rising, and will no doubt fall as slowly. Notwithstanding, however, the chilly air produced by so much moisture, spring advances daily, and promises a season more pleasant. The atmosphere, and the present state of vegetation, have a remarkable resemblance to similar phenomena in lower Louisiana, early in March. From what I have seen, I have no doubt but that June and July are here, as every where else in North America, the most agreeable months in the year

LETTER VIII.

Ogdensburgh, June 28, 1818.

You have, no doubt, seen in the public prints some statements respecting a man of the name of Gourlay, who is now making a political tour through the Canadas. The day before yesterday, a township meeting was called directly opposite our camp, which terminated in a riot, in which Mr. Gourlay was severely beaten. I have not been able to learn, with any certainty, what object this man has in view; no doubt, however, but more is meant than meets the eye. He is not long from England. If any symptoms of revolution should appear in these provinces, the exciting cause must be in Europe. Neither the population or position of the country, are suited to contend with the British Government, unless the other parts of the empire were also in a revolutionary state.

The inhabitants of Canada appear to be very happy and contented with their situation, and with their government generally. What they could gain by a revolution in the present order of things, I must confess I cannot comprehend.

The commerce carried on upon the St. Lawrence is immensely greater than we in the United States commonly believe. The single article of lumber must employ very considerable numbers. Rafts are passing almost constantly. Flour and many other articles are exported to a very great amount. The entire line of the Canada side of the river from Montreal and even from Quebec, is well peopled and cultivated.

Since writing the above, I have seen a National Intelligencer, containing some notices of Gourlay, and explaining who he is and from whence he originated. The substance of this communication is no doubt true, and obliges me to believe that, as I have before stated, there is more than meets the eye in this business. The magistrates of Upper Canada are much at a loss to know how they ought to proceed.*

* This embarrassment does not seem to have been removed, as will be seen by the following extracts from the proceedings of the Colonial legislature of Upper Canada. From the expressions used by the governor in his address, he has viewed the operations of Gourlay as a serious affair, and so it may become, if any very coercive remedy is applied. The governor and his council express respect for the constitutional right of petition, and they are correct in their cautionary proceedings on that subject: any open attempt to abridge the liberty of remonstrance might lead to a recurrence to the last resource of the oppressed. A law of *prevention* may operate by inflaming the malady it will be intended to cure.

York, (U. C.) Oct. 20. The speech of the governor, sir Peregrine Maitland, on the opening of the parliament of Upper Canada, contains the following paragraph in relation to the convention.

" In the course of your investigation you will, I doubt not, feel a just indignation at the attempt which has been made to excite discontent, and to organize sedition Should it appear to you that a convention of delegates cannot exist without danger to the constitution, in framing a law of prevention, your dispassionate wisdom will be careful that it shall not unwarily trespass on that sacred right of the subject to seek a redress of his grievances by petition "

To this passage, the legislative council made the following reply

" We shall at all times feel a just indignation at every attempt which may excite discontent or organize sedition, and if it shall appear to us that a convention of delegates cannot exist without danger to the constitution, in framing a law of prevention, we will be careful that this shall not, unwarily, trespass on the sacred right of the subject, to seek a redress of his grievances by petition "

To the same paragraph, the commons house of assembly reply as follows

" We feel a just indignation at the systematic attempts that have been made to excite discontent and organize sedition in this happy colony, whilst the usual and constitutional mode of appeal for real or supposed grievances has ever been open to the people of this province, never refused or even appealed to, and

My opportunity of observing either the political or moral situation of the people of Canada, has been too limited to enable me to form a very correct opinion upon their views; but from all I have seen or heard, I am inclined to consider, that the temper of the people of Canada is much the same as that of the inhabitants of the colonies, which formed the present United States, previous to their secession from the parent state. Whilst Great Britain, continues to exercise moderation towards her colonies in Canada, so long her power over them will remain unimpaired. Any exertion of authority, however, that will in any manner compromit the rights of the Canadians, will dissolve the spell, that prescriptive habit has formed between the rulers and the ruled. The history of Great Britain would hardly justify an expectation, that the political proceedings of its government, will be conducted prudently, in all cases, towards any people subjected to her power. We would risk little in supposing, that some indiscreet ministry will repeat towards Canada similar folly to that which severed from the mother country the United States. As matters now stand, a serious rupture cannot be expected, nor would be prudent on either side.

There is another light, in which the people of Canada offer an interesting spectacle to those of the United States; that is an approaching union or rivalry. In either case, the latter people will be greatly affected by the former. Though speaking the same language, enjoying a similar system of

deeply lament that the insidious designs of one factious individual should have succeeded in drawing into the support of his vile machinations so many honest men and loyal subjects to his majesty. We remember that this favored land was assigned to our fathers as a retreat for suffering loyalty, and not a sanctuary for sedition. In the course of our investigation, should it appear to this house that a convention of delegates cannot exist without danger to the constitution, in framing a law of prevention, we will carefully distinguish between such convention and the lawful act of the subject in petitioning for a redress of real or imaginary grievances, that sacred right of every British subject which we will ever hold inviolable."

jurisprudence, and regulated in their private conduct by the same religion, yet in political opinion, a wide difference exists between the Canadians and the people of the United States. In the latter country, one generation has passed away since the memorable revolution, that gave them national birth; the men that now act upon the theatre of public affairs have been bred republicans, and such they are in custom, manners and form. The Canadians have been educated, at the same time, in the highest tone of royalty. One party views the trappings of regal pageantry with contempt, the other considers attempered monarchy, as the surest guarantee of private right. Both have a strong sense of human dignity, both consider governments instituted for the protection, and not oppression of society; both feel the *amor patria* with all its force.

If Canada was by any means made an integral of the United States, and like Louisiana, given a legislative equality in the national councils, the force of the preconceived opinions of its inhabitants would soon be felt. By a singular inconsistency, the men who in our last war with Great Britain, were anxious for a conquest of Canada, were also, as a party, those who had every thing to fear from the accomplishment of their own wishes. In case of union, it demands but little foresight to anticipate the consequence.

Many citizens of the United States will smile at the suggestion of rivalry, between their country and Canada. Forty-three years ago, so smiled the ministry of Great Britain. The march of time, and the developement of events, have taught the administration of that haughty government, a lesson of bitter experience. I wish our nation may profit, by one of the most astonishing events in human history; an event that gave it a name on earth, and an event that ought to convince the world, how little dependance there is in the stability of comparative power. Every year gives me more and more scepticism, respecting worldly wisdom. Accident seems to disturb and influence, if not regulate the progress of nations.

The world at this moment, presents very nearly the same evidence that has been given by every country and every age, that wisdom and foresight but rarely have much influence, in producing extensive revolutions. So much depends upon circumstances, beyond all our powers of calculation, that in almost every instance of human history, the events have been productive of consequences, directly contrary to prediction. A few, and a very limited few, have ever possessed talent enough, to form correct estimates of the real bearing of great commotions among mankind. Effects are continually mistaken for causes.

If we date the civilization of those nations from whom we are descended, and from whom we have derived our arts and opinions, from the discovery of the alphabet, there will be exhibited a period of about thirty centuries of accumulated experience. Precepts have been deduced from example, with how little fruit the present moral condition of man, is a melancholy proof. There are many irrefragible reasons, however, to convince an unprejudiced mind, that this apparent hopeless depression of the human intellect, has been produced from causes that admit removal. The exalted elevation of the human understanding, in the principles of many sciences, would warrant the induction, that if ever the most valuable of all sciences, happiness, could be duly comprehended, the means to secure it would become attainable. Hitherto we have been taught to consider our social state, as a remediless scene of suffering. We have bartered the certainty of happiness on earth, for lessons of metaphysics, upon the principles of which no two of our teachers have ever been of accord. We have given the sweat of our brow, to the most idle and useless of our species, and have received stripes and contumely in exchange. We have divided our attention between the wretchedness of the thousand and the glitter of the one. Our ears have been assailed with the cries of hunger and slavery, or regaled with the orgies of pampered luxury.

Let no one deny the truth of the above, and bring the United States as an example of its fallacy. The people of the United States form a very small part of the human family, and are themselves far from being improved to the utmost, or *absolutely* secured against retrogradation. They nevertheless afford evidence of an entire change in opinion, a change against which sceptres and mitres will in vain contend. Europe has by no means recovered from the consequences of the fall of the Roman Empire. Afflicting as it may be, it is a fact, there exists not one well coalesced government in Europe, except France. No other political association, but is composed of shreds of heterogeneous materials, either in a state of anarchy or forced connexion. Nothing has appeared to shew that the monarchs of the day have any adequate conception of producing any better state of things.

It may not be irrelevant to our subject, to view the nations of Europe as they now stand, in relative numbers. To gain any philosophical result, language must be the line of division and comparison; it is the only durable mark of distinction. At this time there are in Europe about thirty millions who speak French; thirty millions who speak German and its dialects; between thirty-five and forty millions who speak Sclavonian and its dialects; twenty millions who use the Italian; fifteen millions of English; about an equal number of Spaniards and of modern Greeks. The Turks, though in Europe for upwards of 350 years, are still foreigners, and few in number.

It is singular that, except the French, none of the nations of Europe are formed out of, and contain masses who speak the same language. The political divisions have arose from blind chance, or the people have been driven together by violence. The art of government, as directed towards its only legitimate ends, the security, protection, and instruction of the great body of nations, is not even in its infancy; as a science it exists not. This is a bold, but unfortunately true assertion. The feudal system reigns in all its pristine strength, as far as the abstract science of government is concerned.

There appears to have been a curious mixture of superstition and ferocity in the character of the northern nations, who overcame the Roman Empire. Either employed in acts of cruelty, or piety—building churches or castles. From this bent of the human mind, has arisen the principle, that produced the present corporate establishments of Europe. Every thing bends either to religion or war. Schools, colleges, and academies, are directed either by soldiers or priests. The revenues of the various states, are expended on schemes of ambition, or paid to men who are worse than idle.

Whole nations, the same in language, customs, manners, and dress, are kept artfully in a state of hostility; such as the Germans, Italians, and now the English. Nations who differ in every respect, have no common interest, are strangers to each other, and who by a difference of language, are prevented from forming any tie of sympathy, are united under one monarch; such are the Germans, Bohemians, and Hungarians; such are the Italians and Germans; such are the Dutch and Belgians; such the English, Irish, and Scotch; such are the Russians, Poles, and Finns, and such are the Turks and modern Greeks.

With such systems of government, can any wonder be excited that hatred and contempt should prevail every where. The people are kept in a state of profound ignorance of their rights, have long abandoned any conception of asserting that, *for* them were all governments instituted, and *by* them ought all governments to be administered. A haughty aristocracy, and cringing hierarchy, possess the execution and fruits of power; the creator of the goods of life, the farmer and artisan, depressed, wretched and poor, have retained the possession of scarce enough of the things they themselves have made, to preserve existence.

The truth of this picture cannot be denied. It may seem difficult to account for such gross ignorance, such apathy, and such forbearance in society; but when the sources from which the instruction of the people are examined, the phenomenon of their degradation vanishes. That German should be arrayed against German; Italian against Italian, and English against English, and that the most enlightened nations of the globe in many other respects, should in the most important of all their concerns, moral government, be still in the most barbarous state, cannot excite astonishment, when it is known how little has been done to instruct, and how much to brutify man.

A few, an invaluable few have existed in Europe, who have labored silently to raise the species from their wretched state, have endeavored to inspire men with ideas of their own dignity, and have been rewarded with persecution from the rulers, and neglect from the ruled. Speculators, innovators, infidels, and all the vocabulary of abuse, have been lavished upon their heads; even the word philosophy itself, has been changed to an epithet, and applied to the most wise and benevolent plans.

The struggle between good sense and power, has continued with daily increasing violence, since the invention of printing. How this contest is to terminate, it is now difficult to predict: but such is the powerful aid given to reason by the press, that the best result may be hoped. The French revolution was nothing more than an effect of this long opposition of prescriptive usurpation, against a relinquishment of power. Those who view the triumph of despotism as complete, know little of human nature, and less of the ordinary course of things in the world. Every symptom evinces an approaching storm, of perhaps tenfold more violence, than the one so lately abated. That the potentates of Europe will be compelled to accede to the wishes of their subjects, and participate, rather than engross the sovereign authority, or again defend their antique rule by the sword, is very certain. Whether, after long and reiterated abortive attempts, the gross of society will crouch to an Asiatic principle of *divine right*, or succeed in forming more rational, and of course more stable forms of government, will be soon determined.

Upon this approaching whirlwind, the people of the United States look with their accustomed indifference, little aware how much their own affairs must be influenced by the issue. Living under a form of government, having many of the most seductive features of the feudal system, we are far from having any other guarantee than our own prudence, against the ordinary ill effects that have been experienced in every instance, where that system has been tried. In our state, and confederated governments, we are feudal in a high degree. If not prevented by a train of extremely fortunate events, our posterity must one day find, that neither similarity of language or opinion, can secure them against the consequences of ambition, pride and violence. Religious or moral precepts, are but feeble barriers against the evil propensities of the human heart. We have, however, two insuperable advantages, that do more for our security than our so much boasted institutions —the PRESS and FREE SUFFRAGE. Whilst legislators and rulers can be dragged before society, and adjudged without evasion, so long will our institutions remain inviolate, and their provisions applied to the intended purpose; but when the right of suffrage is retrenched, and when, if so deplorable an event ever does occur in our history, our *press* is subjected to the control of rulers, then, in crimes, deception, pride, and degradation; in insolence and tears, our posterity will continue to exhibit the same disgusting picture that human nature has afforded, since its acts have been first put on record.

There now exists two English nations, who are, with all their moral resemblance, politically separate, and opposed to each other in views of commerce and national power: and to these may be added another, in Canada. And on this continent, may also be repeated the violent contention of two fragments of a congenerous people. Whether the rivalry or forced union, would be the greatest source of mutual injury, can scarce be made a question. With a very limited share of forbearance, it would be infinitely preferable, for the happiness of each party, to remain independent; and should the folly, ambition, or cupidity of either or both, involve them in national disputes, the transitory evil of war, could not be much worse than that of perpetual mistrust, the necessary consequence of a connection without unity of sentiment.

Canada, with the other British possessions in North America, exhibit, in one respect, a singular contrast with their former colonies along the Atlantic coast. At the moment of their revolt, the thirteen original states of our confederacy, extended in a long, narrow, and very accessible strip, nearly parallel to the shores of the Atlantic ocean. The inhabited parts of Cabotia, or British North America,* on the contrary, presents a very confined and unapproachable front towards the ocean, with an immense line winding far into the interior of the continent. From its local position, if safe from an attack in flank, a much less force would be able to defend Canada, than was necessary to preserve the independence of the United States.

Presenting, in common with the United States, a long and apparently an exposed and weak line of frontier, yet even on that side, the Canadas have been found very defensible: but in front, towards the Atlantic, this country would be extremely difficult to attack successfully. No doubt the day is approaching, when a trial must be made, how far this people are capable of maintaining their claim to nationality.

* Cabotia, in honor of Cabot the original discoverer, is the very appropriate name given by the British geographers, to the vast regions claimed upon this continent by the British crown

You will naturally feel some surprise, at the little notice I have taken of the circumstance of the diversity of nations, which compose the population of the Canadas. In my opinion, that diversity is not of much consequence, in the view we are taking of this country. The descendants of the French do, particularly in Lower Canada, form a large part of the mass of society, but in Upper Canada, and the eastern provinces of Nova Scotia and New Brunswick, the offspring or natives of the British islands, are more numerous than all other classes of society taken together; and in all parts of the British colonies in this quarter, are not only the ruling but the efficient people. At present the French are generally passive, though no doubt in a great measure disposed, if any probability of success offered, to oppose in concert with the other inhabitants, the British government, and will follow the current of events, flow as it may. Active and gallantly, as did the French of Louisiana conduct themselves during the British invasion of that country, and with all their habitual hatred of the British name, I saw enough to convince me, that their conduct would have been very passive, had not gen. Jackson acted with uncommon inspiring energy. Indeed, if I know the French character correctly, the very striking contrast it often exhibits, between extraordinary decision and passiveness, is not confined to the descendants of that nation, in either Louisiana or Canada.

Detesting as I do all conquest, not rendered imperatively necessary for self security, I would always consider an attempt on the part of the United States to conquer Canada, as in the highest degree impolitic; and in any incorporation, without the free consent of the people, excessively unjust. It is a conquest, however, that the British officers seem to consider an object of national policy, on the part of our government. Mr. Bouchette, in his work on the Canadas, page 491, observes that "The views of the United States, " with respect to Canada have been too unequivocally de-" monstrated to leave a shadow of uncertainty, as to their

" ultimate object ; and as the preservation of this valuable
" colony has always been deemed worthy of our strenuous
" efforts, we cannot be too much on our guard against the
" slow working policy, by which that government endeavors
" to compass its ends, or too heedful in adopting precaution-
" ary measures to avert a threatening danger, however re-
" mote it may at first appear."

Bouchette is a respectable writer, and a native of Canada ; he, it appears, has been, however, either deceived, as it respects the real views of the United States, or he charges our government with what, if true, would be gross folly. Canada, with all its loyalty, has been rather a charge than a beneficiary appendage to Great Britain ; to the republican institutions of the United States, it would be a dead weight. Our empire is already too extensive to be easily governed, if the whole surface was well peopled. An accession of territory with reluctant or refractory citizens, would be worse than an unprofitable incumbrance. Adieu.

LETTER IX.

Ogdensburgh, July 17th, 1818.

Dear Sir,

The Commissioners are advancing with the survey of the St. Lawrence river, and its islands, in order to designate the boundary line, between the United States and Upper Canada. The operations of last year terminated about a mile above Ogden's Island, opposite the village of Hamilton, where we commenced this season, and have progressed to a little above this village. The survey is conducted with great precision, but with a consequent slowness, that is extremely incompatible with my views, and induces me, together with some other reasons, to quit the business and proceed on a tour to the westward, through New-York, Pennsylvania, Ohio, Michigan, and Upper Canada. I expect to set out in the Steam Boat to-morrow, on my way to Sacket's Harbor, and Buffalo, and Detroit.

I have already mentioned to you, in a former communication, that the St. Lawrence, properly speaking, commences near this town, as above this place a very slight current is perceptible. I have been engaged in surveying the Gallop rapids and islands, at the head of which the strong currents first commences. A map of this very curious group is enclosed, which will serve to exhibit the peculiar construction of the St. Lawrence islands

Whenever I attempt a general or detailed description of this beautiful river, I feel the difficulty of the undertaking, from its dissimilarity to any other stream with which you are acquainted. I doubt indeed, if it has any near parallel upon our globe. Though I may not succeed in giving you any very precise conceptions of its more minute features, I hope to place before you such a picture of its general physiognomy, as will enable you, with your accustomed force of fancy, to form an adequate idea of its great outline. Though in compliance with the common mode of expression, I call the St. Lawrence a river, yet according to the principles laid down, when speaking of the Hudson, the former stream would be more correctly a strait, uniting the great lakes to the Atlantic ocean, than a river, in the strict meaning of that term. Since my arrival on the boundary, I have several times had arguments with different members of the commission, respecting the comparative volume of the St. Lawrence and the Mississippi rivers. In my statistics of Louisiana, I have calculated the quantity of water discharged by the Mississippi. I shall now for your satisfaction institute a general estimate of, and comparison between those two great North American rivers. I have already premised that when speaking of the quantity of water in, or land drained by the Mississippi and St. Lawrence rivers, all the country is meant, which is watered by their tributary branches.

The following table exhibits the area of the different sections of country, drained by the St. Lawrence.

TABLE

OF THE SUPERFICIES, DRAINED BY THE VALLEY OF THE ST. LAWRENCE RIVER.

	Medial Length	Medial Breadth	Area Sq. Miles
Region lying N. W. of Lake Superior,	300	80	24,000
do. north east of do	400	80	32,000
North of Lake Huron, and west of the sources of the Ottawas river,	200	200	40,000
Peninsula between Lakes Huron, Erie, and Ontario,	200	80	16,000
North-west of St. Lawrence, below the sources of the Ottawas river,	700	220	154,000
Total area N. W. of St. Lawrence,			266,000
Region N. E. of the St. Lawrence, from its mouth to that of the Richelieu,	500	50	25,000
Triangle included between Black, St. Lawrence, and Richelieu rivers,	230	50	16,500
South of Lake Ontario, west of Black river,	200	80	16,000
South-east and south of Lake Erie, and east of Maumee river,	300	30	9,000
Peninsula of Michigan,	250	150	37,500
West of Lake Michigan, and south of Lake Superior,	400	120	48,000
Total south-east and south-west,			418,000
Area of Lake Superior,	300	100	30,000
Huron,	200	100	20,000
Michigan,	270	50	13,500
Erie,	250	60	15,000
Ontario,	180	40	7,200
Allowance for the area of St. Lawrence river, and the smaller lakes,			1,500
			87,200

SUMMARY.

	Square Miles
Total area north-west of St. Lawrence river,	266,000
Total south-east and south-west of do.	152,000
Total covered with water,	87,200
Total area of St. Lawrence valley,	505,200

TABLE

OF THE SUPERFICIES, DRAINED BY THE MISSISSIPPI AND ITS TRIBUTARY BRANCHES.

	Medial Length	Medial Breadth	Area Sq. Miles
Valley of Ohio,	700	300	206,000
do. of the Mississippi proper, above the mouth of Missouri,	750	300	225,000
do. of the Missouri and its confluents,	1350	500	575,000
do. of Arkansaw river,	1100	100	110,000
do. of Red River,	1000	100	100,000
Narrow strip east of the Mississippi, and below the mouth of Ohio	400	70	28,000
Valleys of White and St. Francis rivers,	200	250	50,000
Total area of the Mississippi valley,			1,394,000

Before leaving New-York, and when employed in writing the Emigrant's Guide, I carefully measured and calculated the respective superficies, drained by the St. Lawrence and Mississippi rivers. The former came so near to 500,000 square miles, that I assumed that area in round numbers; re-measuring the same stream by sections, the result is, as you perceive. At the same period I also measured the Mississipi, and found its area varied so little from 1,400,000 square miles, that I assumed that number as sufficiently accurate for general purposes. Calculating again by sections, I found 1,394,000 square miles. From these various estimates. I am confident that neither of these surfaces are essentially incorrect, as far as our maps are entitled to confidence.

The outline of the two streams are respectively as follows: that of the St. Lawrence 3,500, that of the Mississippi 5,600. Of these distances the two rivers have interlocking branches, from the head of the Allegany branch of Ohio, to the sources of the Mississippi and Lake Superior, which following the sinuosities of the dividing line, stretch along 1,300 miles.

Rising from the same vast table land, and having such extended connexion, it is surely worthy of remark, that no two rivers on earth so essentially differ in their general features, as do the Mississippi and St. Lawrence. The former is turbid, in many parts to muddings, the latter unequally limpid. One river is composed of an almost unbroken chain of lakes, the other in all its vast expanse, has no lakes that strictly deserve the name. Annually, the Mississippi overleaps its bed and overwhelms the adjacent shores to a great extent; an accidental rise of three feet in the course of fifty years, is considered an extraordinary swell of the waters of St. Lawrence; this circumstance has occurred the present season, for the first time within the lapse of forty years past. The Mississippi flowing from north to south, passes through innumerable climes; whilst its rival, winding from its source in a south-east direction to near N. lat. 44, turns gradually north-east, and again flows into its original climate of ice and snow. The Mississippi before its final discharge into the gulph of Mexico, divides into a number of branches, having their separate egress; the St. Lawrence imperceptibly expands to a wide bay, which finally opens into the gulph of the same name. The banks of the Mississippi present a level, scarce rising above the superior surface of that stream; those of the St. Lawrence, by a gentle acclivity, exhibit the opposing sides of an elegant basin. Much of the surface, watered by the Mississippi, is a region of grass, where few shrubs or trees rise to break the dull monotony of the face of the earth: the shores that bound the St. Lawrence are, when in a state of nature, covered with an almost continuous and impervious forest. And last, though rather an accidental than a natural distinction, the Mississippi rolls its mighty volume, swelled by more than a thousand rivers, through one empire, and is, as I once before observed, " the largest stream on this globe, whose entire course lies within one sovereignty." The St Lawrence is, for more than thirteen hundred miles, a national limit, and as such, marked with the sanguinary points which distinguish the bounds of rival power. Both rivers have a name in the hearts of the people of the United States, upon both have their arms been wreathed with never fading laurels.

Mr. Bouchette, page 32 of his topographical description of Canada, commences a description of St. Lawrence, which from the extensive local knowledge of this author, is no doubt the best notice of this river that has yet been published to the world. I am ignorant whether you have read Mr. Bouchette's statistics or not; from its voluminous size, it is a scarce and expensive work in the United States. As it would not be in my power to give so extensive, or except in a small part, so accurate a picture of this remarkable stream, I have sent you a copy of Mr. Bouchette's description, with occasional notes from myself, which together will, I trust, convey a tolerable comprehensive view of the most singular object in North American hydrography.

" The river St. Lawrence, (which from its first discovery in 1565, has been called by the inhabitants of the country, to mark its pre-eminence, the Great river,) receives nearly all the rivers, which have their sources in the extensive range of mountains to the northward, called the Land's Height, that separates the waters falling into Hudson's Bay still further to the north, from those that descend into the Atlantic; and all those that rise in the ridge which commences on its southern bank, and runs nearly south-westerly, until it falls upon Lake Champlain. Of these, the principal ones are the Ottawa, Musquinonge, St. Maurice, St. Ann, Jacques Cartier, Saguenay, Betsiamites, and Map couagan on the north; and the Salmon river, Chateaugay, Chambly or Richelieu, Yamaska, St. Francis, Becancour, Du Chene, Chaudiere, and Du Loup, on the south. In different parts of its course it is known under different appellations; thus, as high up from the sea as Montreal, it is called St. Lawrence; from Montreal to Kingston in Upper Canada, it is called the Cataraqui, or Iroquois;* (Cataraqui was the Indian name for the river Iroquois, the name given by the French to the six nations) between lake Ontario and lake Erie, it is called Niagara river; between lake Erie and lake St. Clair, the Detroit; between lake St Clair and lake Huron, the river St. Clair; and between lake Huron and lake Superior, the distance is called the Narrows, or the falls of St. Mary forming thus an uninterrupted connexion of 2000 miles. Lake Superior, without the aid of any great effort of imagination, may be considered as the inexhaustible spring from whence, through unnumbered ages, the St. Lawrence has continued to derive its ample stream. I am not aware that the source of this river has thus been defined before; but examining the usual mode of tracing large rivers from their heads to the estuaries, I venture to believe that I am warranted in adopting the hypothesis. This immense lake, unequalled in magnitude by any collection of fresh water on the globe, is almost of a triangular form; its greatest length is 381, its breadth 161, and its circumference little less than

* Col Ogilvie, the British commissioner on the boundary, informed the author of these letters, that in the old deeds to land granted by the French, soon after their settlement in Canada, the now Ottawa was then called the St Lawrence; but custom has changed this nomenclature. The Ottawa has reassumed its Indian name, whilst Cataraqui has been superceded by the French term St Lawrence.

1152 miles; and as remarkable for the unrivalled transparency of its waters, as for its extraordinary depth. Its northern coast, indented with many extensive bays is high and rocky; but on the southern shore the land is generally low and level; a sea almost of itself, it is subject to many vicissitudes of that element, for here the storm rages, and the billows break with a violence scarcely surpassed by the tempests of the ocean. In the distant range of mountains that forms the Land's Height, beyond its northern and western shores, several considerable rivers, and numerous small ones have their rise, which being increased in their course by many small lakes, finally discharge themselves into lake Superior. To the southward also there is another lofty range, dividing the waters that find their way to the Gulf of Mexico, through the channel of the Mississippi, from those that take a northern course into the great lake; so that its vastness is increased by the tributary streams of more than thirty rivers. On its north and north-east sides there are several islands, of which one, called Isle Royale is the largest, being one hundred miles long and forty broad. Out of Lake Superior a very rapid current is interrupted and broken by several small islands, or rather huge masses of rock, through a channel of twenty seven miles in length, at the end of which it flows into lake Huron. The Falls of St Mary are nearly midway between the two lakes; this denomination, though generally given, but little accords with the usual appellation of Falls, as applied to the descent of large bodies of water precipitated from great heights, that so frequently occur on the rivers of America;* for in this place, it is only the impetuous stream

---

* The French term, *saut*, literally jump, or leap, from the verb *sauter*, to jump or leap, answers rather to the English noun *rapid*, than to an actual perpendicular *fall* of water. The French noun *chute*, is indifferently applied to either a *fall* or *rapid*, but also, more correctly to the latter; *cataract* signifies the same sense in both languages.

of the enormous discharge from lake Superior, forcing its way through a confined channel, and breaking with proportionate violence among the impediments that nature has thrown in its way; yet this scene of tumultuous and unceasing agitation of the waters, combined with the noise and dazzling whiteness of the surge, is not deficient either in grandeur or magnificence."

"Lake Huron, in point of extent, yields but little to Lake Superior, its greatest length from west to east is 218 statute miles: at its western extremity it is less than one hundred, and at about one hundred miles from its eastern shore, barely sixty miles broad; but near the centre it suddenly bends away southward, to the breadth of one hundred and eighty miles; measuring the circumference through all its curvatures, will give a distance of little less than 812 miles; in shape it is exceedingly irregular, yet, with a little assistance from fancy, may be fashioned into something like a triangular. From its western side an extensive series, called the Manatoulin Islands, stretches in an easterly direction for one hundred and sixty miles; many of them measuring from twenty to thirty miles in length, by ten, twelve, and fifteen in breadth, on some of which the land rises into elevations of considerable height. Besides this great chain, there are many others of inferior dimensions, numerously grouped in various parts, rendering the navigation intricate, and in some places, and particularly towards the west end, dangerous. On this lake also, the navigation is often assailed by violent storms, attended with thunder and lightning, more terrific than in any other part of North America. At the western angle of lake Huron is lake Michigan, which, although distinguished by a separate name, can only be considered as a part of the former, deepening into a bay of 262 miles in length by sixty-five in breadth, and whose entire circumference is 731 miles. Between it and Lake Huron there is a peninsula that, at the widest part, is 150 miles, along which, and round the bottom of Michigan, runs part of the chain forming the Land's Height, to the southward; from whence descend many large and numerous inferior streams that discharge into it.* On the north side of lake Huron, many rivers of considerable size run from the Land's Height down to it. One of them, called French river, communicates with lake Nipissing, from whence a succession of smaller ones, connected by short portages, opens an intercourse with the Ottawa river, that joins the St. Lawrence near Montreal.† On the eastern extremity of the lake is

---

*The peninsula between lakes Michigan, Huron, St. Clair and Erie, and the rivers St. Clair and Detroit, now forms the Michigan Territory. It is confidently asserted by many, that, at high floods a communication does exist between lake Michigan and Illinois river. If this assumption be well founded, it affords one of the most astonishing hydrographical anomalies on earth. It has long since been determined that the surface of lake Erie is 565 feet above the level of tide water in the Hudson river at Albany. The difference of level between lakes Erie and Michigan by the descent of the rivers Detroit and St. Clair, cannot exceed twenty-nine feet, if so much. Detroit is 26, and St. Clair river 52 miles in length, and allowing six inches per mile for the perpendicular fall of both rivers, is an ample estimate of their aggregate descent. This computation would yield 594 feet as the elevation of the surface of lakes Huron and Michigan above the Atlantic tides; and if the hypothesis be founded on correct data, of a counter current from the Illinois river into Michigan lake, and vice versa, then the point of separation of those currents is equi-elevated above the level of the gulfs of St. Lawrence and Mexico, and would divide this continent into two vast though unequal islands. Baron Humboldt has established the fact of the existence of a similar interlocutory communication between the waters of the Orenoco and Amazon rivers; and I have in these letters, upon the respectable authority of Mr. Isaac Briggs, published the fact that the waters of the Upper Mohawk do, when swelled by floods, flow partly down the Mohawk and partly down the Oneida rivers.

† It has already been stated, upon the authority of Col. Ogilvie, that the original French term St. Lawrence was continued above Montreal by the stream of the Ottawa. Mr. Bouchette unequivocally establishes the transposition of names, to which I have before alluded.

The Ottawa is a very large and impetuous stream flowing out of the mountains which wind north of lake Huron. The general

the Machedash river, which, though another succession of lakes, separated only by one short portage, establishes a communication by lake Simcoe, Holland river, and Yonge-

course of the Ottawa is tolerably well known, as the traders from Montreal frequently follow that river in prosecuting their voyages to the north-west. For the distance of three hundred miles from its source, the course of the Ottawa is south east to where it approaches within sixty miles of Kingston in Upper Canada; it then assumes a course a little north of east, and flowing in that direction about 200 miles joins the St Lawrence by the lake of the Two Mountains above Montreal. The volume contained in, and discharged by the Ottawa, is immense; few if any rivers on earth of an equal length equal this stream in quantity of water. It is extremely interrupted by rapids and falls, frequently chequered by islands and dilated into lakes of a considerable extent. Settlements have been made upon the Ottawa along both banks between 100 and 200 miles above its mouth; much of the soil is very fertile, and supplied with inexhaustible forests of various kinds of timber.

It has been generally believed that the Ottawa was the largest branch of St Lawrence, but Mr Bouchette gives that rank to the Saguenay; his description of the latter river is in the following words. "The *river Saguenay* which discharges itself into the St Lawrence, at *Pointe aux Allouettes*, is the largest of all the streams that pay their tribute to the *Great river*. It draws its source from lake St John, a collection of waters of considerable expanse, lying in N. lat. 48° 20' W. long 72° 30' receiving many large rivers that flow from the north and north west, from an immense distance in the interior, of which the Piecouganns, the Sable, and the Panboaca are the principal ones. At its eastern extremity two large streams, one called the Great Discharge, and the other the Kinogami, or Land river, issue from it; which, after flowing about 57 miles, and encompassing a tract of land of the mean breadth of twelve miles, unite their waters, and become the irresistible SAGUENAY; from which point it continues its course in an easterly direction for about 100 miles down to the St. Lawrence. The banks of this river throughout its course are very rocky and immensely high, varying from 170 even to 340 yards above the stream. Its current is broad, deep, and uncommonly vehement. In some places where precipices intervene, there are falls from fifty to sixty feet in height, down which the whole volume of the stream rushes with indescribable fury and tremendous noise. The general breadth of the river is from two miles and a half to three miles; but at its mouth the distance is contracted to about one mile. The depth of this enormous

street, with the town of York, now called the capital of Upper Canada: this route would most materially shorten the distance between the upper and lower lakes, and is capable of such improvement, as would render it highly beneficial to Upper Canada,* a subject that will be hereafter adverted to

stream is also extraordinary. At its discharge, attempts have been made to find its bottom, with five hundred fathoms of line, but without effect; about two miles higher up, it has been repeatedly sounded from one hundred and thirty to one hundred and forty fathoms; and from sixty to seventy miles from the St. Lawrence, its depth is found from fifty to sixty fathoms. The course of the river, notwithstanding its magnitude, is very sinuous, owing to many projecting points from each shore. The tide runs about 70 miles up it, and upon account of the obstructions occasioned by the numerous promontories, the ebb is much later than in the St. Lawrence; in consequence of which, at low water in the latter, the force of the descending stream of the Saguenay is felt for several miles. Just within the mouth of the river, opposite to Pointe aux Allouettes, is the harbor of Tadoussac, which is very well sheltered by the surrounding high lands, and has good anchorage for a great number of vessels, of a large size, where they may lie in perfect safety. On the northern shore of the St. Lawrence, and at many places on the Saguenay, there are stations for trading with the Indians for peltry, and for carrying on the whale, seal, porpoise, and salmon fishery; these are known by the name of King's Posts, and are now let, with all their privileges, to the North West Company at Quebec, on a lease at a thousand and twenty-five pounds per annum. An establishment is maintained at Tadoussac, at Chicoutami, on the Saguenay, at Lake St. John, at Les Isles de Jeremie, near Betsiamitis point, at the Seven Islands, beyond Cap des Monts Peles, and at Cap des Monts. At those towards the sea the fisheries are pursued during the summer, and at the interior ones the fur trade is carried on with the Indians during the winter. About the trading post at Chicoutami the land is tolerably fertile, and the timber of a superior quality. In the little agriculture that is here paid attention to, it has been observed that grain ripens sooner than it does in the vicinity of Quebec, although the situation [of the former place] is much further to the northward. Another of the many anomalies that distinguish the climate of Canada.'   [*Bouchette's Canada, page* 563–566

* In the progress of population along the border of the Canadian lakes, an open water route from New-York to the eastern angle of lake Huron, will no doubt be formed, and will more se-

From the extremity of Lake Huron to the southward, the course of the waters are contracted into a river (called St. Clair's) that flow between moderately high banks, adorned by many natural beauties for a distance of sixty miles,* nearly due south, when it again expands into the small lake St. Clair, almost circular in form, its diameter about 30 miles, and about 90 in circuit, too diminutive, when compared with the preceding ones, (and not being otherwise remarkable) to demand a further description. Out of this lake the waters again assume the form of a river, (called Detroit) continuing the same southerly course for 40 miles† into Lake Erie; its stream is divided into two channels from space to

---

riously affect the course of commerce in that quarter, than any improvement within human power, after that of the Grand Canal in the state of New-York. From the post of Michilimakinac to York in Canada, by lakes Huron, Erie, and Niagara river, is 650 miles, whilst it is only 350 miles between those two points by lake Huron and the intended canal by lake Simcoe. How far the intervening country between lakes Ontario and Huron, is favorable to the formation of a canal, I am uninformed, but am inclined to believe that there does not exist any very serious impediment to such an enterprize. Every thing else equal, the inhabitants on the north side of the Canadian sea have against them a difficulty sufficient to prevent a successful competition with their more southern rivals, that is the climate. This is a circumstance affecting the comparative advance of the two countries which must remain unchanged for ever, maugre all human efforts. If an equal share of active enterprize in the great body of the people, and equal protection to person and property in their government distinguishes the contiguous states of the United States, as the British Canadian Provinces, the progress of the former must be more rapid than the latter. The resources of both are, however, immense, and demand for developement only the energetic application of their increasing means.

* The distance is here over-rated considerably. From actual survey, it is less than forty miles from the bottom of lake Huron into lake St. Clair. This subject will be more particularly noticed in the sequel of this treatise.

† This distance is also stated too large, as will be seen by reference to that part of this correspondence relating to Detroit and its environs.

space, by islands of various sizes, the largest being about ten miles long. On the east side of this river the prospect is diversified and agreeable, displaying some of the beauties of an exuberant soil, aided by a very respectable state of cultivation, and enlivened by the cheerful appearance of settlements and villages, gradually rising into consequence by the industry of an increasing population. The Detroit opens into the south-west end of lake Erie This lake extends from south-west to north-east two hundred and thirty one miles, in its broadest part is 63 1-2, and in circumference 658. Near the Detroit it is adorned by many pleasing and picturesque islands, whilst its shores on both sides, have many indications of settlement and cultivation. Gales of wind frequently occur, and bring with them a heavy swell, with every characteristic of a gale of wind at sea; but there are many good harbors, particularly on the northern side,* that

---

* Here the partiality of the Canadian appears. Lake Erie is unfortunately deficient in good harbors on both shores, but if no other circumstance except the confluent rivers existed, that alone would give a decided preference to the southern shore It is a singular fact that the Ouse or Grand river is the only stream of any consequence which enters lake Erie from th Canada shore; whilst on the opposite side enter the Cataraugus, Ashtabula, Cayahoga, Black river, Vermillion, Huron of the state of Ohio, Sandusky, Maumee, Raisin, and the southern Huron of the Michigan Territory; and besides these, many of which afford good shelter for vessels, are the harbors of Dunkirk and Erie, into which no rivers are disembogued. Put-in-bay, in the southern Bass island, is an excellent harbor; perhaps, except Detroit river itself, the best in lake Erie. As the author visited most of these bays and rivers, particular descriptions will be found in the course of this treatise, to which the reader is referred

The Ouse or Grand river rises in Upper Canada, about fifty miles north-west of the western extremity of lake Ontario, and following a south-south-east course of about 80 miles falls into lake Erie 35 miles west of fort Erie; it has a bar at the mouth like all other lake rivers. Interlocking with the Ouse rises the river Thames, the riviere a la Tranche of the French, or Escansipi of the Chippewa Indians. The Thames flows to the south-west, about 15 miles from and very nearly parallel to lake Erie, and finally falls into lake St. Clair about 40 miles east from the

afford protection to the numerous vessels that navigate it. Its greatest depth of water is between 40 and 45 fathoms,* its bottom generally rocky, which renders the anchorage precarious, particularly in blowing weather. From the north-east end of lake Erie, the communication to lake Ontario is by the Niagara river, 36 miles in length, and varying from half a mile to a league in breadth, its course nearly north. The stream in some places is divided into two channels by islands, the largest of which is seven miles in length. The current is impetuous, and being broken in many places by the uneven rocky bottom, is very much agitated. The banks on each side of the river are almost perpendicular, and considerably more than one hundred yards high.† On the western side the road passes along its summit, and delights the traveller with many interesting views both of the river and the country, which is thickly inhabited, and under excellent culture. Here also his mind will be lost in wonder at viewing the stupendous Falls of Niagara, unquestionably one of the most extraordinary spectacles in nature, that presents to the imagination as powerful a combination of sublimity and grandeur, magnificence and terror, as it can well experience. Any description, however animated, whether pourtrayed by the glowing pencil of art, guided by the liveliest fancy, or flowing from the most eloquent pen that embellishes the page of narrative, would, most probably,

---

town of Detroit. Several indentings of the north shore of lake Erie produce harbors, one of which, the North Foreland, has great resemblance to the bay of Erie, though upon a larger scale; some others, like Dunkirk, are open semi-elliptical bays, with no great depth of water. Malden, or Amherstburg, is incomparably the best harbor in Canada, in or contiguous to lake Erie.

* Medium depth about 20 fathoms.

† This is fact only between the falls and Queenstown. Many places above the falls the banks are nearly on a level with, and in others, rising but little above the surface of the river. Below Queenstown, the banks gradually decline, until near lake Ontario, they are subject to occasional inundation.

fall short of doing adequate justice to the reality. The attempt, however, has been so frequently made, and in some few instances with tolerable success, as to convey an idea of its immensity, that, " a description of the Falls of Niagara" has become familiar to almost every general reader. For this reason, and also because in any new endeavor, I should certainly feel but little confident of either reaching the merit of the subject, or contributing to the stock of knowledge already obtained thereon. I will excuse myself from repeating what has been so often related before, and proceed in describing, with my best means, the general outlines of this majestic river.

" Five miles from the great Falls is another, and scarcely less tremendous, natural curiosity, called the whirlpool; it is occasioned by the stream as it passes from the cataract sweeping with impetuous violence round a natural basin enclosed between some rocky promontories, wherein it forms a vortex, that ensures inevitable destruction to whatever comes within its attraction. By thus diverging from its forward direction, and being as it were embayed for a time, the velocity of the current is checked, and subdued to a more tranquil course towards Lake Ontario. Four miles from hence is Queenstown, a neat, well built place, deserving of notice, as being the depot for all merchandize and stores, brought from Montreal and Quebec, for the use of the upper province; but not less so for the romantic beauty and local grandeur of its situation. For seven miles further on, to the town of Newark or Niagara, the river forms an excellent capacious harbor for vessels of any size, exceedingly well sheltered by high and bold banks on each side, with good anchorage in every part. The river of Niagara communicates with the west end of Lake Ontario, rendered memorable by events recently passed, and most probably destined to become the scene of contests, that will be pregnant with momentous import to North America in future ages. In length it is 171 miles, at its greatest breadth 59 1-2, and 467 in circumference. The depth of water varies very much, but is seldom less than three, or more than 50 fathoms, except in the middle, where attempts have been made with 500 fathoms without striking soundings.* Its position is nearly east and west. The appearance of the shores exhibits great diversity; towards the north-east part they are low, with many marshy places; to the north and north-west they assume a lofty character, but subside again to very moderate height on the south.† Bordering the lake the country is every where covered with woods, through whose numerous openings frequent patches of settlements are seen that give it a pleasing effect, which is greatly heightened by the white cliffs of Toronto, and the remarkable high land over Presque Isle, called the Devil's Nose, on the north; the view on the south is well relieved with a back ground produced by the ridge of hills, that, after forming the precipice for the cataract, stretches away to the eastward; the finishing object of the prospect in this direction is a conical eminence towering above the chain of heights, called Fifty Mile Hill, as denoting its distance from the town of Niagara. Of the many rivers flowing into Lake Ontario, if the Genesee

---

* When on lake Ontario, I was informed by sundry captains of vessels, that, after leaving the shores a short distance, the soundings varied from 75 to 89 fathoms, seldom so low as 70 or so high as 90, which would give a medium depth of 82 fathoms. From every information I have received, the bottom of the lakes vary considerably, having hills, dales, and slopes, similar to dry land; but with less abruptness in the ascents and descents. Compared with the surface Ontario is the deepest of all the Canadian lakes, and like Erie receives its principal rivers from the south shore.

† This is only correct as respects the immediate shores; along the south side of lake Ontario runs a narrow strip of land, occasionally rising into banks of 30 or 40 feet high, and often low, and sometimes marshy; but four, five or six miles from the shore the country rises into high hills, with often a very broken and even mountainous aspect. The country near Sacket's Harbor is flat, but resting upon a bed of limestone, with hills of considerable elevation in the rear.

and Oswego rivers be excepted, there are none that lay claim to particular notice, unless it be for the peculiarity of all of them having a sandy bar across the entrance. There are some fine bays and inlets, wherein vessels of every description may find protection against bad weather. Burlington bay is both spacious and secure; but these advantages are rendered of little importance by its narrow entrance being so shallow as to admit nothing larger than boats. Hungry bay, on the contrary, is conspicuous, as affording good anchorage, and safe shelter among the islands to ships of the largest size at all seasons. York and Kingston harbors, belonging to the English, and Sacket's Harbor to the Americans, are unquestionably the best upon the lake, as they possess every natural requisite; the two latter are strongly fortified, being the arsenals where ships of war, even of the first rate, have been constructed by both powers, and from whence have been fitted out those powerful hostile squadrons that have conferred so much consequence upon the naval operations in this quarter.* Very heavy squalls of wind frequently occur, but they are unattended with either difficulty or danger, if met by the usual precautions every seaman is acquainted with.

"Of the many islands at the east end of Ontario, the Grand Isle, lying abreast of Kingston, is the most extensive, and by being placed at the commencement of the Cataraqui river, forms two channels leading into it, that bear the name of the North or Kingston Channel, and the South or

---

* Except the barracks noticed page 72 of this treatise, there exists no defensive or offensive military works at Sacket's Harbor. The temporary lines of defence, erected during the war, are now neglected or removed. It is a position with great natural advantages which might be made, if necessary, very strong. It is also a post of the utmost importance to the U. S. If I was called upon to point out which place, in my opinion, on all the Canadian border, concentrated the most eligible site for a naval and military depot, I would unhesitatingly give the mouth of Black river the preference.

Carleton Island Channel. Cataraqui, from its entrance to the place called Petit Detroit, about 80 miles, is almost filled with one continued cluster of small islands, so numerous as to have occasioned the general denomination of Milles Isles.*

* *Thousand islands.* There is great vagueness in the above description which leaves the commencement of the Cataraqui undefined. Indeed it is very difficult to mark with precision the termination of lake Ontario, or the commencement of the Cataraqui or St Lawrence river. Before reaching Grand Isle, a number of smaller islands chequer the bottom of the lake between Sacket's Harbor and the eastern extremity of the Peninsula of Prince Edward. The lake gradually contracts approaching the west end of Grand Isle, where it is about ten miles wide; three miles farther to the north-east, from Kingston to Cape Vincent, the distance is eight miles in a direct line. Below Kingston, the river, or more correctly, the lake slowly contracts for about fifty miles in a direct line to Brockville, where it is but little above one mile wide. The intermediate space between Kingston and Brockville is an almost continued cluster of islands, but distinguished by very different characters. Grand island, Carlton island and Well's island with some others in their vicinity, are fifty or sixty feet above the level of the water with sloping banks, and a productive soil covered with timber of various kinds, of which pine, elm, maple and linden are the principal species. The banks of the main shore are flat or rise very gradually with a base of secondary or floetz rock. The region known by the distinctive appellation of the Thousand islands is granitic. The islands are mostly small, and many of them naked rock; pine is the prevalent timber. The banks of the main shore often precipitous.

A chain of primitive mountains leaves the elevated country south-west of lake George, and proceeding to the north-west through the state of New-York, between the waters of the Oswegatchie and Black rivers, cross the St. Lawrence between Kingston and Brockville, and continuing into Canada, divides the waters that flow north-east into the Ottawa, from those which flow south-west into lakes Huron and Ontario. The passage of the St. Lawrence over this chain, forms the Thousand islands. Every step I have taken on this stream presents phenomena to demonstrate that this ridge was once unbroken, and that in it, some where existed a cataract, above which the waters of lake Ontario were elevated greatly above their present level. The disruption, or gradual wear of this mass of rocks, let loose the imprisoned fluid, inundated the country below, and then, perhaps, commenced the cataract of Niagara.

I

The distance between Kingston and Montreal is about 190 miles; the banks of the river display a scene that cannot fail to excite surprize, when the years that have elapsed

Below the Thousand islands, commences a secondary region consisting in great part of schistose sandstone, upon which often rests an alluvial deposit. In this manner is formed the unequalled country below Brockville, as far as I have visited the river St. Lawrence. Though not bearing the name, the islands between Morristown and Brockville are formed from similar materials with the Thousand islands. About midway, between and a little below those two towns, occur the last of these granitic islands, and what is very singular, the banks of both shores are formed of floetz or schistose rock. Immediately below Brockville, the Canada shore is formed by a high and perpendicular ledge of the latter formation, and about four miles above Morristown, the margin of the river is a ledge of fine white sand stone in horizontal strata. Below this place, the river is without islands fifteen or sixteen miles, is from a mile to one and half mile wide, with shores rising by a gentle acclivity from the water, and where cultivated, inexpressibly beautiful. The soil exuberantly rich, and covered with a growth of timber, indicative of extraordinary fertility, such as white birch, red maple, sugar tree, elm, linden, hemlock, and white pine.

Four miles below Ogdensburgh, another group of islands commence, but with a physiognomy totally different from any of the preceding. This group is near thirty in number, of different sizes from one and a half mile to twenty yards in length, almost all of an elliptical form, and rising from the water by a globular swell. Such of those islands which have formerly been cleared of timber, and which are now again overgrown by a new generation of trees, are incomparably the most delightful spots I have either seen or whose existence I could conceive. The limpid water that surrounds them, clumps of trees without underbrush, and in summer an air attempered to the most delicious softness. A few days past, our agent col. Samuel Hawkins, gave a *fete champetre*, upon one of them, to the members of the commissions on both sides: the day was, even on the St. Lawrence, uncommonly fine, and amid the groves of aspen, wild cherry, and linden trees, the scene seemed more than earthly. Mrs Hawkins presided, and in the bowers of St. Lawrence, recalled the most polished manners of civilized cultivated society in the crowded city. At the close of evening, major Joseph Delafield and myself, walked over the island, and in full view of the objects which excited our feelings, concluded that no spot on the globe could unite within so small a space, more to please, to amuse and gratify the fancy.

since the first settlement of this part of the country (in 1783) are considered. They embrace all the embellishments of a numerous population, fertility, and good cultivation.* Well constructed high roads leading close to each side, with others branching from them into the interior, render communication both easy and expeditious, whilst the numerous loaded batteaux and rafts incessantly passing up and down from the beginning of spring until the latter end of autumn, demonstrate, unequivocally, a very extensive commercial intercourse. The islands, the shoals, the rapids, with contrivances for passing them, form altogether a succession of novelties that gives pleasure while it creates astonishment."

"Before reaching Montreal, the lakes St. Francis, St. Louis, and des Montagnes, present themselves; they do not admit of comparison with those already noticed, and, can indeed, only be considered as so many widenings of the

---

* The rapid change made upon an uncultivated country by the introduction of the necessary arts of civilized life, never did receive a more striking exemplification, than is now given by the left shore of the St. Lawrence below the Thousand Islands, as far down as Hamilton. Fields joining to fields, farm-houses, with their most attractive decoration, garden, meadow, and orchard, smile along this truly elegant slope. Villages with many of the highest traits of cultivated life, and with all the first principles of civilization, rise along this once desolate waste. Brockville, Prescott, and Johnstown, are now what were once New-York and Philadelphia, what were once Quebec and Montreal, and ranging farther back in the lapse of ages, what was once Athens, Rome, Paris and London.

Many times, when the rising and setting sun spread a glow of golden lustre over this attractive picture, have I demanded of myself, was this country a gloomy forest scene only five and thirty years past? The rich lustre of harvest would have answered, that upon this expanse the labor of ages had been expended; but history faithfully points to the contrary. In 1783 the ax first resounded on these shores; and now, 1818, the world can present but few, if any regions of equal extent, where all that can allure the eye, or gratify the mind, can be found more condensed into one view. Savage life has disappeared for ever, and in its place now stands the residence of the instructed man.

rivers.* They are of no great depth, but form an agreeable variety, by having many pretty islands scattered about them. St. Francis is 25 miles long by five and a half miles broad; the shores in some places are marshy, as they do not rise much above the level of the water. St. Louis and Deux Montagnes, are formed at the junction of the Ottawa with the St. Lawrence; the first is 12 miles long by 6 broad; the latter is very irregular, and in its whole length 24 miles, but varying in breadth from 1 to 6 miles.

" At the confluence of the two rivers are the islands of Montreal, isle Jesus, Bizarre, and Perrot; the first is probably the most beautiful spot of all Lower Canada. On the south side of this island is the city of the same name, and its convenient port, 580 miles from the gulf of St. Lawrence, to which ships of six hundred tons can ascend with very little difficulty.† On the north-west lies Isle Jesus, that, by its

---

* If the first springs that afterwards form the rivers west of lake Superior, are taken into the account then lake Superior itself is nothing more than a dilatation of the waters as they are aggregated in descending from their original source. Lakes Huron, Michigan, Erie, and Ontario, differ in nothing but comparative extent from those of St. Francis and St. Louis in the St. Lawrence river; from lake George and Champlain in the Richelieu; from lake Pepin in the Mississippi, and from lake Leman in the Rhone. The smallest brook, presents all the features of the largest river, where the plain has too little inclination to admit direct *descent*, a pond or lake is formed, and where the *descent* becomes rapid, a flowing stream is the consequence. From these simple principles, arise all the features perceivable from the dimpling pool, to the vast expanse of lake Superior, or the Caspian sea; from the rippling rill to the overwhelming torrents of the Mississippi and St. Lawrence. All streams are, in fact, composed of chains whose links are themselves alternately lakes and cataracts, the cause of the existence of the former, is a greater approach to the curve of the real sphere; the latter is produced by an inclination of more or less obliquity to that curve superficies.

† Compared with any other stream of the globe, the St. Lawrence, when free from ice, certainly affords the best ship navigation. No other river can be ascended so far with equal vessels, and with so little impediment. The only streams that can compete with the St. Lawrence, are the Oronoque and Rio de la

position, forms two other channels of a moderate breadth, one called la Riviere des Prairies, and the other la Riviere de St. Jean, or Jesus. They are both navigable for boats or rafts, and unite again with the main river at *Bout de l' Isle*, or east end of Montreal island. From this city the navigation assumes a character of more consequence than what it does above, being carried on in ships and decked vessels of all classes. In the distance from hence to Quebec, 180 miles, the impediments to vessels of large tonnage sailing either up or down are not many, and may be overcome with much ease, if it be judged expedient that their cargoes should be so conveyed in preference to transporting them in small craft. On either side the prospect is worthy of admiration. The different seigniories, all in the highest state of improvement that the agriculture of the country will admit of, denote both affluence and industry. The views are always pleasing and often beautiful, although the component parts of them do not possess that degree of grandeur which is perceivable below Quebec. Numerous villages built around a handsome stone church, seem to invite the traveller's attention, while single houses and farms at agreeable distances appear to keep up a regular chain of communication. In fact, whoever passes from one city to the other, whether by water or by land, will not fail to have his senses highly gratified, and to meet with many subjects worthy both of observation and

Plate, both in South America. The Amazon and Mississippi can neither present so much facility for internal commerce, as far as the ingress of large ships is concerned. On the eastern continent, the Elbe, Garonne, Wolga, and Ganges, are the rivers that admit the highest descent of ships, neither of which are equal in that respect, to the Hudson or the Delaware.

The beauty of the St. Lawrence islands has been noticed; that of Montreal has the preference of greater extent than any other with equal elegance of natural physiognomy. The scenery around this city is on a vast scale, being bounded by mountains more than eighty miles distant, uniting in itself, a most attractive *local*, with a position equally favorable for external and internal commerce: it now contains 25,000 people.

reflection. About 45 miles below Montreal, on the south side, is the town of William-Henry, or Sorrel, built at the entrance of the river Richelieu into the St. Lawrence, not far from which the latter spreads into another lake, the last in its progress towards the sea: it is called St. Peters, is 25 miles long and 9 broad: like most of the others, this has a group of islands covering about 9 miles of the western part; between them two distinct channels are formed, the one to the south being the deepest and clearest is consequently the best for ships. The banks on each side are very low, with shoals stretching from them to a considerable distance, so that only a narrow passage, whose general depth is from 12 to 18 feet, is left unobstructed. About 45 miles from William Henry on the north side, at the mouth of the river St. Maurice, stands the town of Three Rivers, the third in rank within the province. At this place the tide ceases entirely,* and,

* Or in other words, the town of Three Rivers, stands at the head of tide water in the St. Lawrence. If it is 180 miles from Quebec to Montreal, and 90 from the latter to Three Rivers, than the tides flow 90 miles above Quebec, or nearly 400 miles from the gulf of St. Lawrence, and an unequalled distance into the interior of this or any other part of the earth. Like as in the Hudson, the tides in the St. Lawrence, pass through a chain of primitive mountains, upon the ruins of which stands Quebec. As I have before observed of the chain which passes the St. Lawrence, and forms the Thousand Islands, I repeat respecting that which traverses the same river near Quebec, that it was once continuous, and confined the waters above it, forming a lake, which must have been drained by some of those operations of nature, which impose lasting changes upon our globe.

"When this opening was made by the force of the included water, the land was laid bare on both sides of that river (St. Lawrence,) as far as St. Regis, including the islands of Montreal and Jesus, and by the same operation, the land on both sides of Lake Champlain would be drained as far as Ticonderoga and Whitehall."—*Dr S. L. Mitchill's Notes on Cuvier's Theory of the Earth, page 291.*

This ancient lake was not bounded by St. Regis: at that village there exists no land of any considerable elevation above the level of the water in the river that could set bounds to the included lake. I have already observed that no current of any consequence exists on the St. Lawrence, from lake Erie to the lower extremity of the

indeed, is not much felt at several miles below it: from hence there is scarce any variation in the general aspect of the St. Lawrence, until arriving at the Richelieu rapid (about 52 miles,) where its bed is so much contracted or obstruct-

Thousand islands; consequently the present depression of the river commences at that place. The fall in St. Lawrence, is from the beginning of its current, to tide water 231 feet, (see my letter to Charles G. Haines, Esq.) therefore if any impediment of that height was now raised at Quebec, the accumulated waters would again assume a level to the west end of lake Ontario. It is probable that the outer or Quebec barrier, yielded before the upper, or that of the Thousand islands, and that a cataract of very considerable elevation, existed for a great length of time near where Brockville now stands. The waters, by their abrasion, finally cut the inner granitic chain, and a depression in the depth and great contraction in the extent of lake Ontario was the effect. It appears from the phenomena exhibited by most rivers, that schistose secondary yields more slowly to the action of water, than do primitive rocks, though the latter, are in fact, harder in their texture, than the former. A stream glides smoothly over a bed of horizontal slate, without producing much effect; primitive rocks by their fractured surface, oppose points of contact to the falling fluid which imperceptibly tears away the broken fragments of rock, and finally gains a smooth uninterrupted channel. All the rapids in the St. Lawrence rush over smooth beds of floetz, limestone, or sandstone, which have prevented the stream from producing a greater effect upon the incumbent primitive strata above, towards lake Ontario.

If a similar effect had been produced in the St. Lawrence that has taken place in the Hudson, then would the Atlantic tides have flowed to Niagara. The medium depth of lake Ontario is about 82 fathoms, or 492 feet, and as we have already seen, the difference of level between the surface of lake Ontario, and tide water is 231; of course the bottom of lake Ontario is generally below tide water 261 feet. It is now evident that if the intervening barrier was broken, the lake would again depress 231 feet and leave immense spaces dry land which are yet submerged; though a residue would remain which would still have a depth of 261 feet, far greater than is now the case in lake Erie.

The breadth, strength, and texture of the composing materials in the St. Lawrence, however, renders a farther depression of its volume the work of unlimited ages, and compared with the epocha in human history, the present order of things in that quarter may be considered perpetual. No earthquake, short of a convulsion which would disrupt the earth to its center could reed by huge masses of rock, as to leave but a very narrow channel, wherein at ebb tide there is so great a descent, that much caution, and a proper time of the ebb is necessary to pass through it; at the end of the rapid, there is a good anchorage, where vessels can wait their convenient opportunity. From Montreal, thus far, the banks are of a very moderate elevation, and uniformly level, but hereabout they are much higher, and gradually increase in their approach to Quebec, until they attain the height of Cape Diamond, upon which the city is built. At this capital of the province and seat of government, there is a most excellent port and a capacious basin, wherein the greatest depth of water is 28 fathoms, with a tide rising from 17 to 18, and at the springs, from 23 to 24 feet. From whence, and from Point Levi on the south shore, one of the most striking panoramic views, perhaps, in the whole world, offers itself to notice; the assemblage of objects is so grand, and though naturally, yet appear so artificially contrasted with each other, that they mingle surprize with the gratification of every beholder. The capital upon the summit of the cape, the river St. Charles, flowing for a great distance, through a valley, abounding in natural beauties, the falls of Montmorency, the island of Orleans, and the well cultivated settlements on all sides, form together a coup d'œil, that might enter into competition with the most romantic. At the basin, the St. Lawrence is two miles across, and continues increasing in breadth until it enters the gulf of the same name, where, from Cape Rosier to the Mingan settlement on the Labra-

---

move such enormous masses, and if such a catastrophe ever does occur, an entire change will ensue in rivers and lakes, and produce a new physiognomy on the earth's surface. I have long been of opinion, that the accidental agency of earthquakes and volcanoes, has been overrated, whilst the slow, but constant influence of water has met with too little attention from philosophers and naturalists. This subject will again come in review when we are examining the features of lake Erie and Niagara.

dor shore, it is very near 105 miles wide. A little below the city is the isle of Orleans, placed in the midway, consequently forming two channels; the one to the south is always used by ships, the shore on that side is high, and on the opposite, in some places, it is even mountainous, but in both, extremely well settled, and the lands in such a high state of improvement, that a large tract in the vicinity of Riviere du Sud, is familiarly called the granary of the province. Beyond the island of Orleans are several others, as Goose island, Crane island, and any smaller ones; these two are tolerably well cultivated, but the rest are neglected. At Riviere du Sud, the great river is increased to eleven miles in width, and the country that adjoins it, cannot be easily rivalled in its general appearance. The great number of churches, telegraph stations and villages, whose houses are almost always whitened, are so well exhibited by the dark contrast of the thick woods covering the rising grounds behind them up to their summits, and the termination so completely defined by the distant range of lofty mountains forming the boundary before noticed, that very few landscapes will be found actually superior to it. Beyond Riviere du Sud, is a channel named the Traverse, which deserves mention from the circumstance of the river being here thirteen miles across; yet the Isle aux Coudres, the shoal of St. Roche, and another called the English Bank, interrupt the fair way so much, that this passage, which is the usual one the pilots choose, is not more than from 1700 to 1800 yards between the two buoys that mark the edge of the shoals; it is the most intricate part of the river below Quebec, the currents are numerous, irregular and very strong, on which large ships must consult the proper time of the tide to pass it without accident. On the north shore between the Isle aux Coudres, and the main there is another channel, but the current is so rapid, the depth of water so great, and the holding ground so bad in case of being obliged to anchor within it, that pilots always give the preference to running through the Traverse. Not the smallest difficulty will ever be found in making this passage good, if the bearings and directions laid down upon my topographical map be duly attended to. Passing the Traverse, a very agreeable view of the settlements of the bay of St. Paul, enclosed within an amphitheatre of very high hills, and the well cultivated Isle aux Coudres at its entrance, presents itself. Continuing down the river, the next in succession are the islands of Kamourasca, the Pilgrims, Hare Island, and the cluster of small ones near it, named the Brandy Pots, these are reckoned 105 miles from Quebec, and well known as the rendezvous, where the merchant ships collect to sail with convoy. From hence, at no great distance, is Green island, on which is a light-house, where a light is shewn from sun-set to sun-rise, between the 15th of April to the 10th of December. Near Green island is Red island, and abreast of it on the northern shore is the mouth of the river Saguenay, remarkable even in America for the immense volume of water it pours into the St. Lawrence. Proceeding onwards is Bic island, 158 miles from Quebec, a point that ships always endeavour to make on account of its good anchorage, as well as being the place where men of war usually wait the coming down of the merchantmen; next to Bic island, is the Isle St. Barnabe, and a little farther on the Point aux Peres. From this point the river is perfectly clear to the gulf, and the pilots being unnecessary any longer, here give up their charge of such as are bound outwards, and receive those destined upwards. Below Point aux Peres, are two very extraordinary mountains close to each other, called the Paps of Matane, and nearly opposite them the bold and lofty promontory of Mount Pelee, where the river is little more than 25 miles wide, but the coast suddenly stretches almost northerly, so much, that at the seven islands, it is increased to 75 miles. The settlements on the south side reach down thus far, but hereabouts, they may be considered to terminate, as to the eastward of cape Chat, the progress of industry is no longer visible; on the north side, the cultivated lands extend only to Malbay. In the river itself nothing, (farther) claims our attention, except the separation of its shores to the distance already mentioned, from cape Rosier to the Mingan settlement.

"I must still trepass upon the patience of my readers long enough to mention, that the observations hither made, apply only to one part of the year; and also, to notice, that from the beginning of December, until the middle of April, the water communication is totally suspended by the frost. During this period, the river from Quebec to Kingston, and between the great lakes, except the Niagara and the rapids, is wholly frozen over. The lakes themselves, are never entirely covered with ice, but it usually shuts up all the bays and inlets, and extends many miles towards their centres. Below Quebec it is not frozen over, but the force of the tides incessantly detaches the ice from the shores, and such immense masses are kept in continual agitation by the flux and reflux, that navigation is totally impracticable in these months. But though for this length of winter, the land and water are so nearly identified, the utility of the river, if it be diminished, is far from being wholly destroyed, for its surface still offers the best route for land carriage, (if the metaphor can be excused:) and tracks are soon marked out by which a more expeditious intercourse is maintained by vehicles of transport of all descriptions than it would be possible to do on the established roads, at this season so deeply covered with snow, and which are available until the approach of spring makes the ice porous, and warm springs occasioning large flaws, render it unsafe. When this alteration takes place, it soon breaks up, and by the beginning of May, is either dissolved or carried off by the current.*

* This can only be correct in common years, as instances do occur of the ice between Montreal and Quebec remaining after the first of May. The ice in the Hudson river breaks up always sooner than in the lower part of St. Lawrence, and even in the

"The gulf of St. Lawrence, that receives the waters of this gigantic river, is formed between the western part of Newfoundland, the eastern shores of Labrador, the eastern extremity of the province of New Brunswick, part of the province of Nova Scotia, and the island of Cape Breton. It communicates with the Atlantic ocean by three different passages, viz. on the north by the straits of Belleisle between Labrador and Newfoundland; on the south-east by the passage from cape Ray; the south-west extremity of the latter island, and the north cape of Breton Island; and lastly by the narrow channel named the gut of Canso, that divides cape Breton from Nova Scotia. The distance from cape Breton to cape Ray is 79 leagues, and from Nova Scotia to Labrador one hundred and six."

[*Bouchette's Canada, page 32—33.*

It has already been observed that the St Lawrence was rather a strait than a river; below Quebec it assumes more the character of a bay, than either that of a *strait* or *river*. In such rivers as the St. Lawrence, Hudson, Delaware, Susquehanna, Rio de la Plate, and Elbe, it is very difficult to determine where the river ceases, and the bay commences. Except width, no essential change in the ordinary features of the stream of the St. Lawrence takes place below Quebec. It is perfectly similar at the Island of Orleans, and opposite Cape Rosier.

Amongst the most interesting problems suggested by a review of this mighty river, is the comparative quantity of water contained in its volume or discharged at its mouth. No river of this globe can differ so much in the mass of contained fluid and its expenditure as the St. Lawrence I have already given a table of the area of this river and its

former, the ice not unfrequently continues firm late in April, as was the case in 1818, the present year. The occurrence of rain has the greatest agency in producing the removal of ice in spring, in any river subject to be frozen in winter,

lakes, expressed in square miles; and have also observed that the depth of the lakes was very unequal, and difficult to reduce to a medium. Without pretending to a very strict accuracy, I will endeavor to estimate the quantity of water contained in the St. Lawrence and its lakes, assuming my former superficies as data for the surface, and estimating the depth from the best information in my reach. It appears from the united information of all those who have made the necessary experiments, that lakes Superior and Huron are vast, and in some places unfathomable gulfs; that of all the great lakes that of Erie is the most shallow, not exceeding an average of more than 20 fathoms; and that Ontario varies from 75 to 89 fathoms, with a medium depth of 82 fathoms. The St. Lawrence itself varies very much in depth, and exhibits phenomena that shew its bottom to be excessively uneven. In order to be within the limits of reality, I have assumed a medium depth of 20 feet, for all the surface contained in the last item of my estimate, of 1,500 square miles for the superficial area of St. Lawrence river and the smaller lakes. I have also assumed for lakes Superior, Huron and Michigan 150 fathoms or 900 feet, and upon these data have constructed the following:

TABLE

OF THE QUANTITY OF WATER CONTAINED IN THE ST. LAWRENCE, AND ALL ITS CONTRIBUTARY LAKES AND RIVERS.

	Medium Depth	Superficial Area in feet	Solid Contents in feet
Lake Superior,	900 ft.	836,352,000,000	752,716,800,000,000
Huron, - -	900 ft.	557,568,000,000	501,811,200,000,000
Michigan, -	900 ft	376,898,400,000	339,208,560,000,000
Erie, - - -	120 ft.	418,176,000,000	50,181,120,000,000
Ontario, - -	492 ft	200,724,480,000	98,756,444,160,000
St. Lawrence, & other rivers & smaller lakes.		41,176,000,000	83,520,000,000
		2,130,894,880,000	1,742,757,644,160,000

Incredible as it will appear to yourself and most other persons, it is nevertheless a fact that this enormous mass of fresh water is here underrated, and yet amounts to more than one half of all the fresh water on this planet. This unequalled source of water, you will perceive, propels down the St. Lawrence a stream that flows with nearly equable quantity throughout the year. Amongst the many traits of singularity, that give to the St. Lawrence a character of unity, none is more distinctive than the unchangeable quantity and velocity of its current.

Another problem now presents itself for solution, that is the quantum of discharge, which, though very large, does not bear a proportion to the mass contained.

Three places present themselves from where the discharge can be calculated with most precision; opposite Black-Rock, in the Niagara Strait, and above Ogden's Island, at the Narrows, or at Point Iroquois. At all of these places, the whole volume is contracted into less than a mile in width, but flowing with great velocity. In estimating the mean discharge of rivers, a general mistake is prevalent, to assume the upper current as that of the whole river. Allowing the St. Lawrence to be three-fourths of a mile wide at any of the places I have pointed out, and to flow three miles an hour, with a mean depth of fifty feet, the result would be, that a transverse section of the river would contain 105,600 superficial feet, which multiplied by 15,840 the lineal feet contained in three miles, would yield 1,672,704,000 cubic feet as the hourly discharge. This estimate exceeds by more than one half, the quantity I formerly calculated for the expenditure of the Mississippi; (see Appendix No. 2,) and, though contrary to my opinion when I first arrived on the banks of the St. Lawrence, I am convinced falls below reality. The greater surface drained by the Mississippi, is counterbalanced by a much greater evaporation than takes place on the St. Lawrence.

Yours respectfully.

LETTER X.

Sacket's Harbor, July 20th, 1818.

Dear Sir,

I left Ogdensburgh the day before yesterday, and came on in the Steam-Boat to this village, from which I expect to set out in a few hours on my tour or voyage westward. The extracts I have transmitted from Mr. Bouchette, will have given you the general outline of the natural features of the St. Lawrence; it will be only necessary for me to condense a recapitulation of the minute features, to which I have been more particularly a witness.

With partial exceptions, the banks of this great stream rise by acclivities of more or less inclination, from the margin of the water to often half a mile distance, and from thence become more level in retiring farther from the river. The soil, except among the granitic rocks of the Thousand Islands, is extremely fertile.

That part of its shores which I have traversed, lies in the counties of St. Lawrence and Jefferson, in the state of New-York, and is divided into the townships of Houndsfield which includes this village, Lyme, Brownville, formerly Pennet's square, Le Ray, in Jefferson; Rossie, Hague, Oswegatchie, Lisbon, and Madrid, in St. Lawrence. On the Canada shore, in ascending from opposite Hamilton, I traversed the point of the township of Matilda, in the county of Dundas; of Edwardsburg and Augusta, in the county of Grenville, and of Elizabethtown and Yonge, in the county of Leeds.

In many respects this is amongst the most remarkable, and certainly is one of the most diversified tracts on the St. Lawrence. In the whole range from Brockville, in Elizabeth township, as far as I descended, the shores of Canada present one expanse of cultivated land. The farms, from the regular ascent of the ground, have a fine effect when seen from the river or opposite shore. From the season of my arrival and residence, I had a good opportunity to see the rapid advance of vegetation. On the 20th of May, very little progress in the foliage of spring was perceptible, and yet the first of June was ushered in in all the richness of vernal green. I have seen nothing to prepossess my mind with a favorable idea of Canadian farming, yet the crops appear abundant; orchards are neglected, though in apples and pears very productive. Meadows have a peculiar rich aspect, and no doubt reward their cultivators with an overflowing recompense.

The U. S. shore, from its recent settlement, remains mostly in woods, but where cleared presents a similar aspect with the opposing bank. The progress of improvement on the side of New-York, has been no doubt retarded by the land remaining in the hands of a few wealthy owners, who by demanding excessive prices, and by other injudicious arrangements, have contributed to turn the tide of emigration into other channels.

The timber is excessive for its quantity, variety, and gigantic size. I had often an occasion to make a remark on this subject, which I am unable to explain. When I returned to the middle states from the vallies of Ohio and Mississippi, I was every where from Richmond to Boston, struck with the diminutive size of the forest trees. This impression continued until I visited the upper Mohawk, where the trees commenced to present the enormous trunks every where seen on the Ohio and Mississippi waters. As I advanced northwards, and particularly below the Thousand islands, the hemlock, sugar maple, linden, elm, pine, and two or three species of hickory, rose to a majesty of size and elevation sufficient to excite admiration and astonishment. The white pine in the neighborhood of Ogdensburg, affords often masts of upwards of one hundred feet in length.

Oak is rare, and when it occurs does not yield in weight of wood the other trees. Excessive labor is indispensable in clearing from its natural state, land covered with such a dense forest; formidable as it is, it is falling daily before the farmers and the lumber workmen. Though so many more attractive allurements have drawn emigration southwest, yet the banks of the St. Lawrence are peopling slowly. The caprices of mankind are difficult to reconcile. With a soil at least equal, and with a climate incomparably more congenial to their habits, it is curious that the northern emigrant has so often neglected the banks of St. Lawrence to seek those of the Mississippi.

Coldness, barrenness, and asperity of surface, are the features in which the fancy of the people of our middle states have clothed this country. No deception was certainly ever more complete. The reverse is the fact in every point. It is doubtful with me, whether any part of the earth can exhibit a more delicious summer than this supposed region of frost. Spring, in the acceptation of that term as commonly applied in the middle and southern states, does not here exist. The transition from winter to summer occupies but a few days; and all seasons are accompanied with the highest behest of heaven, health. The pale cadaverous visage of hopeless disease is seldom seen. If the inhabitants earn their bread by the sweat of their brow, they eat it with a good appetite. I am confident that the lumber trade has been a severe injury to the inhabitants, and has had no little agency in preventing a more rapid advance of settlement and increase of wealth. I did not converse with one man on the subject that did not give that opinion decidedly, and some even with bitterness. It is a business with excessive labor in its pursuit, and with poverty and hunger for its common reward. Of all the occupations of man, where the soil will admit culture, lumber merchandize is perhaps the most exceptionable; and yet, with all its obvious ruinous consequences, hundreds, upon a soil of exube-

K

rant fertility, spend their lives between cutting and floating timber, and wretchedness and dependence.

Small grain such as wheat, rye, oats, and barley, grow extremely well. Indian corn here, as in most places where late and early frosts frequently occur, must be a precarious crop, yet it is much cultivated, and I am credibly informed often yields a good product of twenty-five or thirty bushels to the acre.

Bottom land, in the sense understood in the middle states, there is none on the St. Lawrence. Upon the banks of the Potomac, Susquehanna, Delaware, Hudson, and some of the rivers of New England, alluvial bottoms are found, composed of the *debris*, carried down by the overflowing of the streams from towards their sources, and deposited in the form of rich flats. This latter kind of soil exists on the Potomac, near Washington City; on the shores of the Susquehanna, near Harrisburg; on the Delaware river, above Philadelphia to Trenton; above and below Albany on Hudson; in Connecticut, on the banks of Housatonick, Wallingford, and more particularly Connecticut river. Viewing St. Lawrence, I have frequently endeavored to imagine a river, with whose scenery you were acquainted, and to which this river bore a strong analogy; but I knew none possessing those strong resemblances, where preconceived images could give an accurate conception of unseen objects. The east bank of Hudson below the Highlands, and both banks of that river from Newburg to Red-Hook; the banks of the Mohawk below the Little Falls, and those of Connecticut river, near Middletown, afford land'scapes whose features have many traits of comparison with those of St Lawrence; yet with a tameness unseen and unknown on that noble stream. It is comparing an infant to a man, a pigmy to a giant, or a rill to a torrent, to compare any of the eastern streams of the United States to the St. Lawrence

I have already shown, that the Mississippi and its confluents present features so different, that nothing but contrast can be drawn between them and the St. Lawrence. In passing from one stream to the other, a new world opens to the traveller, the face of nature changes, the objects are of new species, almost of new genera, and it is difficult to conceive ourselves upon the same planet.

In nothing, however, do the two rivers so essentially differ as in their islands; those of the Mississippi, like the banks of that mighty stream, are flat, many of them subject to overflow, none marshy; those of the St. Lawrence are mostly elevated, never entirely level unless marshy, and always of an exuberantly rich soil. Both rivers are chequered with islands, but those islands have characters essentially different; those of the Mississippi follow the direction of that river, and seldom occur in groups; those of the St. Lawrence lie scattered promiscuously upon the face of its current, and are almost always grouped.

Of the islands of St. Lawrence, after those of the Thousand islands, the most remarkable are the Gallops, and those in their vicinity. You will remember that I have remarked, that the St. Lawrence, from a little below Brockville to three or four miles below Ogdensburgh, was entirely free of islands; then commences a large group, of which that of the ancient Fort Levi is the first in descending, and that of Presque Isle above point Iroquois the last. I notice particularly these islands, as they are a good representation of the islands of that river generally.

When descending the river in the middle of May, I was particularly impressed with the peculiar features of these islands, and being afterwards employed to survey them and the adjacent shores, became necessarily intimate with their position.

Some miles above Ogdensburgh, even opposite Brockville, a slight current is perceptible, which very gradually increases, and at isle Fort Levi has assumed considerable force. In the space between Brockville and isle Levi, the river varies in breadth from one to one and a half miles; but at isle Levi dilates to near two miles wide. To the north of isle Levi lie a number of others, whose names being merely local I omit, but whose situation and appearance are in the highest degree elegant and agreeable. Upon two of this group, our commissioners encamped, and upon one of which was given the *fete champetre* I have already noticed. Still lower down, commences the cluster more particularly designated as the GALLOP ISLANDS. Here the river is divided by the principal island into two channels, in each of which the current runs with great velocity over ledges of schistose limestone. Below the grand Gallop lie scattered ten or twelve more islands, between which, as also along the shore, the stream flows very irregularly and with great velocity. Still lower down than the Gallops, and three miles distant are two islands, past which the river continues to run with the velocity of a cataract. The line between the townships of Edwardsburg and Matilda, and of consequence between the counties of Grenville and Dundas, strikes the river opposite the Gallop islands and rapid. A short distance below this line the river is united again into one volume, which in two places, point Iroquois and the Narrows, is contracted into less than half a mile wide, with a very deep and rapid current. Ogden's island, opposite Hamilton, also divides the St. Lawrence into two unequal volumes, the main stream being on the Canada shore. From this place, though the river presents two parts, as the Rapid Plat and Long Saut, which are marked as cataracts, yet in reality from Hamilton to lake St. Francis, the whole distance is a rapid running with great violence. The 45° of latitude is rendered in a particular manner remarkable, by striking the river at the head of lake St. Francis; here the stream, which, from the head of the Gallops has run with such prodigious velocity, becomes tranquil, and expands into a lake of near thirty miles in length by three or four in width, within many parts, low marshy shores. Lake St. Francis contracts at its lower extremity into the rapid of the Cedres, below which, though the river occasionally flows with much rapidity, it gradually loses its current in the level of the tides.

Between Montreal and Ogdensburgh, the navigation of this great river is laborious, in some measure precarious, and, without much skill and care, dangerous. It is a compliment to the vigilance and foresight of the boatmen who conduct the various rafts and vessels, that so few accidents occur. A kind of keel boat, of nearly equal size prow and stern, is the ordinary mode of transporting merchandize from and to Montreal as high as Kingston. These boats are managed with great dexterity by the Canadians, who handle with equal adroitness poles and oars. The rapids are often so strong as to oblige the boatmen to use a drag line, and it is wonderful the patience with which these men continue their exertions, against the force of the stream. Descending demands little less labor, and more attention than ascending.

Taken as a whole, I cannot conceive of a more pleasing region than that along both shores of the St. Lawrence, and when the United States' shore is as well cultivated and improved as the Canadian, it will be a voyage of real pleasure to pass along its current.

The islands were claimed by the St. Regis Indians, who have made a sale of their right to the soil, to David A. Ogden, Esq. Except Mr. Ogden's own residence near Hamilton, and a few settlements made upon the grand Gallop under lease from the Indians, those incomparably beautiful islands are mostly uninhabited. Their settlement would add very greatly to the decoration of the scenery of the country. Human imagination could not form an idea of places, where more elegance of scite and prospect would be combined, than on almost all of these islands. The fine seat of Mr. Ogden, opposite Hamilton, is an example. Clearing away their shores would also facilitate navigation, by enabling boatmen to take more advantage, than is now in their power, of the opposing eddies and currents.

Yours,

LETTER XI.

Geneva, July 22, 1818.

Dear Sir,

By the route of Great Sodus bay, I arrived yesterday in this village. I left Sacket's Harbor on Sunday, and from adverse winds, could not make Sodus before Monday morning, and was detained there until Tuesday morning. I did not regret the detention, as it enabled me to examine the bay and adjacent shores with some attention.

The bay of Great Sodus, lies partly in Seneca and partly in Ontario counties, the division line running south from the head of the bay, having on the west, the township of Sodus the north-east angle of Ontario, and on the east, the township of Wolcott, the north-west angle of Seneca county; with two villages, Troupsville in Sodus, standing on the point between the bay and lake Ontario, and port Glasgow standing at the head of the bay in Wolcott. Neither of these villages are yet of much consequence, but will no doubt, keep pace with the progress of the adjacent country.

I have seen no map whereon Sodus is very correctly delineated; on both Lay's and Eddy's maps, the mouth is too wide and not represented as much land locked, as it is in fact. Two points project towards each other from the opposing sides of the bay. The western most of these points, is composed of loose sand and pebbles, lie along the lake, and is, indeed, only the rubbish thrown up by the perpetual surf which beats the shore. About half a mile from the extremity of the western point, an island lies in the mouth of the bay, united to the main shore by a natural causeway, also formed, no doubt, by the surf of the lake. The space between the island and point is the entrance into Sodus, has about 8 feet water, and leads into an excellent harbor, safe from all winds.

The shores of lake Ontario, both east and west of Sodus, are composed of vast banks of earth, twenty or thirty feet high, and every where yielding to the abrasion of the waters of the lake. One dense and continuous forest covers the shore, occasionally relieved by new farms. The country is extremely beautiful, picturesque and variegated, around the bay. The soil excellent. At the time I was there, the fields were yet covered with grain, harvest being rather in its commencement than completed. This circumstance gave me some surprize; I had been often told that to the west of Sacket's Harbor, the climate became more mild in a given latitude. The phenomena, visible to me since my arrival here, does not tend to give force to the correctness of such an opinion. Sodus stands in N. lat. 43° 20′ and very nearly due north from Washington City.

July 21st, at 8 o'clock A. M. I left Sodus and proceeded towards this place. I found the intermediate stationary distances nearly as follows :

	Miles.
From Sodus to Griffith's.	—5
Reynold's,	8—8
Village of Lyons,	8—16
Geneva Church,	8—24
Village of Geneva,	6—30

On leaving Sodus, the road follows the bluffs of Ontario two miles, frequently in view of the lake; it then turns to abruptly south, winding along the western side of Sodus bay, and thence over the ancient alluvion of lake Ontario to Reynold's. What is called the ridge road or natural turnpike is passed at Griffith's. Contiguous to Sodus the surface of the ground is broken, the vallies are, however, only the fissure worn since the recession of lake Ontario;* as when the height of the table land above the bay is attained, a plain of great extent commences with very little asperity of surface. It is evident that lake Ontario has receded at different times. The natural turnpike is upon the alluvial plain; upon this ancient shore of the lake its waves must have beat many centuries, and yet incontestible document exists to prove, that, for perhaps as many or more

---

* FROM THE ROCHESTER TELEGRAPH.

"*Something for Geologists.*—In sinking a well at Carthage, a short time since, the workmen discovered twelve or fifteen frogs, embedded in a layer of close compacted marl, about nine feet below the surface. Particular care was taken to discover whether any communication with the surface could have existed; but it was satisfactorily shewn that there was none. They were of a light brown color, apparently about half grown, and very active. They were in a kind of nest, like mice, and appeared to be isolated from the rest of animated nature. We have heard of frogs being discovered in trees, and in rocks; but have never before witnessed them so far under ground. In sinking the same well about four feet farther, several more frogs were discovered in a layer of loose sand, totally disconnected with the superincumbent stratum or with any possible communication with the exterior. It is believed by the writer, that they have existed there from the period of the recession of lake Ontario, which is probably not less than a thousand years: if so their longevity surpasses that of Thomas Parr of the moderns, or Methuselah of the ancients, and deserves to be recorded. The doubter is challenged to produce his reasons.
X.

"*Carthage, Nov.* 7, 1818."

Though I do not believe the last recession of lake Ontario to have taken place within a thousand years past, I have published the above as a curious fact, both in the revolutions of our globe and in the laws of animal life. Many instances are however on record of cold blooded animals existing in marl, limestone, and marble.

centuries, this lake must have had a surface twenty or thirty feet above the natural turnpike.

At Reynold's the alluvial plain terminates, and a very rugged, hilly region commences. The transition is abrupt, and here from every appearance, was the original south shore of Lake Ontario; at times the remoteness of which I have not the temerity to attempt a calculation. Above Reynold's, the road leaves the alluvial plain and ascends the hills by a gorge, over the mouth of which is a natural causeway, which was evidently formed by a process similar to that which formed the points of Sodus bay and the natural causeway, though at least thirty feet above the latter.

The timber from Sodus to the hills is generally composed of hemlock, sugar maple, red oak, black oak, elm, and linden, the soil extremely fertile though too flat; and very much mixed with rounded granitic pebbles.

The face of the country from Reynold's to Lyons is excessively broken, the hills are not very elevated, but extremely abrupt and steep with a fertile soil. Lyons stands upon the bank of the outlet of Canandaigua lake, a short distance below where that outlet joins Mud creek. The village occupies the verge of the hills, and stands upon a very broken site. The route of the grand canal is traced through Lyons, and up the valley of Mud creek to its source. The outlet is a large creek, with banks much more resembling a bayou of lower Louisiana than a water course of the state of New-York. Lyons has a flourishing appearance amid a fine increasing settlement.

Crossing the Canandaigua outlet I found myself upon a country generally level, but not so tamely uniform as the alluvial plain of Ontario. Cultivation now increased at every step; the soil excellent, fine farms, meadows and orchards on every side, which continued to the village of Geneva.

This is one of the few towns in America named from a town in Europe, where common sense and analogy were consulted in the borrowed nomenclature. Geneva stands in the township of Seneca, Ontario county, at the lower extremity of Seneca lake. It is built along the margin of the lake extending about half a mile in length. The site of the village is truly delightful, standing upon a waving ridge lying parallel to and rising 50 or 60 feet above the water in the lake; the view of which is extensive and romantic. The opposite shore in Seneca county rising gently from the water to considerable elevation, clothed with timber or chequered with farms. To the north and north-east the prospect is also charming, and is now a sea of golden grain, rich orchard or meadow; the houses appear to stand in an ocean of plenty. I have never visited a place which seems to combine in so small a compass so much to please in the softer features of rural landscape. I was detained here one day, and amused myself in walking along the banks of this beautiful lake, and could not avoid exclaiming, that here, with health and competence, could I spend the remaining years of my life, without a sigh to return to the bustling commercial capitals, where for so many years I had scarce enjoyed a quiet day. My reveries were the dreams of fancy excited by a weariness of travelling, the painful recollection of absent family and friends obtruded, with the additional subject of regret that every day carried me farther from that family and those friends.

We are seldom left without some subject of consolation. I had a letter from Gov. Clinton to Col. Robert Troup, of Geneva, which procured me a kind and friendly reception, and every aid in the prosecution of my object. To this candid, gentlemanly and hospitable old soldier, I am under obligations that will carry their recollection to my grave. To meet with such men when far from home amongst strangers, excites feelings that no man need attempt to imagine, who has not been in a similar situation with me, when I met with the venerable Col. Troup.

Canandaigua, July *, 1818.

Yesterday in the afternoon I left the village of Geneva, and proceeded on foot towards Canandaigua; the distance is 16 miles by the following stages—

	Ms.
From Geneva to Reid's,	—01
Parson's,	2—03
Densmore's,	1—04
Torrance's,	1—05
Whitney's,	2—07
W. D. Murray's,	3—10
Hart's & Woodward's	1—11
Canandaigua,	5—16

The day was excessively warm, and towards evening threatened rain. The lowering clouds, however, contributed to give additional amusement to that I enjoyed in viewing the truly charming country through which I was travelling. The face of the earth has in the intervening distance from Geneva to Canandaigua, neither the dead monotony of the alluvial plain of lake Ontario, or the harsh features of the hilly region north of the village of Lyons. Hill and dale now present themselves with diversified but gentle effect.

When I had reached the slope that leads down to Canandaigua lake, evening was rapidly advancing; the black rain clouds gathered heavy over the eminences to the south of the town of Canandaigua, which was now in full view though three miles distant. The scenery every moment became more and more interesting, and my mind more deeply interested. While descending the steepest part of the hill, I was rapidly passed by a man in a single horse carriage, who stopped as soon as he gained the bottom and awaited my coming up, and very frankly invited me to take a seat beside him, which I gratefully accepted. He then drove rapidly forwards, as the rain commenced to fall in large drops When we came to the lower extremity of the Canandaigua lake, and the extensive fields, orchards and meadows near the town came in view. I expressed my admiration at the state of improvement every where visible; my fellow traveller replied—" twenty nine years ago I came up this outlet, " and at that time no mark of the human hand was here to " be seen, except those made by savages, a village of whom " existed on that point,"—shewing me the lower end of the now flourishing town of Canandaigua. I could not doubt his information, though there was something in the shortness of the period, when compared with the effects of human labor under my eye, that seemed almost the effect of magic.

We arrived at the public house, just in time to save ourselves from being drenched in a heavy shower, and after I had returned him my acknowledgements for his politeness, he informed me that his name was Yates, and that he was then in his 72d year. His hale, healthy and firm aspect, rendered this part of his information as remarkable as his short but impressive history of Canandaigua. The whole scene was in fact one of those, which was calculated to exhibit the rapidity of improvement in the United States. This man entered this then wilderness, at an age commonly considered as the meridian of life, 43 years; and while yet in the vigor of his limbs and faculties, a smiling residence for civilized man had arisen under his eye.

I arose this morning early, in order to examine this wonder of western New-York, and was not disappointed in my anticipations; I found it by far the most richly built town of its extent I had ever seen. It does not admit of comparison with Geneva; the two places so essentially differ in their locality and position respecting the lakes on which they are built, that few traits of resemblance exist between them. Both are objects of astonishment when we recollect how short a period has elapsed since a forest occupied their position.

I found the site of Canandaigua to be that of an inclined plane, rising from the lower extremity of the lake of the same name. A valley, or rather bottom, skirts along the south side of the town, beyond which the country rises into hills of considerable elevation; to the north and north-west extends a waving but not hilly country; the east side is occupied by the lake and low grounds of its outlet.

The town extends in a street of upwards of a mile in length from the lake, rising by a very gentle acclivity. Many of the houses would decorate the oldest and most extensive cities in the United States, and from a number of places the view of the lake and surrounding country would reward a tour of considerable distance. I sincerely doubt whether a more desirable village exists in the United States, if in the world *

* On my return from the westward, and during a few days stay at Canandaigua, the following statement made its appearance in the Ontario Repository. I have not the least doubt of its correctness, except as respects the population, which is certainly underrated if any judgment can be formed upon the extent of the town and the number of persons that are to be seen in the streets.

"THE VILLAGE OF CANANDAIGUA.

"A few days since, three gentlemen, from a laudable curiosity, volunteered their services to take a census of the inhabitants residing within that part of the town of Canandaigua, which is incorporated as a village, and to ascertain the number of buildings it contains. It will doubtless be interesting to our citizens, and gratifying to the public, to know the result.

"From the statement it appears, that the village contains 1788 souls, of whom 929 are males, and 859 females, and including 136 blacks, of whom 30 are slaves. Of the whole number, 471 are under the age of 10 years—484 between 10 and 21—and 833 over 21. Of buildings, there are 217 dwelling-houses, 39 stores, 76 shops, 30 offices, and 153 stables. The above are exclusive of the public buildings, viz. one congregational meeting-house, one episcopal church, one methodist chapel; a court-house, a jail, and a county clerk's office; an academy and five school-houses. Of the buildings, we believe not one is vacant, except half a dozen stores. It ought to be added, that besides the academy, which is undergoing a thorough renovation, and the common and Sunday schools, there are two respectable private female seminaries, in which the higher branches of education are successfully taught. The style of building may be said to be not inferior to any, since travellers, who make public their remarks, call our village not only well, but extravagantly built

Canandaigua is the seat of justice for the rich, fertile, and flourishing county of Ontario, and occupies one of the most eligible agricultural and commercial positions in our western country: it has now a water communication with the Seneca river by the outlet of its lake, which as I before observed unites with Mud creek at Lyons, and the united stream meeting the discharge of Seneca and Cayuga lakes, below Montezuma, forms Seneca river. The peculiar construction of this country can only be seen by recurrence to a map: either Lay's or Eddy's exhibits with precision the interlocking waters; but neither have attended with sufficient care to the ranges of high land. The best map, in the latter respect, that I have seen, is that of Mr. John H. Eddy, of the Western part of the state of New-York, published in 1811. As I intend to give you a recapitulation of the peculiar geological structure of the route of the intended Grand Canal, and contiguous parts, I will enter less minutely at present into a topographical review of this neighborhood. You will hear from me again soon after my arrival at Buffalo and visit to the Falls of Niagara. In the interim, I remain, as ever,

Sincerely yours.

"The above surely presents a flattering account of the prosperity of the pleasant village in which it is our happiness to dwell. While other places round about us boast how early they have become great—how by magic their trees have been converted into houses—old Canandaigua has been growing apace, displaying the sturdy vigor and healthful aspect of natural increase.

"But flattering as this account may appear, some danger is to be apprehended from the number of taverns and groceries embraced in the limits of the village. Who, that has not counted them, would suspect that there are no less than *fourteen taverns?* Of groceries there are also too many. The public convenience does not require such a number of inns, and then toleration cannot but be detrimental to the morality of the town. Public officers whose duty it is to regulate these things, should recollect, that it is much easier to prevent, than to root out the evils which grow from such causes."

LETTER XII.

[*The following correspondence took place after my return to New-York, and therefore not in order of time with the other communications made during my tour; but being relevant to the subject of my letter from Geneva and Canandaigua, I have judged it most expedient to insert the subject in this place.*]

New-York, October 2, 1818.

WILLIAM DARBY, Esq.

Sir,—The New York Corresponding Association for the Promotion of Internal Improvements, solicit your aid and patronage towards the great objects of the institution. Will you please to answer the following questions:

1. What canals and water communications could be connected with the line of the great western canal, in our state, for the promotion of internal improvements?

2. What great roads could be united to the line of the western canal, in our state, for the promotion of the same object?

3. What advantages does New-York possess over New-Orleans for supplying the country north-west of the Ohio river, with goods and merchandize?

With high considerations of respect, I am, sir,

Your obd't servant,

CHARLES G. HAINES.

New-York, October 11, 1818.

MR. C. G. HAINES,

Sir—Yours of the 25th ult. was duly received, but the pressure of my private business on my return from a tour of nearly five months, prevented an earlier attention to your communication. You request my opinion in the first instance upon—

"What canals and water communications could be connected with the line of the great western canal, in our state, for the promotion of internal improvements?"

The most obvious, and by far the most beneficial water communication that can be made between the great western canal and circumjacent rivers, is the contemplated canal between the head of Seneca lake and the Susquehanna.* If the two canals were now completed as far as Seneca lake and Cayuga river, the inhabitants of Pennsylvania and New-York states, would exchange their heavy but invaluable articles of coal, gypsum, salt, iron, and pot metal.

Three obvious points of water connexion, between the great western canal and lake Ontario, present themselves—by the Niagara, Genesee and Oswego rivers, all of which are obstructed by cataracts of more or less depression from the lowest part of the plane of the canal to the surface of the lake.

Before proceeding farther in this investigation, permit me to make a few geographical remarks. The commercial facilities naturally existing between the Atlantic states and the valleys of the Mississippi and St. Lawrence,† may be divided into three great divisions; which we will designate as the Northern, Middle and Southern. All that part of the

---

* *Internal Improvements.*—It appears by a report of the commissioners appointed to explore the route of a contemplated canal, between Seneca lake and Tioga river, that there can be obtained a supply of water at the summit level adequate for every purpose—that the fall towards Seneca lake is 117 feet, and will require 37 locks; that towards Tioga river is 43 feet, requiring 7 locks. The length of the canal is estimated at about 20 miles. Among the inducements held forth for opening this navigation, are, the transportation of military stores to the frontier, in the event of future wars, and to send our salt and plaster to Pennsylvania, and to receive their iron and coal in return."—*Niagara Patriot.*

† By the valleys of the Mississippi and St. Lawrence are here meant, all the region watered by the tributary streams of these mighty rivers.

continent of North America, watered by the St. Lawrence river and confluent branches, to the north of the Falls of Niagara, must have a commercial outlet and inlet by that great river, through Montreal and Quebec.—South and Southwest of the Rapids of Ohio, at the town of Louisville, the produce of human industry will pass to New-Orleans, and the articles of necessity and luxury, not found in the country, will be purchased in that city. Between the Chute of Niagara and that of Louisville, from the Allegany mountains to the sources of the rivers of lake Superior, will form the middle commercial district, and New-York, Philadelphia and Baltimore, will divide the profits of exchange; Cincinnati, Pittsburg, Detroit and Buffalo, will be in the middle, what Kingston and York, in Upper Canada, will be in the northern, and what Louisville, St. Louis, Natchez and Natchitoches will be in the southern division. Partial inter-communications may, and no doubt will, daily occur in commercial exchange between the points of contact of these natural sections, but these interchanges must be viewed as exceptions to a great permanent rule formed by nature herself.

In examining the subject of any improvement, MAN ought to seek what is practically useful, and not exhaust upon idle fanciful speculation, what is due to attainable objects of real utility. A water route from the Atlantic ocean to the immense western waters, has now arrested the attention of the most enlightened citizens of New-York and Pennsylvania; and the subject is one, upon which the pens of the ablest politicians or economists of these great states, may be most beneficially employed. It is an object worthy the deepest reflection of a public mind, at once rich in experience and strong in moral youth. It is to be regretted that in the developement of our natural advantages, local prejudices, party and personal animosities should impede the progress of rational research. It is wretched logic, to confound questions of national interest, with the trifling views of faction, or the narrow conceptions of corporation politics.

I have met with two works on a similar subject; one, "A topographical description of the province of Lower Canada, and on the relative connexion of both provinces, with the United States of America." By JOSEPH BOUCHETTE, Esq.

The other, "A Sketch of the Internal Improvements already made by Pennsylvania; with observations upon her physical and fiscal means for their extension; particularly as they have reference to the future growth and prosperity of Philadelphia." By SAMUEL BRECK, Esq.

Whoever reads attentively these two treatises, will I regret to say, find very nearly as much liberality from Mr. Bouchette respecting the United States in general, as from Mr. Breck, when contrasting the city of Philadelphia with the neighbouring cities of New-York and Baltimore, and particularly New-Orleans. The latter writer indeed appears in one point to extreme disadvantage, he seems to consider Pennsylvania as an incidental or secondary object, when included in the same prospect with her commercial capital: Mr. Bouchette, to his credit, extends his views to the causes which may lead to the aggregate prosperity of all the Canadas, and does not confine his anticipations to Quebec

To a reader unacquainted with the relative political position of affairs on this continent, both of these writers would appear to be inhabitants of countries environed with rival and even hostile states. This spirit of rivalry is as injurious as a generous emulation would be beneficial to the progress of improvement. The inherent principles of human nature will, however, operate, maugre all that sophistry can oppose to their progress. Men will carry their superabundance to the best markets, whether in New-York, Philadelphia, Baltimore, New-Orleans, or elsewhere.

Mr. Breck, page 13, anticipates the time when the commerce of the waters of the Missouri and Mississippi, beyond the mouth of Ohio, will come to Philadelphia; in fine, that an era will arrive when human beings will toil 1,600 miles mostly up stream, to obtain a worse market than they could find by floating down stream half the distance. If this prophecy is ever realized, the old proverb, "go farther and fare worse," will receive a very remarkable application.

I notice Mr. Breck's work as it embodies much of the common place philosophy on the subject upon which I am now descanting. To consider that gained to Pennsylvania which is lost by New-York, or vice versa is just about as correct, as it would be for an individual to desire a palace for a residence with mud-walled, thatched-covered, hovels, to decorate the prospect from its portals. In fact, the advance of any city or state of our common country has a reflective effect; the science, wealth, and liberal institutions of any part, must shed their kindly beams upon the whole, and the illumination must be stronger in direct ratio to approximation to the centre of light.

But to return to our subject. The relative territorial extent of the three great commercial sections of the central parts of our continent, is as nearly as I estimate them, as follows:

	SQ. MILES.
Valley of the St. Lawrence below Niagara,	210,000
Middle or central section,	320,000
South and southwestern section,	1,200,000

Each of these grand divisions have their appropriate advantages, which it is, and will continue to be the duty of the inhabitants respectively to improve. Of the three, the greatest number of practical and indispensable canals and roads, can and will be formed in the middle or central section. Until the completion of the great Western Canal between the waters of the river Hudson, and those of lake Erie, that between the Seneca lake and the Susquehanna river, and that between the Hudson river and lake Champlain, no others ought to be ever seriously thought of by the citizens of this state.

Your second inquiry is, "What Great Roads could be united to the line of the Western Canal, in our state, for the promotion of the same object?"

This latter inquisition would admit of a much wider range than the former, if pursued in all its details; there is scarcely five miles upon the whole line of the canal, from which useful and necessary roads may not be drawn; but of these, two obtrude themselves to immediate notice. One to the village of Hamilton upon the Allegany river, in Cataraugus county, and the other between the towns of Buffalo and Hamilton. The lately perceived importance of these two latter places, has prevented their having excited the interest they so eminently deserve. The proper point of contact with the canal, or its confluent waters, by the Hamilton road, is something difficult to fix with precision. Geneva, and Canandaigua, present each some respective advantages of position when contrasted with each other; and have either a decided superiority, as points of departure, over any other places in this state. I have visited both these towns, and from information there received, have no doubt but that excellent roads can be formed, from each to Hamilton, at no extraordinary expense. If I was called upon to dictate a plan upon this subject, I would direct the formation of a turnpike road from both Geneva and Canandaigua, in the direction towards Hamilton. These roads should converge somewhere in the northwest angle of Steuben county, at or near the village of Dansville, or Arkport, and run thence to Hamilton by Angelica. No roads that could be possibly formed in this state, in addition to those already made, would produce so great and immediate benefits, as these I have traced. If this route was laid open by good roads, it would, even independent of the Grand Canal, become *instanter* the thoroughfare between the New-England states and the Ohio Valley. To those who are acquainted with the extent and mass of the tide of emigration now setting southwest, and annually increasing, the advantages of such a route will be apparent. Much embarrassment is now experienced by emigrants from Massachusetts, New-Hampshire and Vermont states, for the want of a direct and easy means of transportation to Pittsburgh. No part of the western territory of New-York is so thinly peopled, as the country included in Steuben, Allegany and Cataraugus counties; good roads would tend greatly to encourage settlement.

Though not equal in importance or necessity with the roads from Hamilton to Canandaigua and Geneva, yet a good solid road from Hamilton to Buffalo, would be of great utility and convenience to the people who inhabit the extreme western section of this state. In a military point of view, the latter road would be of incalculable advantage in a war with Great Britain, in opening more extensively than at present exists, lines of ready communication with our interior and Canadian frontier.

It is much to be desired that a good road was also carried from Hamilton to Pittsburg. In execution of such a work, the people of New-York and those of Pennsylvania ought to act in concert: both parties are deeply interested, though the former rather more than the latter, as the country upon the Allegany is yet but thinly inhabited. From the influence of frost in winter and heat in summer, many of our rivers are rendered useless as channels of communication, often half the year. This is the case with all our interior streams north of Maryland. Durable roads are, therefore, as indispensable as canals, and in places where heat may exhaust or cold congeal water, roads and canals ought to be formed co existent, and made in their turn subservient to the facility of human intercourse, and the augmentation of human enjoyment.

The road from Utica to Sacket's Harbor, though already open, demands very extensive improvements. I travelled this route in the second week of last May, and found many parts in a wretched state. The season was indeed extremely inclement; a time, therefore, that the roads could not be expected to afford pleasant travelling; but if they were well formed and preserved with care, they will at least always secure safe conveyance. It would be waste of time to point out the very high importance of a good road, solid at all seasons of the year, from the interior of the state of New York, to the most exposed and by far the most valuable military and naval station on our Canadian border.

The following are the stationary distances of each of the proposed roads, as near as I have been able to estimate. The distance and stations upon the road from Utica to Sacket's Harbor, were taken from the former to the latter town. The others are taken from Eddy's Map of New-York, a very meritorious work lately published

	Miles.
From Utica, over the alluvion of the Mohawk river,	1 1-2
Height of land between the Mohawk and lake Ontario,	3 1-2—5
Village of Trenton,	8——13
Sugar Creek, one of the head branches of Black river,	23——36

Thus far the road is now tolerable, but from Sugar Creek it follows, generally, the valley of Black river, and is in many places barely passable, in the spring season.

Martinsburgh, seat of justice for Lewis county,	14 3-4—50 3-4
Lowville,	3 1-2—54 1-4
Deer river, a large and impetuous branch of Black river—a good wooden bridge where the road passes,	10——64 3-4
Watertown, on the left bank of Black river,	16——80 3-4
Brownville, right bank of Black river,	4——84 3-4
Sacket's Harbor,	8——92 3-4

A direct road runs from Watertown to Sacket's Harbor, distance 8 miles, but at the time I travelled the country, this latter road was pronounced impassable. I was, therefore, obliged to take the more circuitous route by Brownville, and of course traverse Black river twice. Good bridges have been formed over that precipitous stream, at Watertown and at Brownville.

Route from Geneva to Hamilton.

Height of land between Canandaigua and Crooked lakes,	30
Arkport,	20—50
Angelica,	20—70
Hamilton,	30—100

Intersecting route with the above, from Cannadaigua.

Naples,	20
Arkport,	23—43

From the foregoing it will be seen, that the distance from Geneva is 100, and from Canandaigua 93 miles, to Hamilton. The land distances could be shortened by passing by water from Geneva, through the Seneca and Crooked lakes, and from Canandaigua, by the Canandaigua lake. If the proposed roads were made, it is probable they would intersect near the Conhocton branch of Susquehanna, or between the Conhocton and Arkport. Diverging roads could be easily formed from the main lines to the heads of Canandaigua, Seneca, and Crooked lakes, and thus open still more extensively the channels of transportation, in a very improvable and improving country.

From the head of Crooked lake to Bath or the Conhocton, is only about 5 miles. From Bath, rafts and boats can be and have been conveyed down the Conhocton into the main stream of Tioga, and finally into the Susquehanna river.

Route from Hamilton to Buffalo.

	MILES.
Catarangus Creek,	30
Buffalo,	30—60

This distance is measured upon the map direct; it is not, however, probable, that a road could in reality be made in less than 70 or 75 miles between Buffalo and Hamilton. The face of the country from the Allegany river to Cataraugus creek, and for some considerable distance north of the latter stream, rises into high hills. The road would cross the table land between the waters of the Ohio and those of lake Erie. It may not be irrelevant to remark, in this place, a circumstance of considerable import in the investigation of the subject of the connexion between lake Erie and Ohio river. By actual admeasurement, as reported by Mr. Gallatin, Brownville, or rather the Monongahela river at that town, is elevated 850 feet above tide water in Chesapeake Bay; and by careful measurement made in preparing for the commencement of the great western canal, the surface of lake Erie is elevated 565 feet above the tide water in the Hudson river at the city of Albany. From this data, the Monongahela at Brownville, is 285 feet higher than the surface of lake Erie. I am well acquainted with the Monongahela river between Brownville and Pittsburg, and cannot be induced to consider the waterfall from the former to the latter place above 45 or 50 feet perpendicular; which estimate, if correct, would yield a fall of nearly 250 feet from Pittsburg to Buffalo. This statement will be relieved from all improbability by a very cursory glance upon a map of our continent. The much greater distance from Pittsburg to tide water in the gulf of Mexico, than from Buffalo to tide water in St. Lawrence river will be apparent. It has been found from actual survey, as marked upon Eddy's map of Niagara river, that the difference of level between lake Erie and Ontario is 334 feet. Supposing the gulf of St. Lawrence and the Hudson river at Albany to be on a level, and the distance cannot be considerable, there are 565, less 334, or 231 feet as the fall of water from the bottom of lake Ontario, to tide water in St. Lawrence river; a prodigious depression for the distance, and amply accounts for the rapidity of the rapids at Grand Gallop, Point Iroquois, Rapid Plat, Grand Saut, and St. Mary's Rapid below Montreal.

Assuming the above heights and depressions as correct, there will be about 250 feet from any intervening point more depression to reach the waters of lake Erie than those of the Ohio at Pittsburg. The dividing ridge approaches in Cataragus county, near Portland, within less than five miles of lake Erie. Sailing along that lake, within about three miles from the New-York shore, this ridge appeared to me to be 1000 feet high; some of its points I was then led to believe at least 200 feet still more elevated than the general range of the hills. About 20 miles S. W. of Buffalo this ridge first appears distinctly visible from Lake Erie, and continues in view beyond the town of Erie, and from thence gradually retires into the state of Ohio; in clear weather it, however, remains in sight from the lake, even opposite the mouth of Sandusky bay. Huron and Cayahoga rivers indent it, and when opposite the mouths of these streams it disappears, but in the intervening space rises prominent above the adjacent country.

Your third and last subject of enquiry is, "What advantage does New-York possess over New-Orleans, for supplying the country, north-west of the Ohio river, with goods and merchandize?"

To this interrogatory, I would answer briefly, that as matters now stand, it would be nearly, if not altogether as cheap, to ship goods and merchandize from the former to the latter city, and have them thence transported by water to Cincinnati, or even to Pittsburg, as it would be to convey them by the embarrassing land and water routes now existing between the Hudson and Ohio rivers.* The comple-

* On this subject I have since found that I was mistaken, as the following documents will show. If in the present situation of affairs, goods can be transported as stated from New-York to Pittsburg, consequences flowing from the Grand Canal are easy to foresee—a very great commercial revolution.

tion of the canal from the Mohawk to the Seneca, and a good road from thence to Hamilton, would, if nothing else was done, change the face of affairs. New-York would then enjoy the benefits of her nearer approximation to the water of the Ohio; she would be enabled to counterbalance, by her existing capital, the superior local advantages of New-Orleans; and she would forever preserve her now relative rank amongst the cities of the United States. If a direct water communication was open with lake Erie, the resources of

FROM THE ALBANY ARGUS.

"In our columns of to-day, will be found an advertisement for the transportation of merchandize to the western states and territories, and we have likewise subjoined the printed lists of routes to Pittsburg, through the state of New-York, and cannot but express our astonishment that the efforts of the adventurer to acquire for this state so very lucrative a branch of commerce, have hitherto been unaided by an enlightened public. From the above mentioned list it appears, that by two routes property can be conveyed from the city of New-York to Pittsburg, in the state of Pennsylvania, for five dollars per cwt., by a third at five dollars and a half, and by a fourth, at five dollars and three quarters per cwt. The largest estimate as to time, does not exceed forty days; the residue thirty to thirty-five days.

"It has been said, that the western merchants are generally anxious to buy their goods in New-York, where assortments are more easily obtained, at a cheaper rate, than at Philadelphia; but that the risk and delay of the voyage by sea, or the expense of land carriage, from New-York, compels them to give the former place a preference: in fine, that Philadelphia and Baltimore have regular forwarding establishments on which the western trader can at all times rely; while New-York for want of capital or enterprize, cannot afford them the same accommodation.

"The object of the advertiser appears to be, to convince the merchants of Kentucky and Tennessee, by offering to them the choice of four distinct routes, that New-York possesses advantages superior to those of Pennsylvania and Maryland; that in no case will his charge per cwt. equal that of Philadelphia and Baltimore per hundred pounds; and that if the purchases be made in the city of New-York, the mode of conveyance now recommended, on the score of safety and expedition, must claim a decided preference.

"We confess ourselves converts to the correctness of his opinions—indeed, all doubts are removed by the circumstance of his

the state and this city would be still more enlarged. We have been in the habit of undervaluing the regions watered by the confluent waters of the Canadian lakes. The real fact is, that in many respects the countries, contiguous to the great chain of interior seas, are superior to most parts of our continent of equal extent. The soil is generally good, and every where produce, in abundance, the Cereal gramina. To the west of Niagara, as far as lake Superior, the climate is mild. All the shores of lakes Erie and Michigan,

engagement to transport at those prices; and it is no more than justice to express our conviction, that Mr. Smyth would not undertake what he cannot perform. Apart from the advantages which would accrue to those of our citizens, who are immediately concerned in this carrying trade, the general interests of our state would be greatly promoted by the success of the contemplated project. The mere expenditure of one million of dollars* per annum, at which the transportation from Philadelphia and Baltimore to Pittsburg has been calculated, enormous as the amount may be considered, would be trifling in comparison to the increase of active commerce in our cities—of the immense accession of patronage and support to our steam-boats and other numerous establishments in the interior.

"The trouble and expense of maturing these extensive arrangements, must have been sufficient to appal and discourage an ordinary mind. Mr. Smyth deserves great praise for his enterprize and perseverance, and when we consider the interest which the state has at stake in the success of the undertaking, we most heartily wish that this public spirited individual may fully realize the fruition of his hopes."

"*Albany*, 16*th November*, 1818.

"I take the liberty to lay before you the annexed Advertisement and List of Routes to Pittsburg. In addition to the statements therein contained, allow me to inform you, that during the winter season, transportation to any point west of Albany can be obtained at very reduced prices. If goods therefore were purchased in New-York immediately before the closing of the river, and shipped to this city to wait for sleighing, they can, beyond a doubt, be delivered at Olean for $2 50 per cwt, with a certainty of reaching Pittsburg on or about the first of April. Winter transportation between New-York and Albany never exceeds three dollars, and is frequently no more than two dollars per cwt.

* We have seen this expense stated at three millions of dollars per annum

and great part of those of Huron, will afford fine settlements. With but very few exceptions, those regions are healthy and supplied with excellent water.

Let the produce of their labor pass where it may, the number of human beings that are now daily passing Buffalo will soon dissipate the forests and supply their places with towns, villages, farm-houses, fields, meadows, orchards, and gardens. The beautiful and highly cultivated lands of the strait of Erie, are now a specimen, of what in forty years will be the landscape from Niagara to Chicago.

"Although the navigation of the Allegany, from Olean to Pittsburg, may be depended upon more safely in the spring and autumn than during the summer months, yet a person well acquainted with that river has engaged to convey for me any quantity of property, at least once a week, and appears to feel the utmost confidence in his ability to reach Pittsburg at all times between April and December, in eight days.

"Respectfully soliciting your influence in favor of the undertaking, I remain

"Your most Obed't Serv't.

"CHARLES SMYTH."

"TRANSPORTATION TO PITTSBURG, THROUGH THE STATE OF NEW YORK.

"The subscriber having lately formed a connexion with a gentleman residing near the head waters of the Allegany river, again offers his services to the Merchants of the Western States and Territories, as agent to transport property of every description from the city of New-York to Pittsburg, in the state of Pennsylvania. Assortments of goods, (not single packages, or those whose bulk is out of all proportion to their weight) if shipped at New-York on board the sloops of the 'WESTERN LINK,' will be delivered at Pittsburg for FIVE DOLLARS PER CWT., all charges, except cooperage, included. Six months credit, with interest, will likewise be given, when demanded, for approved New-York or Albany acceptances.

"For more particular information, printed lists of the several New-York routes have been transmitted to Messrs. Richard Bowen & Co. Pittsburg, and Mr. Benjamin Armitage, No. 54 Pine-street, New-York.

"CHARLES SMYTH.

"*Albany, 16th November,* 1818."

It is a very gratifying anticipation, to behold in our fancy the epoch to come, when this augmenting mass of population will enjoy, in the interior of this vast continent, a choice collection of immense marts, where the produce of the banks of innumerable rivers and lakes can be exchanged.

Route	Stages	Mode of Conveyance	Probable time	Highest price per cwt
ROUTE No. 1. Via Hamilton, (Olean.)	From New-York to Albany,	in sloops,	five days,	$0,50
	" Albany to Olean,	waggons,	twenty days,	4,00
	" Olean to Pittsburg.	barges, arks, &c.	five to 8 days,	0,50
			30 to 53 days	$5 00
ROUTE No. 2. Via Erie, Penn.	From New-York to Albany.	in sloops,	five days,	$0,50
	" Albany to Black Rock.	waggons,	fifteen days,	3,75
	" Black Rock to Pittsburg,	lake and river,	twelve days,	1,50
			32 days	$5,75
ROUTE No. 3. Via Erie, by water from Schenectady, [Six months credit, without interest on this route.]	From New-York to Albany,	in sloops,	five days,	$0,50
	" Albany to Oswego,	waggons and boats,	fifteen days,	2,00
	" Oswego to Black Rock, including portage at Lewiston,	lake and land carriage,	eight days,	1,00
	" Black Rock to Pittsburg,	lake and river,	twelve days,	1,50
			40 days	$5,00
ROUTE No. 4. Via Sacket's Harbor.	From New-York to Albany,	in sloops,	five days,	$0,50
	" Albany to Sacket's Harbor,	waggons,	ten days,	2,50
	" Sacket's Harbor to Black Rock, including portage at Lewiston,	lake and land carriage,	eight days,	1,00
	" Black Rock to Pittsburg,	lake and river,	twelve days,	1,50
			35 days	$5,50

on or near the shores of the Atlantic ocean for the conveniences of Europe, and the luxuries of the Indies.

In the Edinburgh Review, for June, 1818, when speaking of Mr. Morris Birbeck's tour in America, and the stream of population passing from the borders of the Atlantic ocean into the region we now call relatively western, occurs this remarkable passage:

"Where is this prodigious increase of numbers, this vast extension of dominion to end? What bounds has nature set to the progress of this mighty nation? Let our jealousy burn as it may; let our intolerance of America be as unreasonably violent as we please; still it is plain that she is a power in spite of us, rapidly rising to supremacy; or, at least, that each year so mightily augments her strength, as to overtake, by a most sensible distance, even the most formidable of her competitors. In foreign commerce she comes nearer to England than any other maritime power, and already her mercantile navy is within a few thousand tons of our own! if she goes on as rapidly for two or three years, she must overtake and outstrip us."

Such are the impressions already made in Europe by our existing state, such the views of our future progress! *The bounds* that nature may have in *preparation*, to limit the *prosperity, wealth, power or science*, of the people of the United States will never be seen by either you or me. With sentiments of sincere esteem, I am, dear sir, yours,

WILLIAM DARBY.

Charles G. Haines, Esq
 Cor Sec'ry. of the Society for the Promotion of Internal Improvements.

LETTER XIII.

Buffalo, July 31, 1818.

DEAR SIR,

On the 24th inst. I left Canandaigua, and arrived here on the 27th. I have, as usual remitted the stationary distances, as by recurrence to particular places I can more clearly convey precise information upon the topography of the country

		Miles.
From Canandaigua to Ross's,		—2
Bates's & Shaw's,	2	—4
Steel's,	1	—5
Loomis's,	1	—6
Carter's	1	—7
Church in Bloomfield,	1	—8
Eggle's,	2 1-2	—10 1-2
West Bloomfield,	3	—13 1-2
Honeoy creek,	1-2	—14
Minor's,	1-2	—14 1-2
Tinker's,	1 1-2	—16
Lima Church,	1 1-2	—17 1-2
Brown's in Avon,	3 1-2	—21
W. T. Hosmer's,	3	—24
Albert Hosmer's,	2	—26
Genesee river and bridge,	3-4	—26 3-4
Sylvester Hosmer's,	3 1-2	—30 1-4
Caledonia,	3 1-2	—33 3-4
Nash's,	2 1-2	—36 1-4
Ganson's in Leroyville,	2 3-4	—39
Clark's,	4	—43
Daniels's,	2	—45

		Miles.
Churchill's,	2	—47
Eggleston's,	1 1-2	—48 1-2
BATAVIA,	2 1-2	—51
McCracken's bridge over Tonnewanta creek,	4	—55
Wilcox's,	2	—57
Touseley's,	2	—59
Murder creek,	6	—65
Holmes's,	4	—69
Porter's,	8	—77
Miller's,	4	—81
Henshaw's,	1	—82
Hopkin's,	1	—83
Atkins's,	3	—86
Averill's,	3 1-2	—88 1-2
BUFFALO,	2 1-2	—91

Leaving Canandaigua, the country along the road for several miles continues flat, and in some places even swampy. The soil exuberantly fertile, timber, sugar maple, elm, linden, white hickory, ash, hemlock, and some oak. The farms have a fine appearance, and the whole country seemed in a state of rapid improvement. The rapidity in which the public houses succeed each other, evince the great publicity of the road.

Great pains have been taken in West New-York, to open and render convenient the highways; but in few countries are the construction of good roads more difficult. The rich fertility of the soil, and its depth of vegetable mould, though so very desirable in an agricultural point of view, oppose very serious obstacles against the formation of roads. In the winter season, unless when the surface is completely frozen, travelling must in this quarter be very difficult and painful.

Approaching Bloomfield, a very great change in the aspect of the ground is visible; the dull monotony now disappears, hills gradually rise into considerable elevation. A circumstance is here apparent that is really a matter of astonishment. As you perceive the surface of the earth swelling into eminences, you find the ridges all lying parallel to each other, and to the chain of lakes which form the Seneca river. This configuration continues to Buffalo, and to the Falls of Niagara. In many parts of the road I found myself continually rising and falling over this chain of ridges; and could not avoid observing, that if their intervening vallies were filled with water, a cluster of islands would be produced, of astonishing resemblance to that of the Gallops in St. Lawrence river. The ridges have the same regular globular swell which you will remember I have noted, as characteristic of the features of the Gallops

Schistose limestone extremely fissured, is the first rock that is seen, overlaid by sand, rounded pebble, and vegetable earth. No farther change worth notice occurs between Canandaigua and Genesee river. That stream has a very diminutive aspect. I am convinced that all travellers are disappointed in their anticipations of its volume. When I passed the Genesee, its waters were rippling over its pebbly bed at the bottom of a deep but narrow channel, of not above 50 yards in width. A good substantial covered wooden bridge has been erected where the road passes.

The west side of this river for about two miles, is formed by what is called the Genesee flats. These are extensive alluvial plains; the part passed by the road is held by the Seneca Indians, and like all lands under the control of savages, lies mostly in its natural state.

Passing the flats, a country commences essentially different from that east of Genesee. Oak becomes now the prevalent timber, a very serious deterioration of soil prevails, every object bespeaks a region of much less productive power, than that which gives bloom to the vicinity of Geneva and Canandaigua. Farms are now less frequent, and have far less prosperous features than those I so much admired to the eastward.

Approaching Batavia, the seat of justice in Genesee county, another change presents its variety—ponds and flats intervene amongst the hills, and give to the bottoms of the Tonnewanta the look of recent and moist alluvion. Batavia is a flourishing village, but to me, neither its improvements or seite was so pleasing as I expected. I remained one night in this town, (July 25th) and on the morning of the 26th sat out for Buffalo. The road follows for some miles the valley of the muddy and sluggish Tonnewanta. Had not the timber prevented such a deception, I might have imagined myself following the sinuosities of a stream of the lower Louisiana; but the dark green of the immense hemlock forests, reminded me that I was tracing another region. Hemlock, beech, sugar maple, and linden, compose the mass of the timber. The soil is excellent, but too flat for either health or very beneficial culture. Schistose limestone forms the base, overlaid as I have before noted.

After passing a short distance over Murder creek, the road leaves the Tonnewanta, and rises into a hilly, broken country, in which, however, some tolerable extensive flats occur. This part of the country is rendered most worthy of remark, from the enormous masses of schistose fissured blue limestone. Many places are seen where this rock covers large spaces, and has every appearance of having once formed the bed of a body of water. I did not perceive the existance of shells in the composition of this stone, but my time and opportunity was too limited to admit extensive research: to note the general appearance of the country was all that was in my power. Timber in this neighborhood, pine, elm, sugar maple; soil fertile, though agriculture must in many places be incommoded by the large bodies of naked or slightly covered limestone.

Water courses all flow north-west into the Tonnewanta, and every where wash the rough surface of the fractured limestone, and before reaching the main stream fall over considerable precipices of the same rock.

Five miles from Buffalo, at Atkins's, near the seat of judge Granger, the last of these creeks cross the road, and within about two hundred yards to the north of where it passes, the road falls down a considerable ledge. The country then assumes a waving rather than a hilly appearance, to within about a mile from Buffalo, when an almost uniform plain commences, which is terminated by the banks of lake Erie.

It was evening when I arrived in Buffalo, therefore unable to gratify my curiosity by a review of the place until the morning of the 28th. The events of the last war between the United States and Great Britain, had rendered Buffalo an object of interest to the American traveller. I also felt anxious to see lake Erie, which in addition to its natural position, had also gained a rank amongst the parts of our country, which during the same war that exposed Buffalo and Washington to the flames of an incendiary, also gave renown to the nation, and left land-marks of glory which will only be effaced by the ruin of the world and human literature.

I arose early in the morning and hasted to examine the village and its vicinity. Like most other new towns, Buffalo is composed in great part by one street following the course of the road towards the eastward, though the town itself lies very nearly in a north and south direction. A few others cross the main street, but are but little improved. But very little appearance remains of the destructive rage of war. Most of the houses are rebuilt, but as in Kingston, some vestiges still exist to attest the fury of invasion. Many good and convenient, and some elegant dwellings and store houses have been erected since the termination of the last war. Three or four excellent inns, and many decent taverns offer their accommodations to the traveller.

The natural situation of the town of Buffalo, though presenting nothing either grand or striking, is nevertheless extremely advantageous as a commercial depot. The attendant diagram will exhibit its relative situation as respects lake Erie, Buffalo creek, and the adjoining parts of New-York and Canada; but cannot convey an adequate conception of the minute features of its *local*. Buffalo creek enters lake Erie meandering over an alluvial plain, whose surface is not elevated above the ordinary level of lake Erie more than four or five feet. This plain extends down the lake and Niagara river, terminates above Black Rock, and is about 300 yards wide. Rising above this plain fifteen or twenty feet, extends another level composed of sand, rounded pebble, and a substratum of vegetable earth. Upon the latter stands the town of Buffalo.

The creek is formed by the union of Cayuga, Seneca, and Cazenovia branches; which rising in the hills to the south east, approach Buffalo by a very rapid current, which, however, subsides before the united waters reach lake Erie. Seneca and Cayuga creeks rise in the township of Sheldon, in Genesee county, interlock with the Tonnewanta, and flow nearly parallel to each other towards the north-west, enter Niagara county, and continuing the same direction about twenty miles in comparative course, turn to the west, and unite five miles a little south of east from the town of Buffalo. Cazenovia creek rises in the south-east angle of Niagara county, interlocking with the head waters of Cataraugus, flows nearly parallel to Seneca, falls into the united streams of Seneca and Cayuga three miles south-east of Buffalo, and from thence to their junction with lake Erie take a common name with the town.

The harbor formed by this creek is excellent and perfectly safe from all winds; but from the shallowness of the bar at its mouth, will only admit small vessels of four or five feet draught. A light-house is now standing upon the point between the lake and creek, and is certainly a great convenience to persons navigating the lake. The creek is navigable for boats to the first forks above its mouth, from whence upwards it is interrupted by falls.

Large vessels are obliged to be anchored out in the lake or laid down below Bird island in the mouth of Niagara river. The current commences to be apparent opposite the mouth of Buffalo creek, but is there very gentle, gradually and imperceptibly augmenting as the strait contracts, until opposite Black Rock, where the whole volume is less than a mile wide; the velocity of the stream cannot be less than five or six miles an hour, with a medium depth of from twenty to thirty feet.

I walked down the beach from the mouth of the creek to the village of Black Rock. The greatest part of the distance (two miles) is a sand bank. From the mouth of the creek about half a mile the shore is low, but then rises into a ridge of at least ten feet perpendicular height above the water. This enormous bank of sand and flat pebbles has been produced by the dashing of the waves for unlimited ages, and is no doubt daily accumulating. Its elevation must originate with the winds unaided by the water, as no storms that could now occur, would ever raise the surge of the lake to the higher part of the bank.

Bird island is nothing more than a mere ledge of rocks rising above the surface of the water, but admirably situated to shelter vessels from almost all winds that could much affect them in this place.

Ever since my arrival on the St. Lawrence waters, I have been impressed with reiterated facts, which combine to prove the general prevalence of a current of air which moves in the same direction with the waters. So incessant is the prevalence of this wind upon the St. Lawrence, below the Thousand islands, that the entire forests have a visible bent to the north-east. The same effect is very perceptible near Sacket's Harbor, and after crossing the Genesee river travelling westward, becomes more and more apparent as lake Erie is approached. The orchards are particularly influenced by this current, and between Batavia and Buffalo are so regularly and so uniformly bent eastwards, as to appear almost the effect of design in those who have planted the trees. Near the beach of lake Erie, this, I may say, almost unchanging wind has forced the forest trees to assume a stooping posture.

July 29th I visited Black Rock. This is a small but apparently a thriving village, two miles north of, and built upon the same plain with Buffalo. Here the banks of the Niagara river or strait, present a very exact resemblance with those of the St. Lawrence, from Brockville to Hamilton. Rising by gentle acclivity from the water; both sides of the river being cultivated afford a fine prospect, though from its longer settlement, the Canada shore is much more improved than that of New-York. Unless in a cataract, I never before witnessed so large a mass of water flowing with such prodigious rapidity. The bottom of the river is composed of smooth rock, over which the water glides. If the stream flowed over broken masses of stone it would be impassable.

After viewing Black Rock I took advantage of a boat going down, and hasted towards one of the great objects of my journey, the Falls of Niagara. The day was intolerably warm, with scarce an air of wind to move a leaf. I found the river much more winding than I had expected from the maps I had seen. Our boat followed the west channel, leaving Grand island to the east. Passing this island I was struck with its remarkable resemblance to many of the St. Lawrence islands, having a similar swell rising from the water. Some new openings are now making, but the greatest part of its surface is yet forest. I had no means of examining the timber, but at a distance the trees had a similar mixture with the opposite shores, hemlock, sugar maple, elm, oak, and linden.*

* Since my return to New-York, the following appeared in the

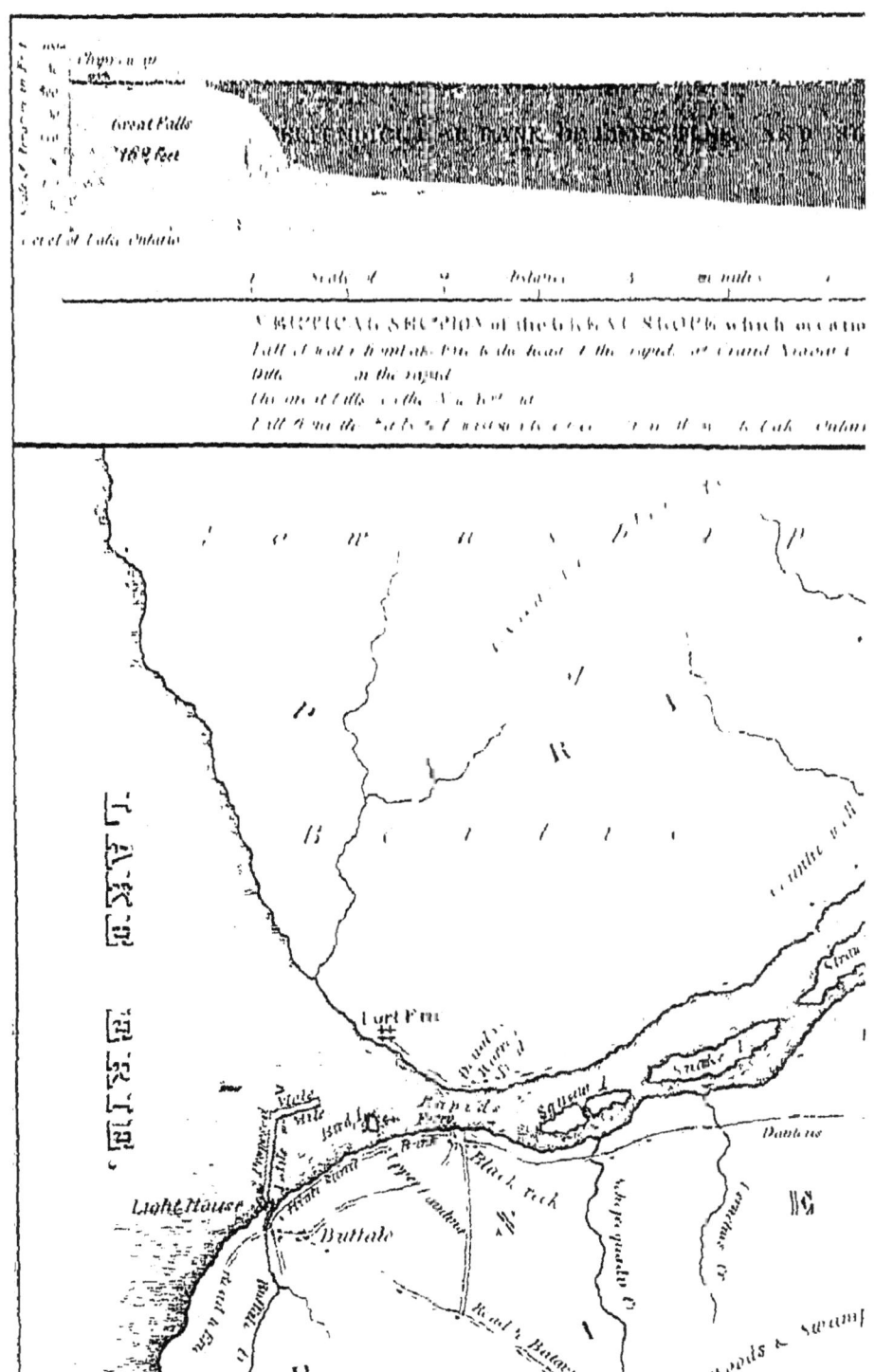

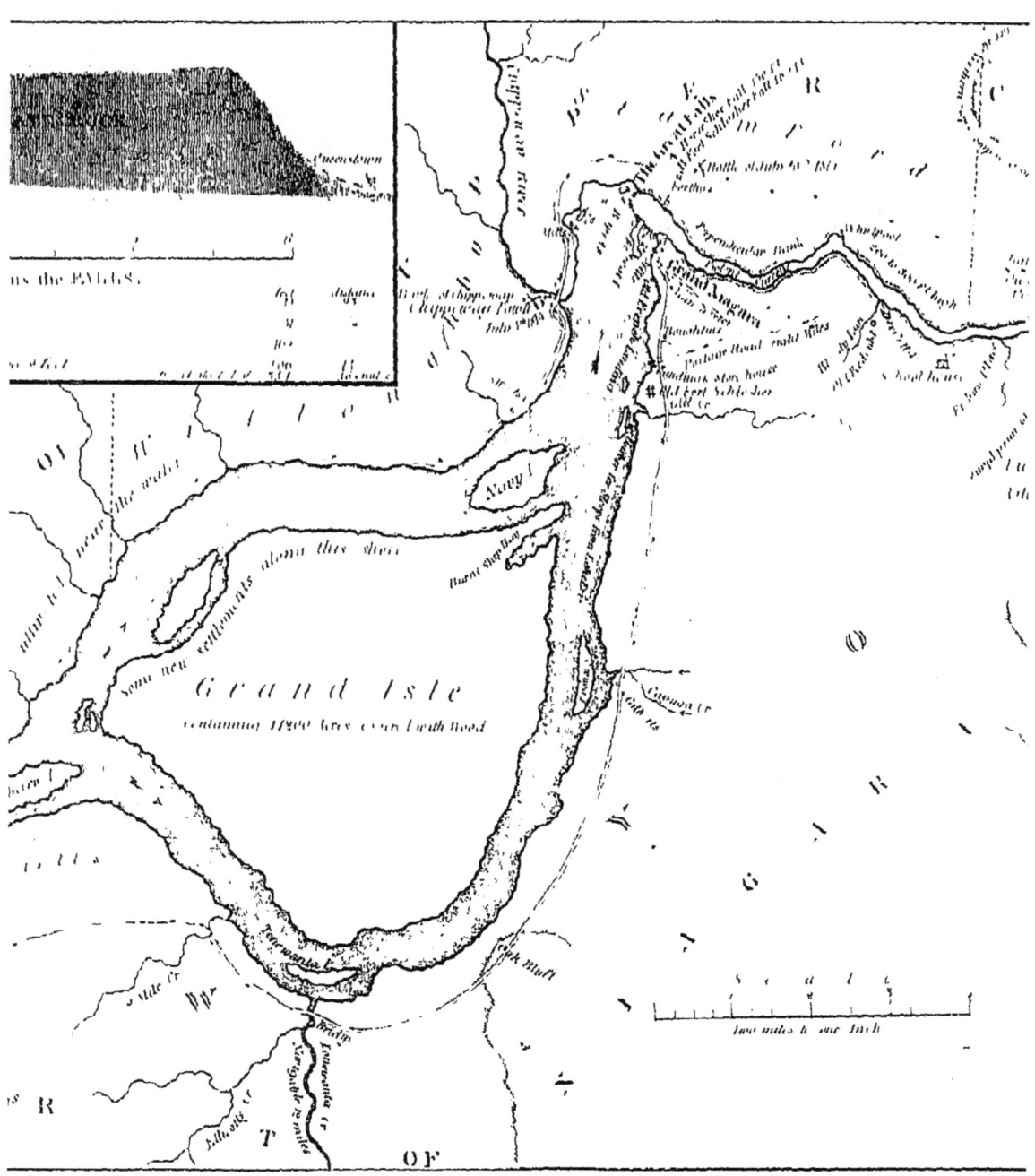

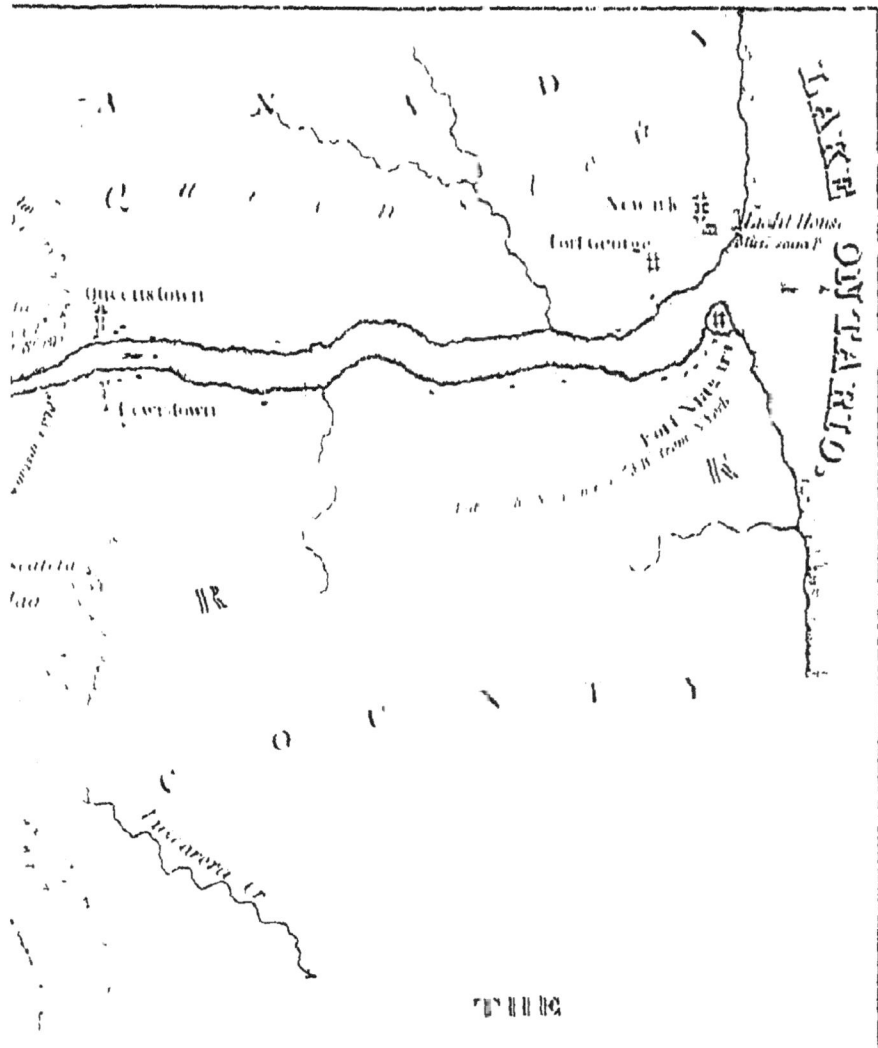

Tonnewanta and Ellicott's creek enter the east channel of Niagara strait very nearly opposite to the middle of Grand island. Extensive marshes and swamps skirt the Tonnewanta from its mouth, for more than twenty miles upwards. This creek or rather river, rises in the town of Orangeville, in the south side of Genesee county, interlocking with the sources of Cataraugus and Buffalo creeks, and with some streams which enter the west branch of Genesee river. From its source the Tonnewanta crosses in a northern direction Orangeville, Attica, and Alexander townships, reaches Batavia after flowing about twenty-five miles; it thence gradually curves to the north-west, west, and south-west by west, falls into Niagara river forty miles from Batavia, having an entire course of sixty-five miles. This stream has now become an object of interest, from the circumstance of

public prints, extracted from the Niagara Journal, published at Buffalo.

FROM THE NIAGARA JOURNAL.

"*Population of Grand Island.*— A very considerable settlement of squatters has been made upon this island, principally in the course of the last season. There are now, we are informed, more than one hundred families, collected from all quarters, many from Canada and the middle counties of this state, and considerable improvements are making. The island is situated in the Niagara river, and commences about three miles below Black Rock, and extends to within a mile and a half of the ... s. It is twelve miles long, and from two to seven miles b..d. The whole of it, before the recent inroads, was clothed ... h heavy timber of an excellent quality. The soil is said to be strong and rich, well adapted to cultivation. The title to it has not yet been determined by the commissioners, but it is generally admitted to be within the territory of the United States. Our readers will probably recollect, that the Indian title to this and the other islands in the Niagara was ceded to the state of New-York, by treaty made at Buffalo, on the 12th of September, 1815, between Gov. Tompkins and others, commissioners on the part of the state, and the chiefs, &c. of the Seneca nation. The state paid one thousand dollars down, and secured an annuity of five hundred dollars. This island will probably, at no distant period, become very populous, and highly cultivated."

its bed being for some distance intended as the route of the Grand Canal; the land contiguous to the lower part of its course from Batavia, is, as I have already observed, subject in many places, to submersion by water. It is navigable for boats upwards of twenty miles from its mouth. Between the mouth of the Tonnewanta and old Fort Schlosser, the marshes in some places border the strait; and what is remarkable, the Chippewa river entering the Canada side a short distance above the falls, exhibits in some measure, similar phenomena with the Tonnewanta. Seen from the strait below the lower extremity of Grand isle, the whole adjacent country appears almost level, no elevation being visible that materially breaks the monotony of the landscape. The strait here turns nearly abruptly to the west, and first exposes to view the cloud that constantly rises from the cataract. Nothing is seen, however, that anticipates in any manner the sublime and awful scene below; even the rapid current that sweeps past Black Rock, is now tranquilized; the strait is here nearly as still as a lake on the U. S. shore, and flows gently on that of Canada. Navy island is a small extent of land lying in the Canada channel, at the lower extremity of Grand island, below which commences the rapids that precede the cataract of Niagara. I passed between Navy and Grand islands, and landed near old Fort Schlosser, and walked down the shore to Whitney's, opposite the *falls*; it was near sun-set, silence began to reign over the face of nature. Slowly and at intervals I heard the deep, long, and awful roar of the cataract: my mind which for years had dwelt with anticipation upon this greatest of the world's traits, approached the scene with fearful solicitude. I beheld the permanent objects, the trees, the rocks; and I beheld also the passing clouds, that momentarily flitted over the most interesting picture that nature ever painted and exposed to the admiration of intelligent beings. with more than my common forbearance, I concluded to behold amid the beams of a rising sun the greatest object ever presented to human view. But whilst the stars of the night gleamed through the misty atmosphere of this apparently fairy land, I walked forth to the margin of the cataract, and in fancy conceived the beauties, the horrors, and the wonders the coming morn would produce. That morn opened, (July 30th) it was clear and serene; I hasted to the verge of the cataract; I expected much, and was not disappointed. The point of land above A. is a thick wood standing upon a sloping bank. The noise of the cataract is heard, but its features unseen, until the observer advances to the verge of the fall; it is then seen so obliquely as to destroy its best effect. Defective, however, as was this perspective of Niagara, it presented beauties infinitely transcending any I had ever seen before. I stood upon the very slope over which the torrent rushed, and for many minutes forgot every other object except the undescribable scene before me; but when the fervor of imagination had in some measure subsided, I beheld under my feet, carved on the smooth rock G. D. C.; W. P. and J. B. and many other initials of friends that had visited this incomparable spot, and left these memoria, that friends only could understand. On beholding these recollections of home, you will forgive me when I acknowledge having dropt upon their traces tears, that were rapidly swallowed in the vortex of Niagara. The beams of morning came, and glanced upon the curling volumes that rose from the abyss beneath; my eye searched the bottom of this awful gulf, and found in its bosom darkness, gloom, and indescribable tumult. My reflections dwelt upon this never ending conflict, this eternal march of the elements, and my very soul shrunk back upon itself. The shelving rock on which I stood trembling under my feet, and the irresistible flood before me seemed to present the pictured image of evanescence. The rock was yielding piecemeal to ruin, fragment after fragment was borne into the terrible chasm beneath.

and the very stream that hurried these broken morsels to destruction, was itself a monument of changing power.

I retraced my steps to Col. Whitney's, and after breakfast returned, and descending the almost perpendicular bank of rocks, found myself under the tremendous FALL OF WATER, that even in description has excited the admiration of cultivated man! I crossed the Niagara strait about 250 yards below the chute. The river was in some measure ruffled by the conflict it had sustained above, but no danger approached the passenger. Perpendicular walls of rock rose on both sides, to the appalling elevation of between three and four hundred feet. The trees which crowned the upper verge of this abyss appeared like shrubs. I was drenched to the skin by the spray of the cataract; but the sublime scene towering over my head, was too impressive to permit much reflection upon a momentary inconvenience. The river below the fall flows with considerable rapidity, but with less velocity or turbulence than I had been induced to expect. The opposing banks are perfectly similar, both being perpendicular about half the descent; below which enormous walls extend slopes, composed of the broken fragments that have been torn from their original position by the torrents from above. Most maps of Niagara are very defective, the river being represented too straight. The best delineation of this phenomenon which I have seen is contained in the map of Niagara river, published with Gen. Wilkinson's Memoirs. In that draft, the river above the fall, is represented, as it is in fact, flowing almost westward. Below the *chute* the stream flows abruptly to the north-east, which course it pursues more than a mile, from whence it again resumes a northern direction, which, with some partial bends, it continues to the place of its final exit in lake Ontario.

Between the lower extremity of Grand isle and the mouth of Chippewa river, the Niagara is upwards of a mile wide, but contracts a little as the rapids commence. The banks as high as Chippewa river, are not very much elevated above the surface of the strait, but apparently rise in descending to the pitch or chute. This change of relative height is only a deception in vision, occasioned by the wear of the cataract. After crossing, as I have already mentioned, I traversed the Canada shore to the bank above the grand or Canada chute. On the diagram enclosed, I have marked the letter C. upon the spot, from where the best view can be taken of the falls, rapids and islands. Many persons have insisted that the best view of the falls is to be had from Goat island. At this time I cannot form a comparative judgment, as the bridge built by judge Porter, from the New-York shore to Goat island, was broken by the ice of last winter. I am doubtful of the fact, of the falls being seen to very much advantage from this island, as the perspective must be very oblique. The rapids are, however, but little less worthy of a visit than the falls themselves, and can no doubt be seen with much greater effect from Goat island than from either shore of the strait. The rapids indeed on the Canada channel is a scene of sublimity and grandeur. Tumbling over ledges, many of which are 8 or 10 feet perpendicular descent; these rapids are in fact a chain of cataracts, over which the immense volume rolls its terrific mass towards the still more awful scene below. The New-York channel has also its appropriate beauties and attractions to the traveller; many small islands covered with cedar stand between the main shore and Goat island, round which the foaming surge dashes with endless rage. One of these islets hangs upon the brow of the falls, and produces a small middle sheet of ten or fifteen yards wide, standing in mimic majesty between the two gigantic torrents on each side.

No adequate idea can be formed from description of this wonder of interior North America. Its pitch in feet, its width, velocity, and consequent mass, can be estimated with considerable accuracy; but the effect upon the mind can only be produced from actual view. If the massy walls of rock, and the rapids above are excepted, there is nothing near Niagara that is striking in the scenery. It is left alone in simple and sublime dignity to strike the soul with a sensation that loss of life or sense alone can obliterate, but the nature of which no language can convey. If towering mountains and craggy rocks surrounded Niagara, I cannot but believe that much of its fine effect would be lost; as it exists it is an image whose whole contour is at once seen, and the recollection unbroken by extraneous objects;* even sound is

---

* A few days after my return to the city of New-York, I had the pleasure to read the following lines, from the 4th canto of Childe Harold, by Lord Byron. It is a description of the cataract of Velino. Words of fire! used to paint to the soul an object, no doubt worthy the mighty genius of the greatest modern poet, but an object compared to which, Niagara is as a towering oak beside a rose shrub. If Lord Byron had given intellectual existence to this grand effort of a master mind, under the very spray, in view of the emerald verge, and with his soul aroused to heaven by the sound of the waters of Niagara, his image would not more vividly pourtray this scene, whose traits only a poet can describe.

> "The roar of waters!—from the headlong height
> Velino cleaves the wave-worn precipice;
> The fall of waters! rapid as the light,
> The flashing mass foams shaking the abyss:
> The hell of waters! where they howl and hiss,
> And boil in endless torture; while the sweat
> Of their great agony, wrung out from this
> Their Phlegethon, curls round the rocks of jet
> That gird the gulf around, in pitiless horror set,
>
> And mounts in spray the skies, and thence again
> Returns in an unceasing shower, which round
> With its unemptied cloud of gentle rain,
> Is an eternal April to the ground,
> Making it all one emerald:—how profound
> The gulf! and how the giant element
> From rock to rock leaps with delirious bound,
> Crushing the cliffs, which, downward worn and rent
> With his fierce footsteps, yield in chasms a fearful vent
>
> To the broad column which rolls on, and shows
> More like the fountain of an infant sea
> Torn from the womb of mountains by the throes
> Of a new world, than only thus to be

subservient to the impression made upon the heart, none is heard except the eternal roar of the cataract. I would have been rejoiced to have seen this place in a tempest. The whole time I was there, the weather, though warm, was otherwise serene and pleasant. Amid the howling of the black north-west wind Niagara must have something of more than common interest. I am inclined nevertheless to believe, that winter alone can give all its most appropriate attendant imagery to the falls. But at all times, at all seasons, and I might say by all minds, will this matchless picture be viewed with wonder and delight, and remembered with feelings of pleasure.

Many silly remarks are however made respecting the falls: their plunging into an abyss of which no one knows the depth is one. The waters mostly fall upon an inclined plane, formed by the broken fragments of rocks which have been and are daily falling from the precipice over which the waters are precipitated. Canoes and other vessels being carried to the verge of the fall with persons in them, gliding

> Parent of rivers which flow gushingly,
> With many windings, through the vale —Look back!
> Lo! where it comes like an eternity,
> As if to sweep down all things in its track,
> Charming the eye with dread,—a matchless cataract,
>
> Horribly beautiful! but on the verge,
> From side to side, beneath the glittering morn,
> An Iris sits, amidst the infernal surge
> Like HOPE upon a death-bed, and, unworn
> Its steady dyes, while all around is torn
> By the distracted waters, bears serene
> Its brilliant hues with all their beams unshorn
> Resembling, 'mid the torture of the scene,
> Love watching madness with unalterable mein."

Only with this description, can be compared that of the Charybdis by Homer it cannot be deemed presumption to say it has no other equal in human literature Let any person of warm fancy, read these lines in view of Niagara, in a fine summer morning, and while the Iris beams upon his eye, he will exclaim, ' this indeed is the language of enraptured poetry"

rapidly but smoothly to destruction, is another romance any vessel whatever, would be dashed to splinters by the rapids before coming within half a mile of the *chute*.

Unless it may be from Goat island, which I did not see, the best situation to see the falls, is from the Table Rock,* or to my mind more safe and more pleasant from the hill above. Mr. Whitney is now constructing a stairway from the New-York side, to lead down to the margin of the stream This work, when completed, will afford a more safe and commodious passage than the wretched ladder down which the curious traveller has been hitherto conveyed.†

---

* Before my return from Detroit to Buffalo, a fragment of rock on the Canada side, supposed to be the Table Rock, broke and fell. It was not however the Table Rock that fell, as the annexed extract will explain.

"FALLS OF NIAGARA.

"*Mr Salisbury*—I have seen it observed in your paper, that the celebrated Table Rock, had precipitated itself into the Niagara river. This is not correct. The part that fell did not extend to within 50 yards of the Table Rock; it was about 20 rods in length, and from 1 to 4 in breadth This part, the day previous to its falling was passed over by a large party of visitors Perhaps it would be proper to state, that since that event, (which destroyed the pathway) Mr Forsyth has constructed a new and safe pathway to the Table Rock."—*Buffalo pap.* S.

† "*Goat Island.*—This beautiful Island, which divides the Falls of Niagara, seems to have been rent from the American side by some violent convulsion of nature; the strata of rocks the soil, and the growth of the timber corresponding with those upon the main land.

" The difficulties of approach to this island have, in all probability increased with time, and as the fall has receded; for we are informed, that it was once a place of frequent resort for the French garrisons in Niagara and Schlosser, and of the British who succeeded them There are numerous inscriptions upon the trunks of the trees, some of which are obliterated; the earliest now legible is of the year 1769. The only mode of access in those days, was to drop down the current from Schlosser upon the point of the island, and great care and circumspection were necessary by avoiding the draft of the current, to escape being carried over the tremendous precipice. But in later times, al-

Visitors increase annually. Mr. Forsyth, keeper of the public inn on the Canada shore, has kept a register of the names of persons who have lodged at his house on their visit to Niagara. The number of names are considerable, and each succeeding year the excess becomes greater. In no other situation in the United States can buildings and other accommodations for the use of travellers, be established with more certainty of remuneration. The cause that leads the stranger to this spot is not the acquisition of wealth, nor is it the debates of a legislative assembly that draws him thither; but the attractions that allure him are a combination of many of the most astonishing features of nature, the rich painted landscape, whose outline was traced by the HAND by whom the world was framed, and whose strong con-

though the curiosity of some surmounted the dread of danger, few were hardy enough to adventure.

"A bridge was built last fall, by the hon. judge Porter, and sanguine hopes were entertained that it would have withstood the torrent, but an unusual collection of ice in the spring occasioned it to be carried away. The perseverance of that enterprizing gentleman, however, was not to be discouraged, and a new bridge has been constructed in a more favorable position, which bids fair to brave the dangers which proved fatal to the first.

"The highest praise is due to Messrs. Pierce & Whitney, the contractors, and to Mr. Osborn the builder, for the judicious location of the building, and its remarkable construction. By means of this structure, which few would have designed or executed, Goat island has become the most interesting spot that fancy can depict, as it affords the best and most varied views of that stupendous cataract which "enchants the world."

"The view from Table Rock, on the British side, has hitherto been much admired, but that spectacle is infinitely surpassed by the grandeur of the views from several points of the island, which exhibit the majestic fall, and the surrounding scenery in unrivalled splendor. From the same point the eye embraces the rapids above, dashing with impetuous fury as if madly hastening to precipitate themselves into the yawning gulf, the tremendous volume of water sends its spray to the heavens, and the winding of the foaming torrent below the precipice, no imagination can conceive, no language can describe the wildness and sublimity of the scene."—*Niagara Patriot.*

tour has and will endure through the changes of countless centuries.

July 30th, I left Mr. Forsyth's and traced the shores of the strait to Queenston, a distance seven miles along a road, over a rolling but not hilly country. From the heights above Queenston, a prospect opens only second to that of the falls, though of a character totally different. The wide sweep of the alluvial plain of lake Ontario lies beneath, chequered with meadows and farms; the deep and rapid strait issuing in its dark profound from the shelving rocks above, the two towns of Queenston and Lewiston; and far on the back ground the ocean-like expanse of lake Ontario, closes the perspective.

It is when standing upon the brow of these heights, that the fact becomes demonstrative that here once dashed Niagara, mingling his foaming surge with the wave of Ontario. The rocky bed has yielded to the ever rolling waters, and the cataract has retired to the deep and distant dell where it now repeats the thunders of ages, and continues its slow but certain march to Erie. Time was when Niagara did not exist, and time will come when it will cease to be! But to these mighty revolutions, the change of empire is as the bursting bubble on the rippling pool, to the overwhelming volume that rolls down the steep of Niagara itself. Since this cataract fell where Queenston now stands, have risen and fallen Assyria, and Persia; Macedonia, and Rome; the flood of northern barbarians issued forth from their native woods, and in the storm of savage fury profaned the tombs of the Fabii, and the Scipio's, and in the march of time the polished sons of those mail clad warriors, now seek with religious veneration the fragments of the statues that their fathers broke; and whilst this moral stream was flowing through the wide expanse of ages, has the Niagara continued its unceasing course. Roused from the sleep of a *thousand years*, the energies of the human mind sought another world, and found America; and amid this new creation found Niagara. During the change of nations, religion and language, this vast, this fearful cataract unceasingly pursued and pursues its slow and toilsome way.

But in soberness, no man ever did or ever can trace this ground, without the intoxication of enthusiasm. I retraced my way back to Buffalo, passing along the Canada shore as far as the ferry below Fort Erie.

There is, however, no scene which the traveller visits, that so little answers his expectations as that of a field of battle. In the splendid accounts of the positions chosen, defended, or lost, the movements of armies, the shock of battalions, and the victory acquired, or defeat sustained by celebrated generals, we are apt to consider the ground upon which these events transpired, as offering something of deep interest in review; but when seen this illusion vanishes, and the eye finds nothing beyond the common objects in nature to render conspicuous the scene of the greatest battles.

The last war between the United States and Great Britain, has been rendered forever remarkable by some of those events which continue land-marks in history. The victories of our infant navy gained against the leviathan of the deep, the burning of Washington, and the destructive defeat of a veteran army of 10,000 men at New Orleans by less than half their number of militia, are facts imperishable as the literature of the world. But in no part of the vast theatre of this memorable war, were the operations of the respective armies so sanguinary as on the Niagara river. Perhaps to the number of men engaged, no battles were ever more obstinately contended, or victory more dearly bought, than were those of Queenston, October 8th, 1811, in which gen. Brock was killed; that of Chippewa, July 5th, 1814, and that of Bridgwater, July 25th, 1814. The latter was indeed one of those desperate conflicts, where the officers and soldiers of both armies, seemed to have lost the feeling of every other sentiment except that of victory. Gens. Brown and Scott were wounded, and Gen. Real, of the British army, taken prisoner. The following facts from Gen. Brown's return of this engagement, are amongst the most singular in human history, on the American side the

"Return of killed, wounded and missing, in the above
"action—killed, 171—wounded, 570—missing, 117—total,
"858."

"The British official account of the above action, makes
"their loss as follows, viz:—killed, 84—wounded, 559—
"missing, 193—prisoners, 42—total, 878."

Fay's letters, page 224.

If to these bloody battles are superadded the not less ruinous and destructive operations at fort Niagara, fort Erie, and at Buffalo, every spot of this strait have now become classic ground, and the traveller for ages will seek the hero's grave. As I passed these fields, I could not but contrast the storm that once raged upon their surface with the deep and solemn calm that reigned around me. Fields once covered with the dead and dying soldier, now smiled in golden harvest.

Upon the rising ground near Forsyth's, I stopped to take a parting view of Niagara, gazed a few moments upon its ever pleasing features, hurried on, passed the fields of Chippewa, and about noon of the 31st August, found myself again in Buffalo.

The following are the stages and distances, on the Canada side, from fort George to Buffalo.

	Miles.
Fort George to Queenston,	—7
Stamford at the Falls,	7—14
Chippewa,	3—17
Palmer's,	9—26
Ferry below fort Erie,	6—32
Black Rock,	1—33
Buffalo,	2—35

Detained by contrary winds in Buffalo to the evening of the 2d of August, I had a good opportunity of examining the place. It does not appear to me that the value of that situation has been duly appreciated by our government. Many reasons concur to enforce the necessity of rendering the harbor of Buffalo capable of containing vessels of any size. Such an undertaking is by no means visionary. At less than a mile from the mouth of the creek, there is sufficient water to admit a first rate ship of the line. If a strong mole was constructed running out from above the light house into the lake, a safe shelter for vessels would be formed. In a naval point of view, such a work would be invaluable, and contribute not a little to secure to the United States the safety and superiority of their flag on lake Erie, and to prevent the repetition of the desolating inroads of an enemy in time of war.*

Adieu.

---

* Some facts relative to the operations of Commodore Perry and his fleet in last war, will be found mentioned in the sequel of this work, which will more strongly point out the necessity of some more secure naval station, than any that now exists on the north-east extremity of lake Erie. The following account of the effects of the winds on that lake has been published at the moment of preparing this sheet for the press; I have given it entire, as a specimen of the tremendous gales that sweep over those inland seas, gales that are appalling indeed, where no haven presents its shelter to the wretched mariner.

"*Gale on lake Erie.*—In addition to the loss of the Hercules, heretofore stated, we gather from the Cleveland Register, of Nov. 24, which came to hand this morning, the following particulars of fatal disasters:

"The schooner Independence, of Sandusky, John Brooks master and owner, John Chambers seaman, cleared from the mouth of Black river, on Saturday the 14th inst. for Detroit, loaded with corn, for John S. Reid, esq. who sent his son Cornelius Reid to assist capt. Brooks, and dispose of the corn. The vessel was capsized in a gale—the cargo lost, and every soul on board drowned—the wreck drifted on shore near the mouth of Black river. A wreck of a vessel, bottom upwards, seen off the mouth of Grand river. Schooner Pauline, was driven on shore near the mouth of Grand river and bilged—her crew saved, but her cargo, consisting of salt, lost. Schooner Boxer, lying in the mouth of Grand river, dismasted, bilged, and a complete wreck—crew saved. Schooner

LETTER XIV.

Detroit, August 13, 1818.

Dear Sir,

On the evening of the 2d inst. I left Buffalo for this city, in the schooner Zephyr, capt. Wilcox, and had a tedious passage of eleven days, but at length found myself agreeably rid of the vessel, and on shore to-day. Since it is over, I do not regret having encountered contrary winds in my passage, as the circumstance enabled me to visit most of the towns along the south border of lake Erie.

A gale commenced to blow with great violence from the N. W. soon after we left Buffalo creek, and continued to rage all night. The darkness of the night, and the narrowness of the mouth of the harbor we left, prevented our return; the course of the wind kept us from sheltering under point Abino, on the Canada shore, and of course left us to the mercy of the storm and waves. I have the misfortune to be very subject to sea sickness, and never did I pass so dreadful a night. The short chopping waves of lake Erie give a vessel, during the prevalence of a gale, an unspeakable disagreeable motion; the nature of its shores renders it amongst the most dangerous parts of the earth to navigate.

Wasp dismasted, and driven on shore at the mouth of Cunningham's creek, bilged—her crew saved, but cargo lost. Schooner general Brown was driven on shore near the mouth of Black river, on Wednesday the 18th inst—her crew all safe, but the vessel considerably damaged. Schooner general Jackson left Green Bay for Mackinaw, some time since, and has not since been heard of—fears are entertained for her safety. British brig lord Wellington, of Canada, was driven on shore at point Abino, and went to pieces—crew saved, but cargo lost."

A fine steam boat is now building at Black Rock, and will be an invaluable acquisition when put in motion.*

We made Dunkirk harbor in the evening of the 4th, where we remained wind bound until noon of the 7th. It is a curious fact, that in a distance of 45 miles from Buffalo to Dunkirk, there is no place where the smallest vessel can find shelter, except the mouth of Cattaraugus creek, which affords but little water, consequently useless for vessels drawing more than four or five feet. Dunkirk is in Chatauque county, township of Pomfret. The alluvial bank of lake Erie is at this place about four miles wide, from the inner border of which, rise the hills which divide the waters flowing into the Ohio valley, from those which fall into Lake Erie. This ridge becomes visible from the lake immediately after leaving Buffalo, though from that place they are distant between twenty and thirty miles in a direct course. Following nearly an east and west direction through Genesee, Cataraugus, and Chatauque counties, the dividing ridge approaches lake Erie obliquely, and at Portland eighteen miles

---

* This boat is called *Walk in the Water*, an awkward term given in compliment to an Indian chief lately dead. She left Buffalo on her first trip about the 17th or 18th inst. The following extract from the Buffalo Gazette, shews the result. "The circumstance I have mentioned of the prevalence of S W winds, renders steam navigation invaluable on the St. Lawrence, though *Walk in The Water* is too large, to answer all the purposes to which, from the shallowness of most of the harbors on lake Erie, she might be applied, if her draught was less.

' The steam-boat *Walk in the Water* has returned to Buffalo from her first trip, and is found on trial to equal the best expectations of her builders and proprietors. She reached Detroit, a distance of more than 300 miles, in 48 hours, and afterwards proceeded to lake St. Clair, and brought down a number of troops. May she prove as profitable to the enterprising proprietors, as she is likely to prove beneficial to the public at large.

' Thus there is now established, on the St Lawrence and its waters steam-boat accommodations for about 800 miles, and the distance of these facilities to travel, will probably be doubled in a very few years, by the introduction of these boats upon lakes Huron, Michigan, Superior, &c."

south-west from Dunkirk, reaches within less than three miles of the margin of the lake. The hills seen from the lake appear to rise much more abrupt than they do in fact. Their slope towards the lake, presents an immense forest chequered with comparatively few farms.

Dunkirk is a new village on the shore of lake Erie. A semicircular bay lies in front of the village, formed by two capes, distant from each other about a mile and a half, with a bar extending from cape to cape, over which there is seven feet water. Vessels capable of passing the bar, find good shelter from east south-east, south, or south-west winds, and the bar breaking the waves, the harbor affords a refuge also from the winds blowing from the lake. The bottom of the bay affords good anchorage within two hundred yards of the shore. Dunkirk is invaluable as offering the only port between Buffalo and Erie. A number of gentlemen in Albany are the principal proprietors of this village and its vicinity; they have expended considerable sums in the erection of a wharf, a road to Fredonia, and other improvements. The site is a dead level, which extends back towards the hills two or three miles, before any considerable eminences disturb the monotony of its surface. The soil is composed of sand and a rich loam, forming an alluvion of great fertility. Timber, hemlock, various species of oak, elm, linden, poplar, (lirodendron tulipifera) sugar maple, and beech. The trees of all kinds are remarkable for their extraordinary size.

The day after my arrival at Dunkirk I walked out to Fredonia, formerly Canadaway, four miles. Canadaway creek rises in the dividing ridge, interlocking with the sources of the Connewango branch of the Allegany river, and flowing north-west towards lake Erie, tumbling from precipice to precipice until it reaches the alluvial border of lake Erie, which it joins two miles above Dunkirk bay. Fredonia is built upon each bank of this creek, is a new and flourishing village. The road from Buffalo to Erie passes through and divides at Fredonia, into what is called the lower or lake road, and the upper or Chatauque road. These roads do not again unite until within the precincts of the town of Erie. The settlements follow generally these roads, particularly the former or lake route.

I should have been much rejoiced to have been able to determine the elevation of the dividing ridge above the surface of lake Erie, but could not have that satisfaction, from want of instruments and time. Independent of their apparent height, two circumstances combine to prove that they cannot fall much short of 1200 feet. First, the distance to which they are visible is at least forty miles. Any object capable of being seen upon the curve of the earth's surface forty miles, must be within a trifle of 1100 feet high. The second datum to demonstrate the considerable elevation of these hills, is, that from them flow waters which enters the gulf of Mexico upwards of twelve degrees of latitude distant from its source. The surface of lake Erie is known to be 564.5 feet above the ocean tides, and allowing the dividing ridge an elevation of 1,100 feet, would produce 1664.5 feet as the entire height of this ridge above the Atlantic ocean. Sloping very gradually towards the south, a rapid depression of, as we have seen, 1100 feet takes place on the side of lake Erie. The extreme head waters of Chatauque lake, rises in the township of Portland, within less than three miles of lake Erie, and is the point of nearest approach of the Mississippi waters, to the margin of any of the Canadian lakes.

Canals have been projected to unite the Ohio and St. Lawrence waters, many points have been mentioned, and amongst others by Chatauque lake. You will perceive the obstacles that nature has opposed to the completion of such a project, by the enormous difference of level, and the very sudden depression. It is a subject to me of some surprize, that the Erie chain of hills is, even by many persons of good information, considered as rising but very little above the surface of lake Erie; but no sooner is the real elevation of Erie known, than the conviction must be irresistible, that a very serious rise must be necessary from that lake, to admit a current of such prodigious length as that of the Allegany, Ohio, and Mississippi rivers. If indeed lake Erie was nearly as much elevated as the source of Allegany river, then would the fall of water in the Niagara strait and St. Lawrence river, be as great in less than 500 miles, as that of the Mississippi and its tributaries in six times that distance; the certain consequence would be that either the fall of Niagara would be 800 or 900 feet, or that the St. Lawrence, from its great rapidity, would be unnavigable.

With good roads, and a thriving interior, Dunkirk must advance in a ratio with the neighboring country, being the only port, no rival can be raised to check its progress nearer than forty-five miles. Should the current of commerce turn towards the city of New-York, then would Dunkirk become the shipping port to a semicircle of at least thirty miles radius. At present the village consists of about 20 houses newly built. The proprietors are employed in forming a road, to join both above and below the village with that of the lake margin.

Aug. 6th, in the evening I left Dunkirk, and, as in leaving Buffalo, encountered another gale, but as it came from the north-east, it carried us rapidly forward. The gale set in about three hours before day, and bore our vessel about 80 miles from Dunkirk by morning; as the sun arose the wind abated, and at 8 o'clock P. M. we passed the town of Erie, into the harbor of which we did not enter. Much of the shore between Dunkirk and Erie, is composed of shelves of rocks, twenty or 30 feet high, and extremely dangerous to vessels, as no place of refuge exists even for boats. The dividing ridge is visible from the lake, following a similar direction with its shores. Above the town of Erie the alluvial border becomes wider, and the slope of the dividing ridge less abrupt, and gradually retiring into the state of Ohio, about twenty miles above Erie it ceases to be in view from the lake. Settlements become more rare: the border of the lake presents one vast forest. Thirty miles from the town of Erie and near the mouth of Conneought creek, is the division line between the states of Pennsylvania and Ohio. We passed this place, and also the mouth of Ashtabula river in the night, and at noon of the 8th, we also passed the mouth of Grand river. At 1 o'clock P. M. we were becalmed which continued two or three hours, and was followed by a strong head wind, which forced us back into the mouth of Grand river. The dividing ridge is visible from the lake opposite this place.

Grand river is a stream of some consequence rising in Portage county, flows over the north-west angle of Trumbull county, assumes a north course, enters Ashtabula county, through which it winds five and twenty miles, turns suddenly westward, enters Geauga county, through which it flows upwards of twenty miles, falls into lake Erie in the latter county, after an entire course of more than seventy miles. It is about seventy yards wide at the mouth, with seven feet water on the bar near the entrance into the lake. The east bank rises to the height of 39 or 40 feet, affording a very handsome site for a village. The harbor is excellent for such vessels whose whole draft of water will admit entrance. A village called Fairport, has been laid out on the point below or east of the mouth of the river. Some houses are built, two taverns and three stores have been established, with a warehouse at the bank of the river. Preparations are making to form wharves, extending beyond the bar in such manner as to afford a harbor to vessels of any draft. If such a work is completed Fairport will be amongst the most flourishing villages on the south shore of lake Erie.

The soil is here on the high banks composed of sand, pebble, and vegetable earth, and no doubt very productive, though of that I had no other means of forming a judgment than by the natural growth, as no cleared lands are yet to be seen near the village.

Three miles from Fairport, upon the left bank of Grand river, stands the very flourishing village of Painesville, the richest and most commercial in the county, containing a number of stores, taverns, mills, and other machinery; a post-office, and a fine wooden bridge over Grand river. The soil of this neighborhood is a rich vegetable mould, resting upon rounded pebble or clay. The land in fact of all the Connecticut reserve is fertile, with but partial exceptions. The timber, hickory, sugar maple, black walnut, elm, oak, and other trees indicative of deep, strong soil. Though but little cultivation appears along the lake shore, the interior is rapidly advancing in settlement. Fairport has all the appearance of a commercial place; in infancy it must be confessed, but yet with such marks as will justify the anticipation of vigorous maturity.

Aug. 9th. I left Fairport early in the morning, with a light breeze from the N. E. and at 2 o'clock P. M. reached Cleveland, at the mouth of Cayahoga river.

Cleveland, like Fairport, occupies the eastern point between the lake and river, and is, after Buffalo and Erie, the largest town upon the shores of lake Erie. Similar to all rivers that flow into any of the Canadian lakes, a bar crosses its mouth with a depth of 7 feet. Cayahoga river rises in Geauga and Portage by a number of creeks, which unite at the north-west angle of the latter county, then enters that of Cayahoga, and falls into lake Erie at Cleveland. A road winding up a very high and steep bank leads from the harbor to the town, which stands upon the table land. The situation of Cleveland is the most pleasing of any town I have yet seen on lake Erie. The general slope of the ground plan of the town inclines towards the lake, though elevated perhaps 60 feet above its surface. Cleveland stands higher than Fairport, but both are subject to the serious objection of having banks abrupt and difficult to ascend from the margin of the water in the harbor. That of Cleveland produces, from its inclination towards the lake, a very pleasant and extensive prospect, which adds no little to the airy and healthy appearance of the town and its vicinity. The soil of the neighborhood is extremely fertile, composed as every where else on lake Erie, of sand, clay, and rounded pebble, in different degrees of mixture. For the first time in the St. Lawrence valley, I saw the peach tree with a vigorous, healthy look, in the gardens and orchards near Cleveland; and here also appears more effects of culture, than in any part of the lake shore from Buffalo.

Cleveland is the seat of justice for Cayahoga county, with a court-house, bank, printing office, a number of stores and taverns, and a post office. It is a position of considerable consequence, being in a direct line of communication between Pittsburg and Detroit, 131 miles from the former city. During last war, the mouth of Cayahoga was found to be a port of great convenience for the transportation of stores, provisions, and building of small vessels for the use of the army and navy. Why large vessels could not be as well constructed here as at Erie, I am unable to comprehend; the water upon the respective bars is equal, whilst the harbor of Erie, from its openness, would be certainly less defensible than that of Cleveland, and the communication between Michigan Territory, and the interior of Ohio, Pennsylvania, Kentucky, and Virginia, more direct by the latter than the former port.

We left Cleveland in the evening of the 8th, with a good north-east breeze; we proceeded up the lake with so much rapidity as to be obliged to he to, in order to have day light to enter Sandusky bay. On the morning of the 9th, our vessel was under way at sun-rise; Cunningham's island and point Peninsula in view to the west; the main shore of Huron county, in the state of Ohio, to the south, and Point-au-Ple, in Canada, to the north; the hills towards the sources of Huron river to the south-east; but in every other direction, the adjacent shores and islands seemed level, and to rise to no great elevation above the water

Between seven and eight A. M. I entered Sandusky bay. This sheet of water is formed by the expansion of Sandusky river, and a long, narrow strip of land, which runs from between the mouth of that stream and Portage river. The strip forms the outside of the bay towards the lake, and has received the name of point Peninsula, forms a part of Huron county, and has been erected into the township of Danbury, it is about twenty miles long, and from two to three miles wide. From the eastern extremity of the peninsula, extends a low, narrow point about two miles long, approaching within a mile of a similar low, long, narrow bar projecting from the main shore. The space between these bars is the entrance into Sandusky bay. The point of the peninsula is called point Prospect, the one opposite point Sandy. A small round island lies inside of point Prospect, called Bull island. The points are covered with dwarf trees, and are, though on a larger scale, in every other respect similar to those which form Sodus bay in lake Ontario.

The entrance lies close upon point Sandy, and like almost all harbors in lake Erie, has seven feet water at the shallowest part. Our ship passed Bull island to the westward and proceeded to the custom house, which is now on the peninsula, and kept by a Frenchman of the name of Peter P. Ferry. Whilst our captain was regulating his affairs with the custom house officer, I walked forth to examine the adjacent country. I found the surface rising from the bay by gradual acclivity, to at least 30 feet elevation. Soil a deep black loam, mixed with sand and pebble: timber, black walnut, shag-bark hickory, white oak, elm, linden, ash, and sycamore, with a shrubbery of alder, sumach, and grape vine. On no land of whatever quality did I ever before see so much black walnut on a given space. This tree, whose existence is an unerring proof of uncommon fertility, is here the prevalent timber, and is found of enormous size and height.

Most part of the peninsula is yet unsettled though some farms are commenced, and it is needless to say, after what

I have already stated of the soil, that the crops are very promising, particularly maize or Indian corn. The property of soil to the lands of the peninsula, belongs to those who enjoy the benefits of what is called the fire lands. The nature of that tenure you know arose from a remunerative grant made by the government of the United States, to some sufferers by British depredation, during the war of the revolution, such as the inhabitants of Fairfield, Norwalk, and some other places. Like most public donations for the moderate benefit of the many, the fire grant has made the fortunes of a few; the property has been, perhaps, foolishly undervalued, by most of those for whose use it was originally separated from the public domain.

The town of Danbury or the peninsula of Sandusky, contains at least 40 sections, or about 25,600 acres, sufficient for more than one hundred moderate farms. The land is generally level, some prairie,* the forest land extremely well timbered; it will no doubt become the seat of a flourishing settlement.

I crossed the bay from the peninsula to the town of Sandusky or Portland, as it seems the village bears both names. The bay is here about four miles wide, which breadth it maintains almost to its head, except at the narrows about five miles above the village of Sandusky. The shores are every where but little raised above the water, in some places flat and marshy, soil exuberantly fertile.

It is curious to see in the heart of the continent of North America, a country so perfectly alluvial, as that which encircles the south-west and west part of lake Erie. Except the hill behind the custom house on the peninsula, every other object in Sandusky bay reminded me strongly of some parts of lower Louisiana, and indeed few places can be more similar though so distant, and so differently situated respect-

* Prairie this word is from the French, and signifies literally *meadow*.

ing the ocean. All the rivers which flow into lake Erie are intersected by ledges of rock, at a greater or less distance from the margin of the lake. I have already noticed the alluvial border skirting from Buffalo, along the south-east side of the lake, with more or less breadth; though in some places very narrow, as between Dunkirk and Erie. This alluvial border is continuous, in no place entirely interrupted, and west of Cayahoga river spreads to the width of from five to ten miles. The ridge of hills which separate the waters of Ohio river from those of lake Erie, and to whose phenomena I have drawn your attention, enters the state of Ohio near the dividing line of Ashtabula and Trumbull counties; pursuing a south-west direction it intersects Trumbull and Portage diagonally, giving rise to its south-east slope to Beaver river of Ohio, and from its north-west inclination flow Grand and Cayahoga rivers. From the south-west angle of Trumbull county, the dividing ridge assumes a west direction, which it pursues along the northern border of Stark, and Wayne, and more than half of that of Richland county. From this latter part of the ridge, flow to the south the head waters of Muskingum, and to the north, part of that of Cayahoga, and the sources of Rocky, Black, Beaver of lake Erie, Vermillion, and Huron rivers. In Richland county the ridge turns south-west, which course it maintains through the remainder of the state of Ohio; discharging southwardly the waters of Scioto and Miami, and northwardly those of Sandusky and Maumee rivers. This ridge does not every where appear in the actual form of hills, with intervening vales, but spreads into an extensive table land. It is, however, every where a distinctive land-mark, and forms an important geological feature in the physiognomy of our country. It appears to rest upon, and to be in great part, except the mere surface, composed of micaceous or limestone schist. The rocks forming shelving acclivities, produce the rapids and falls, which are found in all its rivers. The lowest visible ledge of this vast schistose mass, borders the great lake Erie alluvial plain, which I have noticed. The alluvion has all the features of recent alluvion; the streams are sluggish in their motions, their beds having but little inclination; the land along the banks is the highest part of the ground; the intervening spaces between the rivers are low and mostly swampy; much of the entire surface is prairie, and covered with an exuberant herbage; the soil, where sufficiently elevated for culture, is productive to excess; and the inhabitants are subject to intermitting fevers, during the latter part of the summer and beginning of the fall season. These are the attributes of recent alluvion, from the fens of Lincolnshire, and Holland; from the Pontine marshes to those of the Amazon, Oronoco, Mississippi, and the shores of Erie.

The extent, and unhealthfulness of the lake Erie alluvion, has been very greatly overrated. Its greatest positive breadth is at the mouth of Maumee, and there it falls short of twenty miles. Following the curve of lake Erie, from the mouth of Huron river, in Huron county, to Brownstown, in the Michigan Territory, is about 100 miles, and allowing the alluvion ten miles wide, would produce 1000 square miles or 640,000 acres. I am convinced from all I have been able to learn respecting the country, that the foregoing is too large an estimate. Swamps and flats exist above the lower falls in the rivers, but are of a nature essentially distinct from the alluvial plains along the lake shore.

The village of Sandusky contains only a few new houses. The bank slopes from the water edge a short distance, and then becomes an almost uniform level. The depth of soil is not considerable; the bank upon which the town is built rests upon a bed of schistose sandstone, of excellent quality for building and paving. This schistose base no doubt underlays the whole adjacent country, extending under the mass of similar rock over which the waters of the various streams are precipitated in their way from the higher interior region.

I walked from the village of Sandusky to that of Venice, four and a half miles higher up the bay. Quitting the village of Sandusky a very short distance, I was more than ever impressed with the resemblance of the surface of the earth to many places I had seen on the southern waters of the Mississippi. The timber was in great part different from that of Louisiana, but with the exception of sugar maple considerable resemblance exists in the forests of the two countries. I found here upon the Sandusky plain three or four species of hickory, three or four of oak, intermixed with ash, elm, linden, sugar maple, and an underwood of alder and sumac.

I found Venice situated upon the western shore of a muddy creek, upon a bank much lower and more disadvantageously situated than that upon which stands the village of Sandusky or Portland, though the former village is at present much larger than the latter. Each have the appearance of towns in the first stage of their existence. In January 1798, I saw the now flourishing Steubenville, in the state of Ohio, not more advanced or promising than are now Sandusky and Venice. The great fertility of the lands in their neighborhood, and their situation upon one of the best harbors of lake Erie, are propitious circumstances in favor of their future prosperity. The western line of the Fire lands and of the surveyed part of the state of Ohio, crosses Sandusky bay about two miles west of Venice, and continuing north crosses the peninsula and leaves the township of Danbury to the east.

Monday, August 10th, I left Sandusky bay with a breeze from the west, and after clearing the bar had a fine view of the peninsula, Cunningham's island, and the southern Bass island. With a light wind upon our quarter we sailed to the north west, between Cunningham's island and the peninsula, the channel about three miles wide. I had a very fair view of the adjacent shores, and found them composed, as I had formerly heard them represented, of schistose sandstone and crumbling limestone; the latter frequently white as chalk, and appears worn into chasms by the surf of the lake, and rising from one to ten feet above the water. Cunningham's is the easternmost and largest of the lake Erie islands, is about 8 miles long by one medial width, or covering perhaps two thousand acres of land. Some settlements were formerly made upon this island, but the inhabitants were obliged by the savages to abandon their farms during the last war.

Passing Cunningham's, the Bass islands came in view to the N W. about eight or ten miles distant. Approaching the southern Bass, the first prominent object that is now seen, is what is called Edward's clearing, or Put-in-bay. The west wind prevented me from visiting this noble harbor, decidedly the best in all lake Erie, and dear to the American heart, from the events of last war. It was from here, that on the morning of September 10th, 1813, Commodore Perry led his fleet, to obtain the first naval victory, in squadron, ever obtained by the United States; and it was into this bay, that on the evening of the same day, the captured British fleet was conveyed by its intrepid conquerors. You have so often read, and so well remember the detail of this event, that a repetition here would be lost time to us both.

I passed the eastern mouth of Put-in-bay at the distance of half a mile; its form and situation are both admirable. The Bass islands form a group of seven, lying about three miles from part of the Sandusky peninsula, and, as I have already observed, seven or eight miles north-west of Cunningham's island. Put-in-bay, is formed by a curve of the largest and most southern of the Bass groups, having two entrances, one from the east and the other from the west. The bay is very finely land-locked. The second large island of the group, stretching from east to west across the widest part at half a mile distant, and one of the smaller islands lying opposite each channel. The three main islands do not differ much in extent, though that in which is Put-in-bay is the largest. All are uninhabited, and covered with a dense forest. I had no means to determine their area with certainty, but judged the three main islands to average about one and a half miles long, and half a mile wide, and may cover from 2500 to 3000 acres taken collectively, resting upon a solid mass of schistose rock in great part limestone. From here limestone, for the purpose of making lime, is carried as far as Detroit and Cleveland. The soil is excellent, and would admit a little settlement of thirty or forty families. But every object of utility to which the Bass islands could be applied, yields to the importance of Put-in-bay. This fine haven admits entrance and anchorage for vessels of any supposable draught, safe from all winds. It must become, from its position and depth of water, an object of great national value. No harbor in lake Erie, or in its connecting waters, except in Erie strait, can in any respect compare with it; its occupation as a naval and commercial station must one day take place.

The wind continuing light, we passed the Bass island slowly, sailing north, and when opposite the north-westernmost of the group, could also distinctly see point Pele island on the Canada shore. Clearing the Bass islands, we turned again north-west, but were almost becalmed all the afternoon; we, however, passed the group of small islands, called the Hen & Chickens, consisting of four, lying in a kind of crescent, five or six miles north west of the northern Bass. We left the Hen & Chickens to the north, and in the evening had the Bass islands to the south-east, the Hen & Chickens north-east, and the eastern Sister island to the west. We were now upon or very near the scene of Perry's battle; the evening was serene and beautiful; our little bark glided smoothly and slowly over the waves, where exactly five years, less one month before, the United States' flag was hoisted over the British ensign. I do not remember to have ever spent an evening at sea with so much pleasure. I literally fell asleep on deck, listening to a sailor repeatedly singing a rude song, commemorative of this event of national glory. The songster had himself been in the battle, and seemed to feel a strong emotion of national enthusiasm in passing the now peaceful scene, where he saw the humbled pride of the enemies of his country.

There are three islands extending south west from the Hen & Chickens, and stretching towards Maumee bay, they are called the eastern, middle, and western Sister, though in fact they lie from each other north-east and south west; they are all small, neither exceeds twenty or thirty acres. The eastern Sister, the smallest of the three, being about three acres, on which a considerable part of general Harrison's army, the same which reconquered Michigan, and defeated general Proctor on the Thames, was encamped from the 25th to the 27th September, 1813. It was, in all human probability, for that length of time, the best peopled island that ever existed on our globe.

On the afternoon of the 11th, I arrived in the city of Detroit, considerably fatigued, and very willing to enjoy solid land, though so short a time in the vessel. You will hear of me again in a few days.

Adieu.

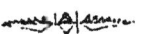

LETTER XV.

Detroit, August 13, 1818.

DEAR SIR,

I HAVE now been three days in this city, which for many reasons has excited and continues to excite more attention than its apparent magnitude would seem to justify. The events of last war contributed to render both the city and country objects of great interest to the American people. Like most events that have taken place in the world, where so much passion was excited, I am convinced that those in this quarter, and the operations of affairs here, have never been given to the world in all the naked purity of truth This much may be said, without once attempting to call in question the veracity of any individual. Much distortion of judgment may exist without a breach of rectitude. It would perhaps be dangerous to offer an opinion in mitigation of the conduct of general Hull, and yet if the expressions of those most concerned and best informed on this subject, that is the persons who were here before the war, and remained here to its termination, deserve any weight, that unfortunate officer was rather incapable than treacherous, rather borne down by the weight of the difficulties that environed him on all sides, than disposed to sacrifice either the interest or honor of a country, in whose service he had grown grey. And yet if these mitigating opinions be founded upon reality, general Hull, if his days were not abridged, the remaining years of his life were doomed to be passed in bitterness and regret, for causes over which he had no control, for calamities in which he himself was a sufferer, and without the power to produce a preventive or remedy.

Detroit, politically and commercially, is separated by an expanse of water, and by an uncultivated waste, from the other parts of the United States, and remains, together with the little community in its environs, an isolated moral mass, having few sympathies in common, and but a slight tie of interest to unite it to the sovereignty of which it forms a part. Much of the association is formed with, and great part of the trade of Detroit is yet carried towards a foreign state This separation of sentiment and action, is daily becoming less distant between the great body of the United States community, and a small but important member. The savage tribes are retiring, and civilized man extending his dwelling over the wide expanse, from Ohio river to lakes Michigan and Huron.

Many years past, when I resided in Louisiana, and when by a freak of folly so common with Spanish officers, the port of New-Orleans was closed upon the interior commerce of the United States; I well remember that the two great political parties, into which our country was then divided, though discussing warmly the most proper means of procuring this commercial key, in one circumstance they were of accord, that was, that the surplus produce of all our states and territories, situated upon the tributary streams of the Mississippi, must find a vent by that great outlet; and politicians of all parties conceded that the power, whether that of Spain, France, Great Britain, or the United States, which possessed New-Orleans, must, with that city, secure also the political and moral government of the inhabitants of countries, whose vital interests were there concentrated. I have heard and read many reasons given for and against the Grand Canal of New-York, but the most potent incentive to its completion, that ought to influence those who are employed to carry that vast project into execution, has been generally overlooked. If such a channel of commerce was open, the consequence would be, not only to secure to the United States the benefits of the produce of its own industry, but also to secure the moral attachment of the inhabitants of some of its remote, and, as matters now stand, most detached parts. Above the falls of Niagara, Canadian commerce would also flow with the most open, unobstructed current, and give to the people of the United States an irresistible influence over the widest extent, and most fertile part of Upper Canada. Buffalo, Detroit, Michilimakinac, and Green bay, would form an immense chain of inter-communication, and by Fox and Ouisconsin rivers, the commercial rivalry of New-York and New Orleans would come in contact in the heart of our country.

Detroit is now a place of extensive commerce, with all the attributes of a seaport; it forms the uniting link between a vast interior, inhabited yet, in great part by savages, and the civilized Atlantic border. You here behold those ponderous packages of articles destined for Indian trade, and while viewing those bales of stroud and blankets, I could not avoid calling to recollection the time when I beheld the same objects upon the Ohio, at Pittsburg, Wheeling, Marietta, Cincinnati, and Louisville; places, where at this time, those rude articles are replaced by objects to satisfy the wants, or gratify the luxury of a polished people. The resident society of Detroit, has all the exterior features of a flourishing and cultivated community, as much so, equivalent to numbers, as any city of the United States. I particularly remarked the great resemblance between the current of business and mixture of people here, and at Natchitoches on Red river, in Louisiana. Each place occupies the point of contact, between the aboriginal inhabitants of the wilderness, and the civilized people, who are pressing those natives of North America backwards, by the double force of physical and moral weight. In each place, you behold at one glance the extremes of human improvement, costume, and manners. You behold the inhabitants in habiliments that would suit the walks of New-York, Philadelphia, London or Paris, and you also behold the bushy, bare-headed savage, almost in primaeval nudity. In the same store-house, you see placed upon the same shelf, objects to supply the first and last wants of human nature.

The city of Detroit is situated upon the right bank of the strait of the same, which unites lakes Erie and Huron;* N. lat 42° 15′ 36″—W. long. from Washington city, 5° 56′—or 82° 36′ west from London. The strait (Detroit) is of very unequal breadth, its narrowest part is immediately op-

---

* *Detroit*, is the French for *Strait*, and literally signifies *Narrow*; from which change of an adjective to a noun, comes the name of *Detroit*.

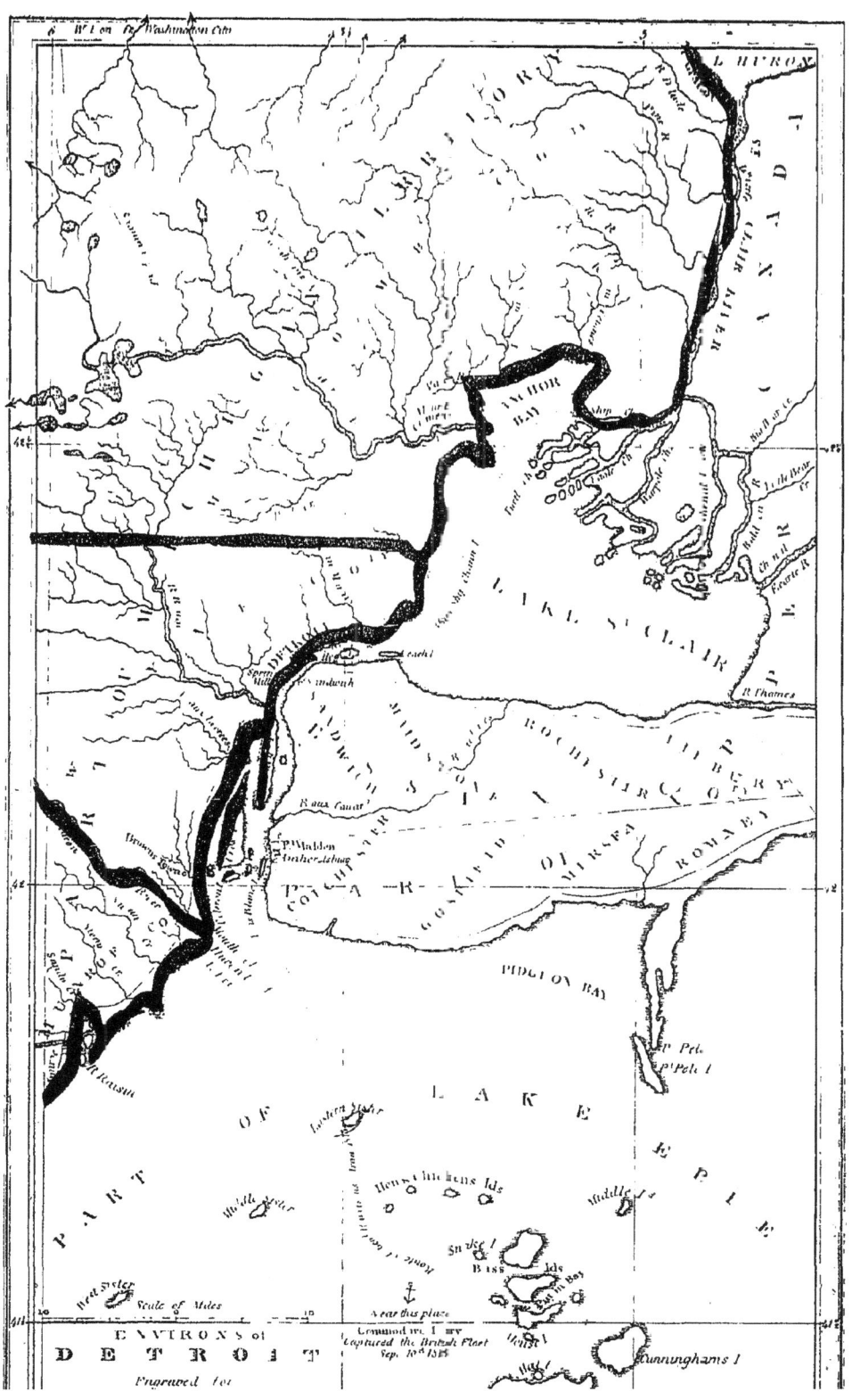

posite the city of Detroit. I had letters to Peter Audrain, esq. Register of the Land office in this city, which procured me access to the maps in his office, amongst which is an excellent representation of that part of the Michigan Territory which has been surveyed, together with the straits of St. Clair and Erie, and Lake St. Clair, connected with the adjacent shores of Canada. I have copied this map, from which the following table is extracted:

TABLE
OF THE STATIONARY DISTANCES FROM LAKE ERIE TO LAKE HURON, WITH THE WIDTH OF THE STRAITS OPPOSITE EACH STATION.

Station		Miles	Breadth
Huron river, U. S. shore,			5
Lower extremity of Celeron island,		2	4
Mouth of Brown's creek, U. S. shore,	1	3	4
Bois Blanc island, opposite the lower end of Gros isle,	1	4	4
Upper end of Bois Blanc,	1 1-4	5 1-4	4
Amherstsburg, and Fort Malden, Canada,	1-4	5 1-2	4
River aux Canards,	3 1-2	9	4
Lower end of Grand Turkey island,	1	10	4
Upper end of Gros island, U. S. shore,	2	12	4 1-4
Mouth of the river Ecorces,	2	14	5
Upper end of Grand Turkey island,	3	17	2
River Rouge, U. S. shore,	1	18	1 1-4
Sandwich in Canada,	2	20	1
City of DETROIT,	1 1-2	21 1-2	3-4
Lower end of Hog island,	2 1-2	24	1 1-2
Upper do. do.	2	26	2
Lower end of Peach island,	1	27	1 1-2
Upper do. do.	1	28	
Mouth of Huron river, of lake St. Clair, and entrance to Anchor bay,	19	47	
Mouth of St. Clair river,	7	54	1
Outlet of the Eagle channel,	4	58	1
Outlet of the Walpole channel,	3	61	1
Outlet of the Chenail Ecarte,	2	63	
Mouth of Belle Riviere,	4	67	
Mouth of Pine river,	8	75	
Lower end of isle aux Cerfs,	4	79	
Upper end of do.	2	81	
River Delude, U. S. shore,	5	86	
Fort Gratiot, M. T. and entrance to lake Huron,	3	89	

These distances are not taken with precision to small fractions of a mile, but measuring the entire distances by five mile sections taken from the scale, the respective results are sufficiently near as to answer all general purposes, and will suffice to enable you to form an accurate idea of the relative position of the places named. I have not given in the table the breadth of St. Clair river, above the Chenail Ecarte,* as it is uniformly about three fourths of a mile.

Approaching the mouth of Detroit river, the shores on all sides are low, no land is seen that rises to any considerable elevation above the water. The ship channel being on the Canada side, vessels pass close upon the cape below Amherstburg; the shores rise here very gently from the lake, soil sandy, but appear well settled and cultivated. Huron river of lake Erie† enters from Michigan Territory, where the lake is so contracted as to render it a suitable point to commence the name of the strait, though no perceptible current appears below the bottom of Bois Blanc island. A group of small islands encircle the lower end of Gros isle, of which Celeron, Hickory, Sugar, Fox, and particularly Bois Blanc, are the principal. The latter is indeed of great consequence. It is high, dry, and fit for culture, covered with timber, soil extremely fertile; but what renders it a particular object of interest, is the circumstance of its completely commanding the main ship channel to Detroit. A much wider expanse of water lies between Bois Blanc and Gros isle, and between Gros isle and the continent of Mi-

---

* The term *Chenal*, or more correctly Chenal Ecarte, signifies literally dispersed or scattered, and is very well applied to the outlet of rivers; but the same name is given in several instances in Canada to waters flowing into others, therefore very improper.

† There are three rivers of this name, two of which enter lake Erie, and one Anchor bay in lake St. Clair. It is extremely perplexing, such repetition of the same names for places so near each other.

chigan Territory, than flows between Bois Blanc and the Canada shore, but the latter, though not above one quarter of a mile wide, is deep enough for the largest vessel, whilst the others are shallow, and perplexed with small islands and sunken bars.

During last war, a small battery was erected on the lower point of Bois Blanc, which is now deserted, and the island now serves as a camping ground for the savages who visit Amherstburg. This island will be one of the most important points which the commissioners, under the treaty of Ghent, will have to determine. At Amherstburg the banks have gradually risen to fifteen or twenty feet above the water, sloping by very gentle acclivity. The town contains from 250 to 300 houses, mostly of wood, and perhaps twelve hundred people. The harbor is excellent, the water continuing deep to very near the shore. Some fine ware houses line the banks, and with the shipping give a commercial air to the place. The adjacent farms have an elegant appearance, and follow each other without much interval of uncleared land.

Fort Malden, by which name Amherstburg was formerly known, stands above the town, but is now in ruins, only some dilapidated breast works and barracks remain, to be perhaps never repaired.

Gros isle is a fine body of land, eight miles long by a medial width of one and a half miles, contains about twelve sections of a mile square, or 7,680 acres of excellent land. Several farms have been opened on this island, but the greatest part of its surface continues under a heavy forest. From the upper point of Bois Blanc island, the ship channel gradually leaves the Canada shore, and passes between Gros and Grand Turkey island, the main channel about two miles wide. Turkey island is about seven miles in length and one mile medial breadth, much of its surface marshy. The riviere aux Canards or Duck river, falls into the strait from the Canada side, one mile below the lower point of

Grand Turkey island; the riviere aux Ecorees or Bark river from Michigan Territory, enters something above its middle, or two miles above the higher point of Gros isle; riviere Rouge or Red river, falls into the strait, also from Michigan Territory, four miles above the riviere aux Ecorees, and one mile above the higher extremity of Grand Turkey island. Above the latter island, the strait suddenly contracts from four to one and a quarter wide, and continues becoming narrower to the city of Detroit, where its width falls short of a mile.

In coming up the strait, when the woods of Gros isle are cleared, both shores exhibit lines of farm houses, interspersed with orchards and gardens. The settlements on the United States side, continue up the rivieres Ecorees and Rouge, which, together with those along the shore of that strait, present a country in a high state of culture. The Canada shore is not less improved than that of the United States; farm follows farm upon both banks, which, with the houses, wind-mills, and vessels on the strait, afford a fine picture of agricultural and commercial prosperity.

The banks upon the United States shore, rise from the water less abruptly than those of Canada, except at the spring mill, three miles below the city of Detroit, where the former rises to the height of twenty or thirty feet, appearing as a comparative hill as seen from the strait. All the rivers and creeks enter from both sides, through low, swampy land covered with folle avoine, or wild oats. This aquatic grain, though thus named, is nevertheless essentially different from either oats or rice; no vegetable that I have ever seen, has a more beautiful appearance than is exhibited by the immense marshes, covered with the folle avoine; it is now in blossom, exhaling a peculiarly pleasing fragrance.

Sandwich is a small town, though the seat of justice in Essex county, Upper Canada; it stands upon the banks of the strait, one and a half mile below Detroit. I walked down yesterday to the ferry opposite, and crossed over to Sandwich, and returned to this city in the evening. I found it a village built principally of wood, composing a single street running parallel to the strait, with about as many stores and taverns as would be found in a place of similar size in the United States. The banks slope gradually from the water, though immediately above the town, they rise abrupt, and appear considerably higher than those opposite, upon which the city of Detroit is built. The shores of the strait on both sides are cleared of timber from one and a half to three miles from the water, giving the country in the rear of the front farm houses a naked appearance. The woods, where not cut down, is excessively dense, and the timber large. The soil, if any judgment can be formed by the aspect of the crops, is very productive. The bank of the strait has been vaunted, I believe correctly, for its fine orchards; fruit trees, apples, pears, peaches, and plumbs, have a very healthy appearance.

The city of Detroit is exceedingly well situated for a commercial port; the banks rise gently from the water, affording an easy communication with the store-houses in the city. Several wharves have been extended to considerable distance into the stream, the largest and best of which was made by the officers of the United States troops, for the use of, and in front of the garrison. The streets are laid out at right angles to each other, but are all inclining from the banks of the strait. The main-street leaves the strait in front of the garrison, but at the upper end of the city has two other parallel streets between it and the wharves. The cross streets are not of much consequence at present, having but few houses built upon them, except near the main-street. Leaving the lower end of the city, it is difficult to know where it terminates, as the farm houses are so closely united to each other. Above the city, though the margin of the strait is well cultivated, the farm houses do not stand so compact as they do below.

I have found two men here, from whom I have received much useful information and polite treatment, governor Cass and judge May, the latter of whom has resided at Detroit forty years, and possesses, perhaps, more correct knowledge of its history, than any man living. Gov. Cass resides on the banks of the strait below the garrison. To these two excellent men I am under very great obligations. The governor leaves this city on the 16th to meet the governor of Ohio, in order to hold a treaty with the Putawattamies, Wyandots, Senecas, Weas, and other nations of Indians.*

* This treaty resulted in the following cessions of land, with the annexed reservations. The cessions are of great consequence to the frontiers of Ohio and Michigan, as it tends to remove the savages to a greater distance westward.

"CINCINNATI, OCT. 15.

"*Treaties with the Indians.*—Our correspondent at St. Mary's has furnished us with the following hasty sketch of the treaties concluded with the Indians by our commissioners. The treaties were signed on the 6th inst. By these treaties the United States have secured more than seven millions of acres of land.

"We learn from our correspondent that the Miamis manifested a great deal of duplicity in their negociations.

"To the states of Ohio and Indiana these acquisitions are of immense importance. In a few years these almost interminable forests will be converted into flourishing towns and villages, and cultivated farms; the silent footsteps of the savage will give way to the resounding of the axe, the din of industry, and the bustle of commercial enterprise.

"REVISION OF THE TREATY OF 1817.

' Additional reserves by the Wyandots at Upper Sandusky, on the north side between the Cherokee Boys reserve and the 12 miles 640 acres, connecting the two; and on east side of the 12 miles, 55,680 acres.

To the Wyandots, residing at Solomon's town, 16,000 acres to centre at Big Spring, between Upper Sandusky and Fort Findlay, and 160 acres lower side Mrs. Whitaker's reserve at Lower Sandusky, reserved for a ferry or crossing place for the Indians.

" To the Shawanoes on the east side of the former reserve at Wapakanetto, 12,800 acres.

" To the Shawanoes and Senecas on the west side of Lewis' reserve of 7 miles, 8,960 acres; all to be equally divided east and west the north half for the Senecas, and the south half for the Shawanoes.

Respecting the present state of the population of the Territory of Michigan, I do not expect to receive much positive information, not contained in the census of 1810. Of the position of the settlements, and the quantity, quality and

"To the Seneca Indians adjoining south of their reserve of 1817 on each side Sandusky river, 10,000 acres

"*Additional Annuities.*— To the Wyandots, 500 dollars; Shawanoes and Senecas of Lewis' town, 1000 dollars; Senecas on Sandusky river 500 dollars; Ottaways, 500 dollars, perpetually to be paid annually. All, together with annuities heretofore granted, payable in specie.

"TREATY OF 1818.

"The Puttawattamies cede from the mouth of Tippecanoe river up the same to a point that will be 25 miles from the Wabash on a direct line; thence parallel with the general course of the Wabash to the Vermillion river, down the same to the Wabash, thence down the Wabash to the place of beginning (supposed to be 50 or 60 miles,) all their title south of the Wabash, for which they are to receive $2,500 in specie, annually forever, to be paid equally at Detroit and Chicago, also annuities heretofore granted to be paid in specie

"Grants to the following persons, half bloods, James, John, Isaac, Jacob and Abraham Burnet, two sections of land each; and to Rebecca and Nancy Burnet, one section of land each—half of the same on the lower side of the mouth of Tippecanoe river, on Wabash, and the other half on Flint river

"640 acres to Peerish, a Puttawattamie chief, on Flint river, at his residence.

"640 acres to Mary Chattalie, on Wabash, below the mouth of Pine river.

"The Weas cede their whole interest in Ohio, Indiana and Illinois—Reservation of 7 miles square on Wabash, above the mouth of Raccoon creek. The United States to pay them a perpetual annuity of 1150 dollars, which, added to annuities heretofore, makes 3000 dollars annually, all payable in specie

"The Delawares cede all their claims in Indiana on White river. The United States to furnish them lands to settle on west of the Mississippi, on the Arkansas, pay them for their improvements where they now live in 120 horses, not to exceed 40 dollars in value each; furnish perogues for transportation, provisions for their journey, permit them to occupy for three years hereafter their farms on White river, and to pay them a perpetual annuity of 4000 dollars, which, together with annuities now existing are payable in specie—Also to furnish them with a blacksmith when they settle west of the Mississippi. They reserve two and a

locality of the cultivatible soil, I have procured considerable document not hitherto made public. Our ordinary maps are deplorably deficient respecting the peninsula of Michigan, some of the most important rivers are slightly marked or wholly omitted. Before proceeding to give you a detail of the extent, position, and respective quality of the soil, I will present you with the result of what I have learned in general, respecting the geological structure of the peninsula, contained between lakes Michigan, Huron, St. Clair, and Erie, and the straits of Erie and St. Clair.

It is most probable that the entire region above the Thousand islands to lake Superior, reposes upon a bed of floetz or schistic rock, of various component parts. I have already noticed the phenomena which came to my knowledge, along the south and west of lake Erie, and pointed out their effect upon the structure of the rivers of that tract of country. Beyond the Maumee to lake Huron, all the streams, without exception, which draw their sources from the interior part of the peninsula, are precipitated over considerable falls before arriving at their mouths. You will perceive by the notes extracted from Audrain's map,* the materials which compose the rocks, over whose ledges these falls of water are thrown. It appears also that at the distance of twenty

---

half sections of land at First creek, above Old Fort and are to receive 13,320 dollars for the liquidation of debts owed by them to traders, &c.

The Miamies cede their interest to the country east of the Wabash, south of a line from Fort Wayne west to the Wabash; reserving one tract of 30 miles square on the Wabash, besides a great many others of less magnitude. The United States to pay them $15,000 per annum, perpetually, in specie

* I have given this map the name of Audrain in the text, as it was from Mr. Audrain I procured a copy; but in justice it ought to be noticed that the map was constructed by Mr. Greely, the United States' Surveyor in Michigan Territory, and those useful notes were made upon the original map by Mr. Greely, in his own hand writing.

or twenty-five miles from the extreme depression of the valley of St. Clair and Erie, that the table land of Michigan becomes flat, and covered with innumerable ponds and interlocking water courses. The rivers have their sources upon this extensive flat, and flow south-east into St. Clair and Erie, and north-west into Michigan, passing over an arable border of about twenty-five miles wide, which skirt the lakes and straits from Maumee to Calumet. Some of the interior *plateau* is described as good land, but the face of the country is generally too level, and of course subject to immersion in wet seasons.

The length of the rivers which flow from this table land is remarkably equal, and their banks composed of very similar soil, and covered with timber of correlative species. Extensive tracts, are open natural meadows or prairie.

From the foregoing you will perceive that the peninsula of Michigan is a vast cape, projected northwards from the elevated region, from which flow the Wabash, Maumee, and the eastern streams of the Illinois river.

In executing the surveys in the Michigan Territory, a meridian line has been drawn, commencing on the river Raisin about five miles above its mouth, and continuing from thence due north seventy-two miles, from whence was drawn another line due east fifty-two miles, which intersects the head of St. Clair river at Fort Gratiot. I do not know in what manner the surveys were made, but this is their outline, as they stand represented in the land office in the city of Detroit. Bounded west and north by these lines, and upon all other sides by St. Clair river, St. Clair lake, Detroit river, and Lake Erie. The ancient settlements were formed along the water courses, and continue to be in most part the only establishments yet made in the territory.

The superficies included in the surveys, does not vary much from 2,500 square miles or 1,600,000 acres. Some part of the United States land in this area has been sold, but the sales did not operate to add much to the population of the country. The valuable fractions of sections were in a great share purchased by the resident inhabitants, and annexed to lands already in their possession. Though the soil is good in general, some of it excellent, and all parts well situated for agriculture and commerce, some causes have hitherto operated to prevent any serious emigration to the Michigan Territory. For upwards of a month that I have been travelling between this city and Geneva, in the state of New-York, I have seen hundreds removing to the west, and not one in fifty with an intention to settle in Michigan Territory. By the census of 1810, the inhabitants then were 4,762, falling short of 5,000. I cannot be led to consider this enumeration correct, there were in all reasonable modes of calculation, more than 6,000 people in this territory at that period. I cannot consider the present number short of 10,000, though since 1810, no increment has been added of consequence to the mass, except that of natural increase. The city of Detroit contains at least 1,200 people, and it does not include more than one eighth of the whole body.

The lines of settlement extend along the river Raisin, Huron of lake Erie, Detroit river, riviere aux Ecorces, river Rouge, lake St. Clair, Huron of St. Clair, and St. Clair river. Many other minor streams are also lined with settlements. I have already observed the great uniformity in the quality of the land. In no country in which I have travelled, are there to be seen so much sameness in that, and indeed in many other respects. This monotony does not, however, extend to the productions of the soil, which are as varied as the climate will admit; small grain of all kinds that can be cultivated north of lat. 42°, can be reared in abundance. Fruits are remarkably productive.

The climate, at least as far north as Fort Gratiot, is as temperate as that of the western parts of the state of New-York, and perhaps more healthy. It is conceded that the seasons are much more mild at Detroit than at Buffalo, the difference is greater than could be expected from the small difference in latitude, less than one degree. The phenomenon may be, and I believe it is produced by the prevalence of westerly winds, which crowd the ice continually into the N. E. angle of lake Erie.

The following notes I extracted from the map in Mr. Audrain's office; they will afford you some knowledge of parts of our country hitherto unknown.

"Riviere aux Raisins, (Grape river) is a rapid stream of about 150 miles in length, and generally four chains in breadth. During the time of freshets, large rafts of timber can descend the river from the confluence of the Neemscon, a considerable branch, about 20 miles from lake Erie. Six miles above the mouth of the river Raisin, its rapidity is such that it can only be ascended with light canoes; at the mouth it has a sand bar, which obstructs the entrance of vessels drawing more than two feet water.

The banks are clothed with heavy oak, hickory, ash, elm, linden, yellow wood (*liriodendron tulipifera*) the latter answering well for boards; the soil is a black loam."

"Huron of Erie, can be ascended 150 miles to a portage of about 3 miles, into a stream called the Grand river, entering into lake Michigan. The river Huron is about 200 miles in length; course from the west, and general width four chains 88 yards.

Vessels drawing four feet water can enter and ascend four miles. The land is generally hilly on the southern border, having good timber and rich soil; and on the northern border extensive prairies, light sandy soil."

"Riviere Rouge is about two chains in width, discharging into the strait of Erie about four miles below the city of Detroit; it is navigable for vessels drawing 16 feet water, four miles from its mouth to the ship yard; thence for craft drawing 3 feet water, 8 miles, it then branches into considerable streams, upon which the lands are excellent. The timber on the banks of this river is oak, sugar maple, elm,

P

bass wood, (linden) poplar, (liriodendron tulipifera) and oak. The soil is a black loam."

"Huron of lake St. Clair, is generally about three chains (66 yards) in width, and navigable for boats drawing three feet water ten miles, to the first branch. The main branch interlocks with the northern branches of the river Rouge. The border of this river is covered with excellent white oak, and the soil is equal to any in the territory."

These notes were taken by me from the original map, in the surveyor's, Mr. Aaron Grely's own hand writing. I deem them of statistical importance, as being made from actual observation under the authority of the United States government, and as they tend to establish the great general features of the rivers of Michigan Territory.

It may be observed as a curious geological coincidence, that the Michigan peninsula is contrasted with another projection of land, of a similar general form and very nearly equal extent. The Canadian peninusula is, however, more insulated than that of Michigan. The former is also distinguished from the latter by some other peculiar features. The river Thames (la riviere a la Tranche) of the French or Escansippi of the savages, rises in very near the centre of the Canadian peninsula, runs to the south-west, having also another parallel and almost equal stream to the Chenal Ecarte, flowing both into the eastern side of lake St. Clair.

It is remarkable that these two streams are without falls or rapids in all their course ; the Thames about one hundred, and the Chenal Ecarte eighty miles in length. This exemption from rapids is the case, however, with all the known streams of this part of Canada, and proves that its surface is much lower than that of the Michigan peninsula. The soil of the former, from all the concurrent accounts I have seen is even still more fertile than that of the latter.

Mr. Samuel R. Brown, author of the Western Gazetteer, speaking from personal observation, having been in general Harrison's army when that officer pursued general Proctor up the Thames, states that, "The land in this part of the "Upper Province is uncommonly fertile, and admirably cal- "culated for farms. On the river there are extensive bot- "toms, then a gentle rise of beautiful timbered land, to "which succeed openings well calculated for wheat."

[*Mr. Brown's pamphlet*, Troy, 1814. *p.* 65.

Smith's Gazetteer of Upper Canada, describing the Thames, observes that, "It is a fine inland canal, and capa- "ble of being greatly improved. The lands on its banks "are extremely fertile."

Mr. Bouchette gives a richly coloured, but I am induced to believe a true sketch of this charming country.

"Along the northern part of the Niagara district runs a ridge called the Queenstown heights, stretching across the river Niagara, and away eastward into the state of New- York; the altitude of this range in any part of it, does not exceed 160 yards above the surface of the lake, (Ontario.) This space containing the Newcastle, the Home, and the Nia- gara districts, is watered by a great number of streams, both large and small, that greatly contribute to its fertility; in the latter district is the Welland, formerly called the Chip- pewa, a beautiful river, flowing through a remarkable fertile country for about forty miles, and wholly unobstructed by falls; also the Ouse or Grand river, a stream of much great- er magnitude, rising in the interior of the country, towards lake Huron, and after winding a long and picturesque course, falls into lake Erie: across its mouth there is a bar, but always with eight feet water upon it. It is navigable for small vessels from the lake many miles upwards, and for boats to a much greater distance.

"The land through the whole of the last mentioned dis- trict is uncommonly rich and fertile, with a considerable por- tion of very flourishing settlements upon it. From the river Ouse, proceeding along the shore of lake Erie, up to the lake and river St. Clair, the whole space is extremely even, with scarcely a league of it but what displays excellent situa   ons for settlements, and in spots where the land is already under tillage ; finer crops or more thriving farms are not to be met with in any part of either province.

"The portion of the western district, lying between lake Erie and lake St. Clair, is perphaps the most delightful of all the province. The fertility of the soil, the richly diversified and luxuriant beauties that every where court the view, the abundant variety of excellent fish that teem in the rivers, and the profusion of game of different species that enliven the woods, the thickets and the meadows, combine to insure a preference to this highly favored tract for the establishment of new settlements.

"From the Ouse to lake St. Clair, the space is occupied by the London and Western districts : it is watered by many small streams falling into lake Erie, besides the river Chenal Bearte, and the exquisitely picturesque river Thames, formerly called the riviere a la Franche. The latter rises far in the interior, about the township of Blandford, and after pursuing a serpentine course in a direction nearly south-west, discharges itself into Lake St. Clair. It is navigable for vessels full twenty miles from its mouth, and for boats and canoes nearly up to its source, but little less than one hundred miles. The river Chenal Bearte runs, almost parallel to the Thames, at about ten miles from it, and also falls into Lake St. Clair. The portions now described are those only that are more or less settled upon. In the rear of the townships are large tracts of land stretching far to the northward, covered with immense forests, and little known except to the Indians ; but it has been ascertained that there are many wide spreading extents of rich and fertile soil, particularly bordering upon the south-west bank of the Ottawa river. Through these regions, as yet unexplored by civilized man, there are many streams, and some of great size that flow both into lake Huron and into the Ottawa river but none of them have been sufficiently traced to admit of being delineated on any map. Timber is almost every variety is found in the greatest profusion; the oak, beech, walnut, (hickory) ash, maple, elm, pine, sycamore, birch, and many other sorts are of peculiar excellence, and of capital dimensions. The climate is so peculiarly salubrious, that epidemic diseases, either amongst men or cattle, are almost unknown; its influence upon the fertility of the soil is more generally perceptible than it is in Lower Canada, and supposed to be congenial to vegetation in a much superior degree. The winters are shorter, and not always marked with such rigor as in the latter; the duration of the frost is always accompanied with a fine clear sky and a dry atmosphere; the spring opens, and the resumption of agricultural labor takes place from six weeks to two months earlier than what it does in the neighborhood of Quebec: the summer heats rarely prevail to excess, and the autumns are usually very friendly to the harvests, and favorable for securing all the late crops. In fact, upon so good a soil, and under such a climate, industry and an increase of population are only wanting to render this colony flourishing and happy."

[*Bouchette's Remarks upon Upper Canada, p. 592.*

The valley in which flow the river Thames and Chenal Ecarte, in Canada, occupies the same relative part of the peninsula, in which it exists, as does the table land of that of Michigan, giving great advantage to the former. In point of soil and climate no particular difference can be perceived between the opposing banks of the straits of Erie and St Clair. All the Canadian, and most of the Michigan peninsula, are south of the forty fifth degree of north latitude; considerable difference in the seasons exists between the northern and southern parts; spring is much earlier, and autumn more protracted at Detroit, Sandwich, and Amherstburg, than at York and Fort Gratiot.

Taken as an entire whole, I very much doubt if any part of the earth does greatly exceed the St. Lawrence valley, in the natural benefits which, judiciously cultivated, seems the happiness, comfort, and indulgencies of human life. The summers are to a proverb delightful, the winters are cold, when compared with those of even our middle states, but a Canadian winter if cold, is uniform to a degree inconceivable, to most of those who are acquainted with the changeable seasons below the forty-second degree of north latitude. In the meaning of the term Canadian winter, I do not simply intend those of Canada only; it applies with equal force to nearly, if not all the countries drained by the St. Lawrence, of course includes immense tracts comprised within the territorial limits of the United States.

I am now upon the eve of returning to the city of New-York, of retracing my steps, and of bidding, perhaps an eternal adieu in a few days to a country, where the pain, anxiety, and vicissitudes of travelling, did not prevent me from beholding and admiring the face of nature in her richest garb. I have endeavored to convey to the friend of my heart the impressions I have received. You know how far I have succeeded. I now turn "*a longing lingering look*" towards home, and the dearest associations of life; I hope in less than one month to again embrace those friends, whom, amid even the wonders of Niagara, or the storms of Erie I could not forget. I hope to leave this city to-morrow, in the mean time,

Adieu,

LETTER XVI.

Buffalo, August 31, 1818.

DEAR SIR,

As I informed you in my last, I left Detroit on the 23d inst. and have arrived here yesterday. I took my passage in a lake schooner. The steam-boat Walk-in-the-water was impatiently expected at Detroit, but did not arrive until after I left that city; I did not see her, but learned at the town of Erie that she was gone up and performed well, though drawing rather too much water to suit entirely the navigation of lake Erie. She stranded in about seven feet water on Erie bar. A more fatal fault in the construction of any vessel to be used on lake Erie could not be easily committed, as that of too great draught of water. The harbors are few, narrow, and difficult to enter, and the intermediate shores dangerous in the extreme. With the exception of the Niagara river below Bird island, Put-in-bay in the southern Bass island, and Detroit river, there exists no harbor in lake Erie that can be safely entered in a swelling sea, with a vessel drawing seven feet water. To the number of vessels which are actively employed, I am convinced there are many more wrecked on lake Erie, than on the coast of the United States, dangerous as is some parts of that coast. Dunkirk is an open harbor, but for suitable vessels can be, except Put-in-bay and Detroit river, most easily entered of any in the lake; and next to Dunkirk in facility of entrance, are Maumee and Sandusky. The bays are indeed generally more easy of approach than are the rivers.

I was much pleased to find that the schooner in which I performed my passage, was to take Maumee bay in its course, as that and Erie were the only places of particular importance, along the United States shore of lake Erie, which I had not visited going up.

Our vessel fell down Detroit river with a fine light breeze, which died away in the evening and left us lying quiet most part of the night; but on the morning of the 25th a light N. W. wind sprung up, which increasing with the rise of the sun, carried us finely along. I had a view, though at a distance, of the mouth of the rivers Huron and Raisin, the houses of the inhabitants standing like white spots upon the disk of the horizon. Leaving the western Sister a small distance to the east, about 5 o'clock P. M. our little bark was safely at anchor in Maumee bay.

The whole coast from Amherstburg to Maumee is an undeviating flat. Approaching Maumee bay, I sought on all sides for some eminence, or some distant range of hills, to break the monotony of the perspective, none such appeared; one dead uniformity, one narrow line of woods, or the endless expanse of water marked the horizon. Maumee bay is formed with some resemblance to that of Sandusky, though the former is neither so wide or long as the latter. The Maumee river after tumbling over a ledge of rocks near Fort Meigs, gains the level of the great alluvial plain, noticed in my last, over which it meanders a few miles, expands to two or three miles wide, and opens into the extreme south-west angle of lake Erie. An island in the form of a crescent, about three-fourths of a mile long, lies very nearly midway between the two exterior capes of the bay, of course two channels lead into this harbor. Behind the crescent island, vessels find safe shelter and excellent anchorage. I had no means to measure the exact distance from the island to the opposing capes, but would judge about three miles, and very nearly a similar distance to a part of the shore to the east of the mouth of Maumee river. Like most of the harbors of Erie, Maumee has seven feet water on the bars east and west of the crescent island. Our vessel passed into the bay the west channel, close upon the point of the island, and anchored in the bay formed by its curve.

I landed upon the crescent, and found it a beautiful sand bar, about one hundred and fifty yards wide in its broadest part, and covered with dwarf bushes of different kinds. Near the middle, and consequently widest part, the two sides of the island are higher than the center, leaving the latter a pond of water, in which are growing rushes, and other aquatic plants. Many years past I witnessed the same feature in the structure of the islands between New-Orleans and Mobile bay. I have in fact found an astonishing resemblance between the appearance of much of the coast of the Mexican gulf, and the shores of Erie, from Cleveland to Detroit. Crescent island no doubt, like the points which enclose Sandusky bay, has been formed by the meeting of two currents; it is now an admirable natural mole to secure the mouth of Maumee, and forms for the depth of water, one of the best harbors in this lake of storms.

As I did not attempt to penetrate the country, I remained upon the island and in the ship, whilst our captain went up the Maumee river to transact his affairs, and on his return left the bay on the 26th. We sailed nearly east, having the coast of Maumee to Sandusky bay on our right, and the sisters and Bass islands to our left; clearing the narrows between the southern Bass and a cape of the Sandusky peninsula, we veered to the south-east between Cunningham's island and the eastern extremity of the peninsula, and held upon that course until opposite the mouth of Sandusky bay, we then changed to a little north of east, and having a fine steady south-west breeze, we hove to on the 27th about noon, opposite the mouth of Ashtabula river. Some of our passengers, beside myself, went on shore; little is here to be seen. Ashtabula is a small and unimportant river, rising about thirty miles from the lake, in the state of Ohio, giving name to the north east county of that state. Vessels of five feet draught of water can enter Ashtabula two or three miles. Only a couple of farm houses can be seen at its mouth, hills appear rising almost from the margin of the lake: here indeed is one of the narrowest parts of the lake Erie alluvial border. Ashtabula enters the lake obliquely, the river running to the north-west, leaving a high sandy point projecting between the river and lake.

Not having any particular object of detention, our vessel left Ashtabula at 2 o'clock P. M. and being detained by a calm, did not reach the harbor of Erie before about sunrise on the 28th. I hasted on shore, as I had long desired to see that place.

The town of Erie, formerly Presque isle, stands at 42° 7′ N. lat. 3° 7′ W. long. from Washington city. The bank upon which the town is built, rests upon an immense schistose mass of rock, surmounted by a stratum of clay, rises in bluff and broken abruptness to the height of 30 or 40 feet, from whence it spreads into a level plain, with no great inclination in any direction. A small drain which traverses the town, has cut a deep ravine, which, near the bay, exposes the solid rock. The main street runs at nearly right angles to the bay shore, a little N. E. of the ravine. So much sameness prevails in all small towns, that little description suffices to those who have seen but a few of such places. Erie, like almost all other villages, is composed in great part by one main street built along the principal road; Erie has, however, some cross streets, upon which are good substantial buildings. The town has a very neat appearance, many of the houses are elegant, with trees planted in front. I have seen very few places of its extent, which exhibited so much of the air of a commercial depot. It is the seat of justice for Erie county, has a good substantial court-house and its attendant a jail, many good stores and taverns, blacksmith's, hatter's, shoe-maker's, and taylor's shops.

The bay or harbor of Erie is formed by the shore, and a long, narrow, low, sandy isthmus, which projects from it two miles south-west from where the village now stands. Towards its termination the isthmus inclines a little towards the main shore, giving an elliptical form to the bay. The bar runs out from the isthmus some distance above the point, and has barely 7 feet water. The channel is very winding, until about half a mile below the town, where the water deepens to twenty feet or more. No winds, except those from the north-east could affect ships at anchor in this bay, and even from that quarter the swell would be broken on the bar. On all sides it is effectually land locked. The isthmus is not more than four or five feet above the water, is overgrown with cedar trees, and cranberry bushes.

In a cove of the isthmus now lie the hulks of Perry's squadron, and his captured British ships. The Lawrence and Niagara now lie very quietly beside the Detroit, Queen Charlotte, and Lady Prevost. You are no doubt acquainted with the fact, that the strongest part of the squadron was prepared at Erie, which produced this great national victory; the Lawrence and Niagara were both built here, and were taken over the bar by a curious contrivance. The captain of the schooner in which I came from Detroit, was then (1813) a shipwright, and assisted to transport these vessels into the lake, which, as he described the means and process to me, were the following: Two large flats or scows fifty feet long, ten wide, and eight deep were prepared, laid along side one of the vessels, filled with water, and fastened to each other and to the vessel by large beams of hewn timber run through the port holes; then the water pumped from the scows, which, as they became empty, buoyed up the vessel, and the whole machine rendered capable of passing the bar. By good fortune, the British either cou'd not, or they neglected to oppose this operation, and lost the naval superiority on lake Erie. The same fleet which conquered Barclay's squadron, carried general Harrison's army to the city of Detroit, produced the re-conquest of Michigan, and the chastisement on the Thames of the sanguinary and ferocious Proctor.

A few hours enabled me to see Erie and its environs, and to leave me at leisure to desire to be again on my way towards Buffalo, which was the case, at about an hour before sun-set of the same day we arrived. Nothing worth notice intervening until the morning of the 30th, (Sunday) I gladly found myself at Mr. Isaac Kibbe's tavern in Buffalo.

One of the first pieces of news which reached me on my arrival, was, that the table rock at Niagara had fallen a day or two before. This was a projecting shelf of slate rock on the Canada side, where curious visitors went to view the falls. The certainty of its stability had been doubted for some time past, not without foundation it appears. Fortunately it fell whilst no persons were upon it, for if such had been the case, some amiable human beings would have been plunged to swift destruction. I will be detained here a few days, perhaps three or four. I intend to return by the Cherry Valley route. You will hear from me again at Albany.

Adieu.

LETTER XVII

Albany, September 15, 1818.

DEAR SIR,

After a long journey of twenty-one days, I arrived here the day before yesterday from Buffalo; I left that town on the 27th ult. and came by the route of Batavia, Canandaigua, Geneva, Auburn, Cazenovia, Cherry Valley, and Schenectady. Over this tract as far as Geneva I had been before, but from that place to Schenectady, the intermediate country was new to me. With renewed pleasure I re-visited Canandaigua, again reviewed this extraordinary production of a few years past. When passing that village on my way to the westward, I had a letter from governor Clinton to Mr. Gideon Granger, who was at that time absent. At the time of my return I was more fortunate: I found Mr. Granger, and received from that excellent man a reception that, to a stranger, was sincerely gratifying. Mr. Granger's elegant mansion stands upon the highest part of the plain, upon which Canandaigua is built, and adds considerably to the decoration of that unequalled village. This expression you may say is extravagant; it is not, however, inaccurate. Viewed in all respects, I am persuaded that no village in the United States can compare in the beauty, variety, and taste of its edifices. The gentle slope of the ground upon which it is erected, contributes to give full effect to the perspective. The main street is wide, with paved side walks, and planted with trees. Many of the houses are seated at some considerable distance from the street, with wide, well shaded side walks in front. To my eye, this mode of constructing dwellings in towns, villages, and even in cities, has a very pleasing appearance. It gives an air of comfort and quiet—that must always constitute much of the satisfaction we feel, when viewing the dwellings of man. That of Mr. Granger, splendid as it is, gains another interest, more gratifying than the mere admiration of architectural magnificence; the generous politeness of its owner, and the friendly deportment of his family. Princely wealth, is here combined with the warmest feelings of hospitality. It is such men, who render the possession of the gifts of fortune in their hands a public benefit.

I left Geneva on the afternoon of the 10th, and proceeded down the outlet of the Seneca lake. A water communication with lake Ontario now exists by this route. At Waterloo, five miles from Geneva, the Seneca outlet is obstructed by falls, or rather rapids, past which locks have been constructed. Below the falls, the Seneca outlet runs north-east ten miles, and joins Cayuga outlet at the lower extremity of Cayuga lake. The united stream winds in a northern direction five miles, receives from the west the Canandaigua outlet.* At the junction of those streams it is intended to pass with the grand canal. The country near the outlet, between Geneva and Cayuga, is not so uniformly level as I expected to find; there is, however, no striking objects of much interest. The road crosses the outlet of the falls, and proceeds

---

* Facts are daily transpiring which tend to exhibit the rapid improvement of this part of the state of New-York. The Canandaigua outlet, is like that of Seneca, precipitated over ledges of rock. The following extract is interesting, but by no means sufficiently explicit. It is much to be desired, that those who write on statistical subjects, would be more particular in describing local objects. It will be seen by referring to my letter from Canandaigua, that a considerable stream is formed by the junction of Mud creek with the outlet of Canandaigua lake; this stream is now rendered of more importance by the removal, or rather obviating an obstruction in its bed, in the township of Galen, Seneca county.

FROM THE WATERLOO GAZETTE.
"NEW LOCK NAVIGATION.

"*Mr. Leavenworth*—It is with extreme satisfaction, that through the medium of your press, I can inform the public, that on the 19th ult. the first heavy laden boat passed the Lock, lately constructed on the Clyde, near the new milling establishment of the Messrs De Zeng, at the village of Clyde, in the township of Galen. This valuable improvement completes an excellent Durham boat navigation, through perhaps the most fertile sections of Seneca and Ontario counties, for upwards of forty miles west from the Seneca river, and creates an eligible scite for all kinds of hydraulic operations, at a point where it has hitherto been considered utterly impracticable to raise a sufficient head of water.

"Besides, it is not the least pleasing reflection, that in the course of a very few years, this stream may become a most important link in the chain of our western inland state navigation.

"In justice to an undertaking of such magnitude and utility, I am proud to acknowledge the enterprize of the Messrs De Zeng, advised and directed by the skill of that able architect, and mill-wright, Mr. James Valentine. May success reward their efforts.   "A SENECA FARMER."

thence east to Cayuga bridge and village. This bridge is, perhaps, the longest in the United States, situated at any considerable distance from the sea board: it exceeds a mile by a small fraction, is formed of wood, upon a frame resting upon the bottom of the lake. The outlets of all the chain of lakes, of which Cayuga is one, have great sameness. Cayuga is the longest, and no doubt contains more water than any of the others; Seneca approaches nearest to it in magnitude.

Fall creek rises in the township of Homer, in Courtland county, flows south into Virgil, turns to the west and enters Dryden, in Tompkins county, receives a large branch from Locke, in Cayuga, then assumes a south-west course to Ithaca, in Ulysses, where it receives a number of other streams, and turning abruptly to the north, suddenly expands into Cayuga lake. The sources of the Fall creek are very considerably higher than the lake into which their waters are discharged;* this is the case also, with all the tribu-

---

* I have inserted the following extract, as it illustrates the structure of the country, and opens to the curious traveller a source of instruction and amusement. The scenery of our country has been too much neglected. Many very interesting objects in the best settled parts of the United States, are scarcely known beyond the neighbourhood where they exist.

"*Ithaca, (N. Y.) June 16.*
"OUR CATARACT.

"The numerous and magnificent cataracts in our country, have been themes of wonder and delight, and are considered as a peculiar feature in the physiology of the western part of this state. Niagara has long been viewed as the greatest natural wonder of the world—and for sublimity and grandeur is doubtless unrivalled.

'The falls of the Genesee, the Cohoes, the current on the Black river, have all been noticed by the traveller and journalist. But the falls near this village, which next to the Niagara, do not yield in point of sublimity, beauty, and extent, to any in the state, are scarcely known out of their vicinity. Fall creek, on which our falls are situated, rises in the north east corner of this county, and, after a course of twenty miles, empties into the head

tary waters of the other lakes contiguous to Cayuga. The relative size of Seneca and Cayuga lakes is not materially different, the former is thirty-three and a half miles long, from Salubria to Geneva, the latter thirty-five and a half, from the mouth of Fall creek to that of Seneca outlet; the widest part of each of these lakes is opposite Romulus, in Seneca county, and is nearly equal, three miles. Both lakes diminish very gradually towards their respective extremities. The advantage of these lakes to the agriculture and commerce of the country in which they are situated is incalculable: and when their outlets are improved in such

of Cayuga lake. When it arrives within three miles of the Cayuga lake the chain of falls commences, and continues with little interruption, about one mile and a half, when the water is precipitate over the last and grandest fall, to a level with the lake. The whole descent of water in this distance, has been estimated at *three hundred and fifty feet.* The view of the precipice from the bridge at the foot of the falls is the most grand and picturesque I ever beheld. The water falling nearly perpendicular, from the height of about *ninety feet*—the steep and craggy banks towering to an almost equal height above, and crowned with evergreens, give a wild and romantic effect to the scenery, unequalled by any thing that can be imagined. After clambering up the rocky banks, another fall presents itself to view, of about half the height—and ten or fifteen rods above this, the stream pitches about forty feet, presenting the form of a half circle, in its descent over the broken and craggy rocks, tumbling and foaming with inconceivable velocity."

"ITHACA, SEPT. 30.

"*Census of Ithaca.*—A friend has favored us with a census of this village taken during the past week. By this it appears, that the village contains a population of 611 persons, of which 313 are males, and 298 females—186 are under the age of ten years, 143 between ten and twenty; 269 between 20 and 45, and *thirteen only* over forty-five. The buildings are 226 in number, comprising a church and court-house, 77 dwelling-houses, 4 inns, 19 stores, (2 vacant) 7 groceries, 28 mechanic's shops, 8 offices—and out-houses to complete the estimate."

This is the clearest and most satisfactory, of all the recent enumerations of the population of the villages in west New-York, that I have been able to procure.

a manner as to admit an uninterrupted communication with Seneca river, and ultimately with the grand canal, the whole will present a picture of convenience of intercourse, that may challenge an equal in any part of this earth, so far removed from a sea coast. And as if nature intended to lavish the richest and most essential of her gifts upon this favored region, salt and gypsum abound. It would in fact be a tedious and useless task, to enumerate a small part of the various advantages possessed by the inhabitants of this singular country. I must draw your attention to some facts, respecting the geology of the region watered by the Seneca and Oswego rivers. The peculiar features of the former stream, will best appear from inspection upon a good map. You will perceive that it is formed in most part by the outlets which we have been noticing, and that its general course is from west to east, at right angles to these outlets and their parent lakes. The lakes themselves occupy the base of very deep vallies. On this latter circumstance I had, until this period, very erroneous opinions. I had conceived that the spaces between the lakes were plains, or at least very little elevated above the surface of the water in the lakes: I now find that so far from being plains, those intervals are elevated to an astonishing height, from which the streams rush with an impetuosity in proportion to their rapid descent.

Independent of the long ridges which rise between the lakes, another of more elevation winds between the waters of Susquehanna river, and the streams which flow northward towards lake Ontario. In reality the latter ridge is the spine of this country, from which the former diverge like the ribs of an animals. The descent from the parent ridge is very gradual to the southward, but to the northward is abrupt.* How far the peculiar features of the intermediate country will contribute to facilitate or impede the intended

---

* See page 156, note upon Internal Improvements

water communication between Susquehanna river and Seneca lake, I am not prepared to decide.

I stopped on the morning of the 11th at Auburn. This village has for many reasons become an object of considerable attention. It stands upon the outlet of Owasco lake, in the township of Aurelius in Seneca county, upon a bottom or level piece of ground. The village of Auburn is more recent than either Geneva or Canandaigua, and in point of population, I would suppose exceeds the former place.* The country in the vicinity of Auburn seems to be well cultivated. The houses in the village are many of them well, and some expensively built; many good taverns and stores, are interspersed amongst the other buildings.

The circumstance which contributes most to render Auburn an object of attention, is that of its being the site of the second penitentiary erected within the state of New-

---

"*Auburn, October 7.*

* "The village of Auburn contains 2017 souls—641 males, and 423 females—466 males, and 443 females, under the age of eighteen—free blacks, 35 males, and 29 females—slaves 8 males, and 2 females. Whole number of families 294. One Presbyterian church, one Episcopal church, and a house of public worship for the Methodists, a court-house, a county clerk's office, and state prison, 241 dwelling-houses, 12 offices 23 stores, 2 market-houses, 16 groceries, 74 mechanic's shops, 10 mills, 6 stills, and 164 out-houses, making an aggregate of 525 buildings.

"Among the 150 labourers on the state prison, 75 are supposed to be transient residents.*

"It is worthy of remark, that among a population of 2017, two persons only were confined to their beds.

"This village contained, in April, 1817, a population of 1506, increase in 17 months, 541."

The foregoing census is another instance of the want of precision in the most necessary details. I cannot avoid expressing a hope, that as public attention seems now turned upon such subjects, that more perspicuity will be used than is now frequently the case; the true benefits of such publications must be lost, in proportion as the subject-matter is unconnected, or inconclusive.

---

* We presume it will be understood, that the state prisoners are not numbered in our census.

York. I went, together with some other travellers, to see this house of punishment, and found it a large oblong building, enclosed within a strong stone wall. We were conducted over the building by the keeper. Every necessary attention appears to be paid to the safeguard and health of the convicts. I have always considered that the best lessons that the United States ever gave to the world, was upon the subject of crimes and punishments.

Between Auburn and the outlet of Skeneateles lake, the country continued to present no very striking changes of scenery, from that between Geneva and Auburn. At the village of Skeneateles, the outlet leaves the lake, and continues to flow northward about fifteen miles, then falls into Seneca river. After crossing the outlet I turned southward up the lake. The Skeneateles is in form similar to those of Seneca and Cayuga, but of much less extent than either of the latter, being fifteen miles in length, with a medial width of less than one mile.

The space between Owasco and Skeneateles rises rapidly from each lake, to a ridge of at least four hundred feet high, mostly covered with an enormous forest; some farms are seen, but the greatest part of the surface is yet in woods. East of the Skeneateles the country is more improved, but also presents an immense and very much inclined plane, rising gradually from the water. The road winds along this slope, about half way from the lake to the apex of the hills; the farms have a curious aspect when viewed either from above or below the road. The soil is good, but very stony, and in many places must be inconvenient to cultivate, from the very great steepness of its surface. The timber is composed of hemlock, sugar tree, elm, several species of hickory, and oak. The whole country is well supplied with excellent spring water.

The lower half of Skeneateles lake lies in Onondago county, and the higher moity forms the demarkation between the township of Sempronious, in Seneca, and Spafford, in Onondago county.

I remained the night of the 11th near the head of Skeneateles, in Spafford, and on the morning of the 12th set out, crossing the country towards Otisco lake. No roads are yet formed in this part of Onondago except the common country roads. I traversed the ridge between the lakes, and found it elevated to an astonishing height, when contrasted with its representation upon a map. Farms chequer the hill sides in their steepest parts, and spread along the bottoms, in every direction. The settlements are less frequent, and have the appearance of being much more recently established, than those to the northward near the great western turnpike. After clambering the Skeneateles and another very high and steep ridge, I found myself upon the Skeneateles turnpike road about two miles above Otisco lake. I found the turnpike leading eastward through the south parts of Onondago and Madison counties. The country improved at every step, though continuing hilly and broken. The weather was dark and gloomy. I felt weary, and for the first time I was seriously indisposed since my leaving New-York. I got to my lodgings, near the church of Cazenovia a little before sun-set, having travelled on foot over a very rough country more than thirty miles.

Sept. 13th. I found myself considerably refreshed and renewed my journey eastward. The road passes along the dividing ridge between the head waters of the Chenango branch of Susquehanna, and the Chittinengo river flowing north into the Oneida lake.

At Cazenovia church,* the character of the country is es-

* Strangers from the southern and western states are not unfrequently embarrassed when travelling in the state of New-York, and to the eastward of that state, by the common custom of naming the villages from the townships in which they are situated. This is the case with Cazenovia. I did not personally visit the village of that name, but passed through the southern part of the township. The custom of publishing the progressive

sentially different from that westward through which I had been travelling the three preceding days. The regular and almost artificial aspect of the hills and lakes from Geneva to Otisco lake, gradually yielded to a more irregular though still broken country. With the exception of some vallies, which I crossed at nearly right angles, I found no level country between Skeneateles and this city. The many flats, lie upon the head waters of the Chenango, but are mere bottoms between surrounding hills;* the soil every where fertile, and in many places well improved.

Advancing eastward through Hamilton and Brookfield, forming the south-east angle of Madison county, the face of the country becomes extremely hilly, rocky and generally of recent settlement. I had travelled through no part of the state of New-York, where the hand of man had made so little change in the primitive rudeness of nature.—The road in this quarter crosses the sources of Chenango and Unadilla rivers; the latter forming the boundary between the southeastern part of Madison and the northwestern of Otse-

---

population of our new settlements is laudable, but editors of public prints ought to be careful to procure correct data on that subject I have in this treatise appended as notes, as many of these enumerations as have met my eye relating to places upon, or near the line of my route.

"*Cazenovia.*—The village of Cazenovia, in Madison county, New-York, was first settled in May 1793.—In 1806, it had 212 inhabitants—in 1810, 440 inhabitants—and it now contains 709 souls—It has three churches, several manufactories, and all the appendages of a thriving village."

* While the above notes were in the hands of my printer, I was told that a valley existed, out of which the waters of the Chenango flowed south, and those of Oneida north, without any elevated intervening ground between the sources of these streams If this information is correct, it is of great importance, and may ere long lead to the formation of another link in our interior communication. A minute and skillful examination of the interlocutory branches of other streams, with those of the Susquehanna, is really an object of great import in the adjustment of some of the most serious questions in our internal policy

go county. The road keeping so near a dividing ridge, passes, I am inclined to believe, the least attractive parts of Otsego, as from every information I received, the average improvement in this county would very much exceed what would result from an estimate founded upon the part over which I travelled.

Rising one hill after another, I found myself at about four miles west of Cherry Valley, where I spent the night, and about two hours before day on the 14th, resumed my journey. During my whole tour, this was the only instance in which I travelled in the night; the moon shone very clear, and either from the elevation of the country or the advance of the season, the air was keen and sharp, with a white frost. I walked on and passed Cherry Valley before day. I regretted the circumstance, but my mind became daily more anxious to regain my home. I could by the clear moonlight perceive the general aspect of the place. The village is seated between the base of a high and very steep hill, and a small creek, the source of a considerable stream, from the name of which, that of the village is derived. The hill, or rather mountain, rises east of the village, and is a part of the same chain which forms the Little Falls in the Mohawk river. Seen by day light, I have no doubt but that the vicinity of Cherry Valley would have a wild and romantic appearance; to my eye it presented that contrast every where found in New-York, in the towns and villages of ancient date; the low Dutch built mansion and the stately modern edifice; and also like almost all towns laid out by the original settlers of this state, the streets follow the inflections of the roads. In opposition to common opinion, I have been led to consider the right angled mode of laying out cities as inconvenient and unnatural, where neither the varieties of the ground or facility of intercourse with contiguous places are consulted.

The road towards Albany leaves Cherry Valley, winding up the steep ascent of the mountain, for two miles before it attains the summit level. Day light began to appear over the verge of the highest peaks, before I gained the extreme height, and before reaching the opposite slope, the sun had risen over the valley of the Mohawk. The morning was remarkably clear, and gave to the perspective all its extent. The richly cultivated vale lay before me, scattered peaks of the Cherry valley mountain extended along my right, terminated by the blue apex of the Catsbergs, on my left as far as the eye could reach, arose the broken fragments of the chain through which the Mohawk breaks at the Little Falls. Far distant upon the disk of the horizon, arose the elevated hills of Montgomery county, between the Mohawk and Sacondago rivers. To the eastward towards Schenectady, was spread an endless variety of hill and dale; fields, meadows, orchards, farm-houses, and copses of wood, varied to almost infinity, by the charming irregularity of its features, I gazed upon this truly expansive prospect, and pronounced it by far the finest landscape I had ever seen. There was an extent and striking contrast of parts, that rendered the whole a picture that must attract the entire attention of every beholder. The southern extremity of Herkimer and the southwest angle of Montgomery are the points where the waters of the Susquehanna make the nearest approach to those of the Mohawk. In the townships of Litchfield and Columbia, in the southwest angle of Herkimer, the sources of the Unadilla river rise within eight miles of the banks of the Mohawk at the German Flats. In the townships of Columbia and Warren, are also the extreme north sources of the main branch of the Susquehanna river, which rise within less than ten miles of the Mohawk at the Little Falls. The chain of mountains which passes Cherry Valley, and as I have observed forms the Little Falls, leaves Otsego county in the township of Springfield, and enters Herkimer county dividing the township of Warren from that of Danube.

I have observed in my Emigrant's Guide, page 190, that hills and mountains are not only specifically but generically distinct. It is commonly considered that mountains and hills are mere relative terms, but the philosophy of such an opinion is not founded in fact. In the United States instances are numerous where the chains of hills and mountains pass each other at a great diversity of inclination. I have already pointed out the remarkable chain of hills which separate the waters of St. Lawrence from those of the Ohio valley. You will perceive, that the same ridge which winds along the south shore of lake Erie, continues through the state of New-York, by an inflected line. This ridge leaves the state of Pennsylvania, in the north-east part of Erie county, and following nearly the general course of lake Erie, and within five or six miles of the shore of that lake, winds through Chatauque into Cattaraugus county; then turns south-east about twenty miles, reaches within ten miles of the bank of Allegany river, at the mouth of Little Valley creek. Turning to the north-east, through the residue of Cattaraugus, the ridge enters Allegany county; upon the west border of the latter county it assumes a south-east direction, between the waters of the Genesee and Allegany rivers, enters Pennsylvania in Potter county, through which it curves, and again enters the state of New-York, in the south-west angle of Steuben county. It then pursues a north-west course, again enters Allegany county, turning by an elliptical curve returns into Steuben county near Arkport, and following a north-east direction enters Ontario county in the township of Springwater, but enters rapidly again into Steuben county, and winding through the latter to the south-east, enters Tioga county discharging to the south-west the creeks of the Conhocton branch of the Susquehanna, and to the north-east streams flowing into Canandaigua, Crooked, and Seneca lakes. Winding along the northern border of Tioga county, through the townships of Catherine, Cayuta, Danby, and Caroline, attains the north-east extremity of the county, and turns to the north, forming the east border of Tompkins, and the south-east of Cayuga, reaches the head of Skeneateles lake, in the

north-west angle of Courtland county; from the [...]
the ridge assumes a course east-north-east [...]
Argos, in Madison county, where it attains [...]
point. From Argos the course of the ridge is [...]
to its intersection with the prolongation of the Catsb[...]
near the village of Cherry Valley. Uninterrupted by the
Catsbergs this remarkable ridge continues down the Mohawk river, and is gradually lost between Schenectady and
Albany. The Schoharie river is the only stream which
actually crosses the ridge in all its length.

It is really an object worthy of great attention, the uniform character of this singular spine south of lake Erie;
where dividing the Mississippi waters from those of St
Lawrence river; and where separating the numerous branches of the Susquehanna from those of the Mohawk, its features have a striking similitude. Sloping imperceptibly to
the south, and falling abruptly to the north, is the peculiar
trait in the natural history of this ridge, which will have the
greatest influence in the operations of human improvement.
It may be observed also as not the least wonderful trait of
this ridge, that it forms a limit between that part of the continent of North America, remarkable for the magnitude
and abundance of its lakes, and that part as remarkable for
the almost total want of lakes.

The Mohawk river flows along the eastern part of the
ridge we are noticing, at a medium distance, above Schoharie river, of from ten to twenty miles. The natural structure of the Mohawk is little less peculiar than the ridge itself. Occupying the narrow vale of two exhausted lakes,
this stream rises in the secondary region west of the granitic ridges, which form the nucleus of the Allegany mountains, with its sources so nearly poised, as to leave the waters at liberty to flow either towards the Hudson or St Lawrence. Flowing from this table land with a very uniform
current, between perfectly alluvial banks, for thirty five

miles, the Mohawk meets its first considerable obstruction, by intersecting the Catsbergs at the place now called the Little Falls. Here the stream pours over a ledge of primitive rocks, and enters a region which, in soil, timber and geological structure, differs very essentially from the country west of the Catsbergs: the stream, however, again flows with a very equable current about sixty miles, to the Cohoes Falls, over which its waters are literally plunged into the Atlantic tides. You will perceive that the elevation of the summit level of the Mohawk, south of the village of Rome, following the report of the canal commissioners, page 68, is above tide water in the Hudson river, near Troy, within a small fraction of 419 feet. Of this depression 132.8 feet, including the Little Falls, are found between Rome and Schoharie creek, and 286 feet between the latter stream and the level of Hudson river, below the head of tide water.

The range of the Catsbergs being in some measure an anomaly in our geography, has given rise to considerable ambiguity in our maps, and are not strictly correct on any representation with which I am acquainted. The late excellent, and much to be lamented John H. Eddy, left that part of his map of the state of New-York unfinished at his death. I was employed by Mr. Thomas Eddy, to sketch these mountains, which I did, following the best information I could procure. I found the Damascus mountain, in Wayne county, Pennsylvania, marked upon Mr. Eddy's map; but to the east of the Cochecton Falls, in the Delaware, the map was a blank, as respects the very distinctive chain which forms those falls. I sketched the mountain ridge which winds from the Cochecton Fall, through Susquehanna and Ulster, to the borders of Greene county, in the state of New-York, and which, in the latter county, rises into the remarkable Catsbergs, whose conic summits have so fine an aspect, seen from the Hudson river. The center of Greene county is formed by a curve of this chain, out of which flow the sources of the Schoharie. Viewing a map of this part of the state of New-York, it would appear that the sources of the Schoharie ought to flow into the Papacton branch of the Delaware river; but after pursuing a north-west direction, within the curve of the mountains, the various branches of Schoharie unite in the township of Windham, and entering the southern angle of Schoharie county, pierces the Catsbergs, and assuming a northerly course, crosses Schoharie and part of Montgomery counties, falls into the Mohawk river opposite Tripe's hill.— The origin and course of the Schoharie river, very remarkably exemplify the little influence of the mountains of the United States upon the direction of the streams. No part of the valley of the Schoharie is less than 286 feet, and its sources are 2,800 or 3000 feet above tide water in Hudson river. The country watered by this small but beautiful river, below its passage through the Catsbergs, is amongst the most charming regions of the United States. I passed through the townships of Cacajoharie and Charlestown, in Montgomery, and Duanesburg and Princeton, in Schenectady county, and found the country on both sides of the road well cultivated, and extremely pleasing to the eye. If any part of this region deserves a preference in soil, variety of site, and general improvement, it is that near the Schoharie river.

Entering Schenectady county, the country insensibly deteriorates both in soil and cultivation, and contrary to what might be expected, the approach to Albany is over a tract of land, in great part in a state of nature, covered with a forest of evergreen trees, growing in a loose, sandy soil. Norman's Kill rises in Schenectady county, and flowing south east falls into the Hudson river below Albany. The country watered by this creek is mostly broken, rocky, and along the stream often precipitous, giving to the traveller a striking contrast to the fine region along the Mohawk.

Drenched by a heavy rain I arrived in Albany, Tuesday, Sept. 15th, 131 days from my departure from that city. I have now, strictly speaking, closed my tour; the remaining part of the distance I have to pass over in order to return home, is too well known to you to render any farther observations necessary. You will see me in New-York in a few days. I expect to remain in this city three or four days in the mean time

Adieu,

ADDENDA.

NO. 1.

EXTRACTS FROM BOUCHETTE'S CANADA.

"IN forming the plan of government for Canada, the general principles of the English constitution were introduced, wherever it was practicable: in the Upper Province no impediments to this course of proceeding were met with, but in the Lower one some small deviations from them were found necessary, in order to reconcile it to the genius of a people so long accustomed to a different regime. The civil department is administered by a governor, who is generally a military officer and commander of the forces, a lieutenant governor, an executive council, a legislative council, and a house of assembly, or the representatives of the people. The governor and lieutenant governor naturally exercise their authority under the royal commission. The members of the executive council, amounting to seventeen, derive their appointment from the king, and this body exercises a direction over the concerns of the province, nearly similar to that of the privy council in the affairs of England. The legislative council, by the act of the constitution, consists of fifteen members, (although at present that number is increased,) all of whom are appointed by mandamus from the king, and may be termed the second estate of the province; and, with the third branch or house of assembly, forms the provincial parliament. The governor is invested with power to prorogue, and in the exercise of his own discretion, to dissolve the parliament, to give the royal assent or refusal to bills passed by it, or to reserve them in case of doubt or difficulty, until his majesty's pleasure be known thereon. Such acts as receive the governor's assent are usually put in immediate force, but he is enjoined to have copies of them transmitted to England, that they may receive the approbation of the king in council, and his majesty has the right, with the advice of his council, to cancel any act so passed by the provincial parliament within two years from the date of its arrival in England, but hitherto its wisdom has been so well directed, in the arduous task of legislating, that there is no instance on record, of this prerogative ever having been exercised. The acts that emanate from the provincial parliament, are all of a local nature, such, for instance, as providing for the internal regulation of the country, through the various departments, for its defence, as far as relates to enrolling and embodying the militia, and imposing taxes for raising the necessary supplies, to defray the expences of government. But any acts, having for their object the alteration, or repeal of any laws existing antecedent to the constitution granted in 1791; the tithes; grants of land for the maintenance of the Protestant clergy; the rights of presentation to rectories, or the endowments of parsonages, whatever relates to the exercise of religious worship, or disqualification of religious tenets, the rights of the clergy; to changes or modifications of the discipline of the church of England, or of the royal prerogative on the subject of waste crown lands, must, after having passed the provincial parliament, be submitted to the British parliament, and receive the royal assent before they can pass into laws. The house of assembly is composed of fifty-two members, and is a model, on a small scale, of the house of commons of the imperial parliament; the representatives are extensive proprietors of land, and are elected for the districts and counties, by the votes of persons being actual possessors of landed property, of at least forty shillings clear annual value: for the city of Quebec and the towns, they are chosen by voters, who must be possessed of a dwelling-house and piece of ground, of not less annual value than five pounds sterling, or else have been domiciliated in the place for one year previous to the writ of summons issuing, and have paid one year's rent, not under ten pounds sterling, for a house or lodging. There exists no disqualification either for the electors or elected on account of religious tenets, for, in this country, where toleration reigns in its plenitude, every one, whatever may be his faith, is eligible to fill any office or employ, provided the other qualifications required by law are not wanting. The sittings of the house begin in January, and all the public and private business is usually gone through by the latter end of March, about which time it is prorogued, so that the session never exceeds the term of three months, between January and April. Should parliament not be dissolved by the governor, a circumstance that, indeed, very seldom occurs, its duration is limited by the act of the constitution to the period of four years, when its functions expire, and writs are immediately issued for the election of another. At such a crisis the independence and energy of the various voters, the professions and humility of the candidates, are as strikingly pourtrayed as in the more turbulent contests, that take place on similar occasions in the country.

"The criminal code of the United Kingdom extends to Canada, and is carried into effect without the slightest variation. For the administration of civil justice, there is a court of appeal, in which the governor presides, assisted by the lieutenant governor, not less than five members of the executive council, and such of the principal law officers, as have not had cognizance of the previous trial; against the decisions of this court, as a final resource, an appeal may be made to the king in council. A court of king's bench, a court of common pleas, with each a chief justice and three puisne judges. Quarter sessions of the peace held four times a year, besides a police and subordinate magistrature for determining affairs of minor importance.

"By far the largest portion of inhabitants* are descended from French ancestors, the reader will readily surmise that the prevailing religion is Roman Catholic; of this persuasion, there is a Bishop of Quebec, a coadjutor with the title of Bishop of Salde, nine Vicars General, and about two hundred curates, and missionaries spread over the different districts of the province, by whom the tenets of their religion are inculcated with assiduity

* Only correct as respects Lower Canada, the fact is the contrary in the Upper Province.

and devotion, but little tinctured with bigotry or intolerance, unhappily so frequently characteristic of the same faith in the old world. Exercising their sacred functions under the auspices of a Protestant government, they feel the value of mildness in their own conduct, and strenuously endeavor to repay its protecting power by a zealous performance of their duties, and by instilling into the minds of their flock, a grateful obedience to the laws, with a reverence for the constitution, as well as the obligations imposed upon them in their character of good citizens. They are also chiefly employed in the important cares of education, of which they acquit themselves in a manner that reflects the highest credit upon their exertions. To this fact the seminaries of Quebec and Montreal, and the college of Nicolet, bear a powerful testimony. In these establishments, where the higher and more abstruse sciences yield to those of more extended and primary utility; professors are employed to teach the various branches of the classics, mathematics, and belles-lettres, whose learning would acquire them reputation in any country. In communicating their instructions, the French idiom is in general use, but in the college there is a professor of the English tongue, an example worthy of being followed by the two former, as this language now becomes an essential part of youthful studies. The revenues of the Catholic clergy are derived from grants of land made to them under the ancient regime, and the usual contributions ordained by their ecclesiastical government, which are, perhaps, more cheerfully paid by the Canadians, and collected in a manner much freer from vexatious exactions than in any country whatever.

"The spiritual concerns of the Protestant part of the community are under the guidance of the Lord Bishop of Quebec, nine rectors, and a competent number of other clergymen, who are supported by annual stipends from the government, by the appropriation of all granted lands as provided for in the act of the constitution, and the other sources of revenue peculiar to the church of England. In a degree of moderate affluence, exempt on the one hand from inordinate impropriation, and on the other from penurious parsimony; thereby giving to the clerical order, the degree of consequence in the superior ranks of society that is due to its ministry.

' In the unrestrained exercise of two systems of divine worship so widely differing in their tenets, it is a pleasing fact, that the discipline of the two churches never encounters the smallest obstruction from each other; on the contrary, the greatest good will and harmony is observed to prevail, as well between the pastors, as the flocks committed to their charge.

' For the defence of the two Canadas, a regular military establishment is maintained by the British government, which, in time of peace, may amount to about six or seven thousand men, including artillery, engineers, commissariat, &c. But when we are at war with the United States, this force is increased as the presence of circumstances demands; and at this period, (1815) I may venture to compute it, although without official documents to fix the precise numerical strength, at from twenty-seven to thirty thousand men in both provinces. In aid of the regular troops, an I in order that, under any exigency, the government may be enabled to bring a sufficient force into the field, the lower province is apportioned into fifty-two divisions, wherein all males from fifteen to sixty years of age, are bound by law to enroll their names every year, with the captains of companies appointed for their parish, within the month of April. After the enrolment is completed, they are mustered four times in a year, either on Sundays or holidays, when they are instructed in as much of the rudiments of military exercise as the occasion will allow; besides these four muster days, they are once in each year, reviewed by the commander in chief, or the officer commanding the division. This is denominated the sedentary militia; and as the average strength of each division so enrolled may be computed about a thousand, it makes the aggregate amount upwards of 52,000 men.* The incorporated militia, by an act passed in the provincial parliament on the 19th of May 1812, is fixed during the war, at two thousand men; but by virtue of authority vested in the governor, it is at present increased to five battalions, or nearly double the number, which, on the re-establishment of peace with the United States, will be reduced to the standard named in the act. This body is chosen by ballot from the unmarried men of the sedentary militia; its term of

* In the Lower Province only.

service is two years. It is also provided that one half of each regiment may be discharged annually, and the vacancies filled up by a fresh ballot; a plan that will have the good effect of extending gradually a certain degree of military discipline over the greater part of the population capable of bearing arms. The battalions thus formed of single men, renders the military service less obnoxious to the individual, and less expensive to the state, by saving the provision otherwise necessary to be made for wives and children of militiamen actually embodied. By the same act, the sum of twelve thousand pounds annually is raised for the maintenance of this constitutional force. The incorporated militia is well equipped and in a state of discipline that merits the highest commendations, by which it has been able to brigade with the regular troops during the existing contest, and to take so distinguished a part in some of the actions fought, that it must press upon the consideration of government, a firm reliance upon its future exertions, and devotedness in the cause of its country.

"In the Upper Province, the same system, with some trifling modification, prevails, but from the more scanty population the force is proportionably much less; however, the militia of Upper Canada had its full share of the hardships of the war, as well as many opportunities of distinguishing itself in presence of the enemy; and the real magnitude of its service may be estimated, when it is considered, that, by availing himself of it, the governor general, Sir George Prevost, was enabled with a number of troops of the line, inadequate according to usual military calculations, not only to repel every attempt of the American commanders to invade the British territory, in the years 1813 and 1814, but to overwhelm the assailants with defeats, that for a long time will leave an indelible stain upon their military reputation."

[*A Geographical Description of the Province of Lower Canada. with remarks upon Upper Canada.—London*, 1815. *By* JOSEPH BOUCHETTE. *Page* 15—24.]

"AMERICA possesses a climate peculiar to itself, the quantity and prevalence of heat and cold, seems to be governed by laws materially differing from those that regulate the temperature of other parts of the earth. It is certain that a person would be materially led astray, were he to form an opinion of the temperature of Canada from the analogy of local situation: it lies, for instance in the same parallel of latitude as France, but instead of exhaling the exquisite fragrance of flowers, and ripening delicate fruits, delicious excellence, as is the case in that country its surface is covered with accumulated snows for nearly one half of the year, and vegetation is suspended for nearly the same period by continued frost. Yet this circumstance is unattended with so much rigor as any one would be disposed to suspect, and notwithstanding the apparent severity, Canada enjoys a climate that is congenial to health in an eminent degree, and highly conduces to fertilize its soil. Heat and cold are certainly to extremes; the latter both for duration and intensity by far the most predominant, is supposed to derive much of its force, from the following cause, viz. the land stretches from the St. Lawrence towards the north pole, which it approaches much nearer to, and with a less intervention of sea, than that on the old continent; it expands also an immense distance to the westward; therefore, the winds between the north-east and north-west passing over a less surface of water than in the same portion of the other hemisphere, are consequently divested of a similar quantity of their intense frigor, and afterwards sweeping across the immense chain of mountains, covered with perpetual snows and ice that intersects the whole of these cheerless regions, they acquire a penetrating severity, by traversing so vast a tract of frozen ground, that even their progress into lower latitudes, cannot disarm them of. Of these winds the north-west is the most rigorous;* and even in summer, as soon as it prevails, the transition from heat to cold is so sudden, that the thermometer has been known to fall nearly thirty degrees in a very few hours. The highest range of the

* This is also the case in all parts of North America, east of the Chippewan mountains; the frigid influence of the north-west current of air is severely felt upon the shores of the gulf of Mexico. Upon the Atlantic slope, east of the Allegany chain, the winds from the northwest are peculiarly piercingly cold

summer heat, is usually between 96 and 102 degrees of Fahrenheit;* but an atmosphere particularly pure, abates the oppressive fervor felt in other parts at the same point. In winter the mercury sometimes sinks to 31 degrees below zero, but this must be considered its very greatest depression, and as happening only once or twice in a season, or perhaps not more than thrice in two seasons, and then its continuance rarely exceeds forty-eight hours; but the general range of cold in medium years, may be estimated from twenty degrees above, to twenty-five degrees below zero. The frost which is seldom interrupted during the winter, is almost always accompanied with a cloudless sky, and pure dry air that makes it both pleasant and healthy, and considerably diminishes the piercing quality it possesses when the atmosphere is loaded with vapours. At the eastern extremity of the province, from its vicinity to the sea, fogs are brought on by an easterly wind, but to the westward they seldom prevail, and even at Quebec are almost unknown. The snow usually lies on the ground until the latter end of April, when it is melted by the powerful rays of the sun, rather than dissolved by the progress of thaw, the air still continuing pure and frosty; when it has disappeared, the spring may be said to commence; and as the ground being protected by so thick a covering during winter, is seldom frozen many inches deep, the powers of vegetation almost immediately resume their activity, and bring on the fine season, that would excite in a stranger to the country the greatest degree of astonishment. Rain prevails most in the spring and fall of the year,† but is seldom violent or

* If the thermometer of Fahrenheit ranges in Canada, in summer, between 96 and 102, the intensity of Canadian heat is greater than in Louisiana; I never was made acquainted with a higher range of the thermometer in New-Orleans, when properly placed, than 94°.

† Taken in the sense understood by Mr Bouchette, when he wrote the above expression, the same observation would apply with equal force to all those parts of North America, included in the Canadas and United States. But, in reality, the rainy season of all these vast regions actually commences about the beginning of November, and continues until the latter end of April. Snow is only water in a state of congelation; and in fact that element falls from the clouds in all states, between complete fluidity, to that of the most solid ice. It is therefore, unfounded in princi-

of long duration in the level parts of the province. Towards the mountains, however, their frequency, and duration are both increased. Bordering on the gulf of St. Lawrence, as the face of the soil is rugged and mountainous, the climate somewhat influenced thereby, participates in its ungenial nature, but advancing to the westward, it becomes more mild, and encourages the resumption of agricultural labours at a much earlier period, particularly in the western district of the Lower, and all the settled parts of the Upper Province; at Montreal, for instance, only 79 geographical miles southward, and 143 miles due west from the meridian of Quebec, the spring is reckoned to commence from five to six weeks earlier than at the latter place. Vegetation is proportionately more luxuriant and vigorous, producing crops of greater increase, by seldom experiencing checks in their early stages from the hoar frost, so injurious to the rising growth wherever it prevails. In a comparison between the climates of Great Britain and the Canadas, some advantages result to the latter, because the prevalence of fine clean weather, and a pure atmosphere greatly exceeds that in the former, besides, the degree of cold is proved by actual experiment, not to be proportionate to the indication of the thermometer, as a corroborating instance, it is remarked, at its utmost severity, which is in the months of January and February, the labour of artisans in out-door employments is rarely suspended many days in succession.

"From the climate of a country, its soil comes under notice by a sort of natural transition. On making a calculation of the superficial contents of the area, enclosed between the two principal ranges of mountains before spoken of, about 16,628,000 square acres may be computed, to include the greater part of the land in the Lower Province yet surveyed, that is capable of being turned to any favorable account in an agricultural point of view. In so great an extent, undoubtedly every gradation of quality, between very bad and very good is to be found, but it would be attended with some dif-

ples of true meteorological philosophy to call spring and autumn our rainy seasons. In all places where winter is of sufficient length and frigidity to permit considerable accumulation of snow, the spring floods in rivers, owe their augmentation, more to the melting of that meteor, than to the rain that falls during the rise of the waters.

ficulty, to state with tolerable correctness the relative proportion of each kind. Sensible that, in thus generalizing the whole, only an imperfect sketch can be given, it is my intention that as much care as possible shall be used to render the subject more clear and familiar, when treating the different districts and divisions geographically. For the present then, it may suffice to say, that, with respect to goodness, the eastern parts are inferior to the western, being of a more irregular and uneven surface, in many places consisting of a light soil, of a sandy nature laid upon a stratum of perfect sand or gravel, in others it is varied with mixtures of clay, loam, and sometimes a good vegetable mould upon a reddish argillaceous bottom, constituting a medium between the two extremes; this latter species is rather supposed to exceed the inferior classes in quantity, and with a moderate degree of careful husbandry will yield the farmer pretty fair returns. In the western part of the province, although the variety is nearly as great as in the other, in its nature it is very superior, the soil most esteemed, is a composition of fine rich loams, both a yellow and bluish colour, with a good black earth, forming a soil, that in the country is supposed to be endued with the greatest share of fertilizing properties of any of the natural classes, and of this sort consists the chief portion of land in the western division. The remaining part is always above mediocrity, in fact, it may be fairly asserted, that through the whole of North America, and indeed in many other countries, it will be difficult to meet with land more inviting to form new settlements upon, or where it is already cultivated, capable of being made more generous and productive, by the introduction of an improved system of husbandry. Its superiority over the contiguous districts of the United States is fully manifest, by the readiness with which American families in considerable numbers, have for years past, abandoned the less fertile fields of their nativity, to settle upon a soil that they are certain will abundantly repay the industry and art bestowed upon it. Undoubtedly the burthen of the taxes and peculiar laws will have had some share in causing these migrations across the borders, into a country where neither would be felt. But be this as it may, many farmers thus changing the scene of their labours, have, either by purchase or by lease, obtained extensive estates and endenizened themselves under the British government, whilst others, as eager to enjoy the same advantages, but less honest in their manner of obtaining them, have selected convenient situations among the reserved lands, wherein they have unceremoniously domiciliated without license or title; and even without the acknowledgement of rent, have continued to cultivate and improve their favorite spots thus chosen.*

"This species of tenure certainly ought not to be allowed by the crown, and means should undoubtedly be taken to eject such tenants, because their prior occupancy, the irregularity of its being generally unknown, deprives the natural subject of taking the lots upon the terms before recited. It is also desirable not to permit the pernicious example of such unauthorised possession of valuable property to communicate its influence, or, indeed, to exist at all. It is much to be wished, that the system of management in Lower Canada was as good as the land, upon which it is exercised; agricultural riches would then flow in a copious and inexhaustible stream; for if the natural excellence of soil and goodness of climate, contending against the disadvantages of a very inferior, not to say bad mode of husbandry, be capable of

* How far a disaffected citizen of the United States, is qualified to make a good British subject in Canada, I am unable to determine. Where Mr. Bouchette is uninfluenced by national or political prejudices, he is a respectable writer; but when descanting upon any subject relating to the United States, he evinces more than the mere partiality of an Englishman. My opinion has been given in the text, that in no part of his Britannic majesty's dominions, except India, are to be found so many persons in proportion to given numbers, averse to the people and government of the United States, as in the two Canadas, New-Brunswick, and Nova Scotia. Great moral change in public feeling, must take place, before the inhabitants of these provinces can relish our institutions. Wise and reflecting men in the British North American possessions, would, to avoid a frequent recurring border warfare, an evil they have experienced, consent if all circumstances were favorable to a separation from Great Britain; but would very reluctantly be amalgamated into the Union of the States. Indeed without violent and repeated infractions upon their personal rights, the people of Canada will long remain as they now are, sincerely attached to the government of the parent state. It was such infractions pertinaciously continued, that produced the United States; let England profit by the folly and crimes of her former rulers.

yielding crops of 15 to 18 to one, what might not be expected from it, were the modern improvement in implements as well as culture, that have been introduced with so much benefit in England, to be applied to it? The Canadian farmer unfortunately, and it is a subject much to be lamented, has hitherto had no means of acquiring instruction, in the many new and beneficial methods, by which modern science has so greatly assisted the labors of the husbandman. Unskilled in any other mode, he continues to till his fields by the same rule that his forefathers followed for many generations, which long habit and an unprofitable partiality engrafted thereon, seems to have endeared to him; knowing the natural bounty of his land, he places his greatest reliance upon it, and feels satisfied when he reaps a crop not inferior to that of the year gone by, apparently without a wish to increase his stores by the adoption of untried means. Apprehensions of failure and consequent loss, operate more strongly than disinclination, for a desire to enlarge his profits is full as lively in him as in other men, which, aided by a genius active in imitating, would certainly impel him to try his success at any innovation, productive of corresponding advantages, that might be introduced by another. Example is the only stimulus required, and it is well worth the attention of those to whom the welfare of the British colonies is confided, and who must be sensible of the importance of this one in particular, to consider of means by which this stimulus could be most effectually excited. Whatever encouragement might be given as an incentive to the industry of the native, or the alien settler, to persevere in an approved plan of clearing, draining, and getting under cultivation the new lands, or of improvement upon such as are already under management, by a reform of the present system, a judicious variation of crops, and the introduction of new articles suitable to the climate, of which there are many, would be attended with so much benefit that in a very few years these provinces must become one of the most valuable of all the exterior possessions of Great Britain.

"The practice of husbandry in Canada is defective in some very principal points: in the first place the use of the plough, which ought to be viewed as the base of all agrarian improvement, is not enough attended to, and where it is applied, it is done in a manner so inadequate to the purpose, that the good intended to be derived from it, is powerfully counteracted; generally speaking, this operation is performed so lightly, that scarcely more than the surface of the ground is broken by it; the weeds that ought to be extirpated are only cut off, they consequently shoot out again and absorb much of the vigor of the soil, that otherwise would nourish the seed and plants committed to it. If the Canadian husbandman could witness the difference between the style of ploughing in England and his own, I am certain that he would readily be convinced of its utility, and willing to adopt a method so much in favor of his autumnal expectations. Another main object in farming improvements, is, the judicious application of the various manures to different soils, in which essential particular it must be admitted the Canadian practice is much in arrear, as it is only within a few years, and in the neighbourhood of the large towns, that it has in some degree been attended to by a few farmers more intelligent than their brethren; this neglect, added to the pernicious practice of sowing the same sort of grain year after year, upon the same land, without other means of renovation than letting it lie fallow for a season, must excite wonder that it should produce such crops as it actually does. When the heart of the land is supposed to be gone, or greatly deteriorated, the remedy is, after taking a crop of wheat from it, to allow a natural layer of clover and grass, which serves as summer feed for cattle. In autumn it receives a ploughing in the usual way, and in the ensuing spring is again put under wheat or oats. This plan is unprofitable and injudicious, the stock derives but little advantage from the herbage, while with a little more care the grounds might be turned to much better account. The introduction of different kinds of grasses and other succulents, regulated by a moderate degree of skill, could not fail being attended with complete success. Among the various sorts, the English red, and Dutch white clover are worthy of notice, being calculated as well for summer feed as excellent winter store. To these might be added the yellow Swedish turnip, a species perhaps superior to any other of its class, as it will endure the most violent frost, and maintains its goodness until the spring, as well as in autumn; that the acquisition of such a plant to a country always subject to a long winter would soon become valuable, does not admit of a question. It is entitled to the farmer's attention, as being a profitable article; from 20 to 25 tons per acre may be raised by careful management, which if housed before winter sets in, would furnish an undeniable food for cattle during that season; by its means he would obtain a beneficial employment in fattening his stock intended for market, and also a large quantity of valuable manure from his farm-yard, ready to be applied to the poor and exhausted lands at the breaking up of the frost. Many other advantages would be the result, if a systematic arrangement in the change of crops were to take place of the undeviating practice at present existing, by it a great progress would be made in the science of agriculture, and a long catalogue of hereditary errors, would no more remain unopposed by any radical improvement. I must again repeat, that example only is wanting to induce the Canadian farmers to explode the unproductive methods they have so long followed, and yield to the admission of profitable innovations. There is yet another article or two of culture of the very first importance to the mother country, which would most certainly prove highly beneficial to these provinces if sufficient attention were to be paid to them. The first of these is hemp, well known to be a native plant of the country, with climate and soil peculiarly well adapted to its growth; in small quantities it has been raised on many farms, though as an object of commerce, the cultivation of it has not been attended with success, notwithstanding it has been tried under the sanction of government, that held out the encouragement of premiums, with the additional inducement of a certain good price, per ton for all such as might be produced fit for its purposes; as so desirable an object hath not been accomplished under these circumstances, it would seem to imply that some insurmountable obstacle opposes it. In reality there is none such, both soil and climate are favorable as nature could form them, and the extensive demand of Great Britain must ever ensure an undoubted market at prices high enough to remunerate the growers very handsomely: the cause of failure in the attempt, must be sought for somewhere else than in any natural deficiencies. That time and considerable sums of money have been wasted is unquestionably true, but it is equally a fact, that the good intentions of administration have been defeated by the inadequate measures pursued in the execution of the plans, and not a little impeded by a want of general agricultural knowledge, in the persons to whom its management was confided. It is not to be denied, but that there are some existing difficulties to be removed before the cultivation of hemp can be made generally agreeable to all persons interested in the agricultural produce of the province: but as the chief of these arise from the discountenance the clergy might show to its introduction on an extensive scale, from a supposition that it would interfere with raising wheat and other grain upon the lands now in tillage, and thereby somewhat diminish their revenues; may they not be surmounted by making it a tithable article, and fixing the rate to be paid as it is in England, namely, five shillings per acre, or otherwise in the same proportion as the contribution of grain is at present taken by them, a 20th part?—Under such a regulation the ecclesiastical body would consult its own interest, by promoting the increase of this production; a measure which could easily be accomplished by the powerful influence that body possesses in all the concerns of the country people, whether temporal or spiritual. I have been unequivocally assured by a gentleman, who has devoted the greatest part of his life to the improvements of growing and dressing both hemp and flax, that he has carefully examined several parcels of the former, sent some time ago from Canada to London, and is decidedly of opinion, that the growth is much superior to what is in general imported from Russia; but on the other hand, from mismanagement after pulling, and from being steeped in bad water, its quality and colour, are greatly inferior to what they would have been, had it undergone a proper process. The management of this plant contains nothing of mystery, and is so plain that it may be carried on by the least intelligent husbandman in the colony, if he be but once put in the proper routine. The choice of a soil fit for the purpose is a leading point, and the kind which is considered the best, is a rich deep loam, whereon a very good crop may be raised without manure, but it may be grown on almost any species not absolutely of a bad quality, if it be well manured, except where there is a cold sub-soil or a very shallow staple. To ensure a good crop, the most careful attention must be paid to ploughing and preparing the land. The tilth should be as fine and as deep as possible, a circumstance hitherto but little noticed by the most part of our Canadian farmers, and in consequence of this neglect, their produce has been most materially reduced in quantity. The seed, of which about four bushels should be allowed per acre, ought not to be put in the ground until the weather is become warm; for the young plants when they begin to shoot up are exceedingly tender, and liable to be injured if night frosts happen in the early period of their growth. May is generally the best month for sowing it; but in Canada this time must be pointed out by a correct knowledge of the climate. After the seed is got in, a light harrow should be used, and nothing more is required until it is fit for pulling; this will be, in from ten to fourteen weeks. In hemp the male and female plants are more distinctly defined than in almost any other species; the former bears a light coloured flower, but never produces any seed, the latter, on the contrary, yields the seed but does not bear a flower. Land is not at all impoverished by the growth of hemp, for after a good crop has been pulled, it cannot possibly be in better condition to be laid under wheat, or indeed any thing else

"The different soils both of Upper and Lower Canada, are likewise admirably well calculated for the growth of flax, an article well deserving the farmer's consideration, from its yielding, with tolerable good management, a larger as well as more certain profit than the greater part of other crops. Loam, loam mixed with clay, gravel, or sand, or clay alone, indeed any land but such as is very wet or very shallow, is good for raising it. On warm, dry soils the sowing may commence in the middle of March, and continue according to the condition and quality of the land, until the first week in May; but with it, as with hemp, the seed time must be guided by a knowledge of the climate. The ground may be prepared by a moderate ploughing, which is not required to be very deep. From two and a half to three bushels of seed per acre may be sown, which must be harrowed in, or bush harrowed, and afterwards well rolled. When the plants are from four to six inches high, care should be taken to have them well weeded, and then no further attention is required until the season for pulling arrives. It remains on the ground from twelve to sixteen weeks, and is sufficiently hardy not to receive any injury from night frosts. Flax and flax seed, as well as hemp, may be produced in Canada fully equal, to say the least of it, to what is obtained from any other country. But they have always been so injudiciously managed after pulling, that their natural good qualities have been seriously deteriorated. From whence one might deduce, that unless a very different system be resorted to, no reasonable expectation of profit from growing it can be formed, and consequently few endeavors will be made to extend the cultivation of these valuable articles. But to combat such a supposition, I feel infinite pleasure in being able to make known among my countrymen generally, that the process of steeping and dew rotting now in practice, whereby the fruits of their labor have been so seriously injured, may be entirely superceded, and henceforward the culture of these important productions may be pursued with an absolute certainty of deriving an ample profit therefrom. However doubtful this assertion may appear to many, it will nevertheless be realised by the use of machines for threshing out the seed, and separating the woody from the fibrous parts, both of hemp and flax, invented by Mr Lee, to whom a patent has been granted for his highly valuable discovery. From a minute and attentive inspection of this machinery, simple in its construction beyond all conception, as well as completely effectual in its performance, and from the ocular demonstration of the perfect success of its operation I have had the satisfaction to receive from this gentleman at his factory, I am warranted in saying with the utmost confidence, that if it be introduced into the British North American colonies, the greatest benefits will be derived, not only by them, but by Great Britain also.* As it will stimulate the occupiers of land to pursue this

---

* I have been more minute in making the foregoing and farther extracts from Mr Bouchette's work, from a conviction that any useful innovation, improvement or invention that can be introduced into the Canadian provinces, can be, with at least as much utility adopted in the contiguous parts of the United States. The culture of flax, has since the extensive introduction of cotton cloths, declined in the United States: but the benefits of the change, in many places may be justly doubted. The invention of the circular saw, for extracting the seed from the fibre of cotton, was the epoch of the extension of that article, and its cheap application to the wants of mankind. How far human genius may obviate the expence to which the culture of flax has hitherto been subject it is impossible to determine; if the statements of Mr. Bouchette are even partially correct, much is already done on

branch of husbandry more than any premiums offered, or means resorted to by government, would be able to do under the old method. By the use of this invention, the necessity of *steeping* and *dew rotting* being avoided, the farmer having pulled his crop, has nothing to do but stack it, when sufficiently dry for that purpose, and let it remain until convenient opportunities occur of bringing it into a marketable state, which may now be performed in a very few hours.

The superiority of this mode of preparation is very great, and the advantages obtained by it in equal proportion. All the labour and attendant expence of steeping, spreading and drying; as well as the losses incident to these operations, is wholly saved. The produce of fibre is fully one-third greater by this than by former methods, while the fibre itself preserves the whole of its natural strength unimpaired by any destructive process. In cleaning flax the whole of the seed is preserved, and some parts of the plant that by steeping are entirely destroyed, are now saved to be turned to a very profitable account. The chaff, for instance, is an excellent food for horses, cows, sheep, &c. and the woody part when separated from the fibre, is a strong manure, particularly good as a top dressing for wheat; both of these have hitherto been wasted. The mode of using the machines is so easy as to be worked by women or even children; they may, without inconvenience to a family, be fixed in cottages, or the out-houses of any description, so as to furnish a constant in-door employment through the winter months. Hemp or flax prepared by this invention is found, from experiment, to be greatly superior in strength to any other. The most impartial criterion, namely, that of suspending a weight by a line made of different sorts, of the same length, thickness and weight, has been had recourse to, when the one prepared in this manner has supported more than double the weight of the other.

" From many conservations I have had with Mr Lee, on the subject of his patent, besides frequent proofs of its efficacy, I feel the strongest conviction that the value of his invention will soon be appreciated when it is introduced into Canada. With

that subject, and serves to shew how slowly the most valuable discoveries find their way into use.

such an impression on my mind, I am persuaded, I shall be aiding to increase both the interest and comfort of my fellow-countrymen, by promoting, as far as lies in my power, the general use of so simple and so well contrived an apparatus. To establish, in some degree, the reality of what has been adduced, I will insert the following estimate of the expences and produce of one acre of flax, which I have been repeatedly assured by the patentee is the result of many years practical experience as a grower, and formed upon such a calculation as any fair average crop, properly attended to, will not fail of realising always, and most frequently somewhat exceed it.

EXPENSE PER ACRE.

	£ s. d.	$ cts.
Rent of land,	5 00 00	22 22
Ploughing and harrowing,	1 10 00	6 66
Sowing, harrowing, and rolling,	7 05	1 66
Weeding by hand,	15 10	3 32
Pulling and setting up,	1 00 00	4 44
Three bushels of seed,	1 11 06	7 00
Cartage and stacking,	1 00 00	4 44
Threshing out the seed, and cleaning the flax fit for market.	8 10 00	37 77
	£19 14 00	$87 51

PRODUCE PER ACRE.

	£ s. d.	$ cts.
30 cwt. at 60 shillings per cwt	30 00 00	133 33
9 bushels of seed at 10s. per bushel,	4 10 00	20 00
Chaff,	1 11 06	7 00
Manure,	2 00 00	8 88
	£38 01 06	169 21
Expence,	£19 14 00	87 51
Profit,*	£18 07 06	$81 70

* I have reduced this estimate to Federal money at an allowance of 4s. 6d. to the dollar. If the data are drawn from correct sources, the benefits of cultivating flax amount to a very seductive aggregate. The value of cotton, to the cultivator, does not

"This account is made out from the ratio of agricultural expences in England. Some of its items are undoubtedly different from what they would be in the colonies; but the excess in one would be balanced, or nearly so, by the reduction of another; and as the prices allowed for the produce are such as the ordinary state of the market will always afford, and after making a reasonable allowance for tythes, freight, and other incidental expences, the general result is sufficient to induce speculation with tolerable fair prospects of success. It must be also taken into consideration, that the expense of the machinery is very moderate; nor should it escape notice that a steady demand will be found in England, both for flax and seed at fair prices.*

much exceed the balance here shewn in favor of flax; and if the ordinary expences of the respective places where these two vegetables can be reared, are taken into account, it would admit doubt which of the two products promise the largest reward to human labor. Rent of land enters largely into the above computation, and though the price of land in the U. S. must be also estimated, the interest of that price would seldom amount to more than one dollar per acre, even with the addition of clearing and fencing: consequently the profit to the citizen of the U. S. would be greater, than to the English farmer, by the enormous difference of more than $20 per acre.

* Flax, is now cultivated in many of the most thickly populated parts of Europe, in places, where from the number of people and scarcity of land upon which to rear vegetables and animals for food, flax would cease to be cultivated could the inhabitants receive in commerce, that material at a moderate price. It is only since the introduction of the saw-wheels for cleaning cotton from the seed, that the use of that excellent vegetable wool has become so prevalent. The plough itself, does not produce a greater comparative abridgment of labour, than does the saw-wheels. Four horses, two men, and one boy will cleanse, pack, and enclose in bales per day at least six hundred pounds of clean cotton, with a common cylinder of fifty saws; in the ancient mode of extracting the seed by hand, four pounds of clean cotton was an excessive quantity to be cleaned in one day by one person. If the value of the machinery and attendance are assumed at an equivalent of ten full grown workmen, there remains a difference of fifteen to one in favor of the use of the saw machinery in cleansing cotton. It is very probable that flax and hemp admit a rapid transition from the crude plant to use, in an equal ratio.

"With respect to hemp, it can never be doubted but what his majesty's government will be again ready to lend every support and encouragement to the production of an article in our own dominions, that we have long been forced to purchase from strangers; which cultivation meeting with success, in a few years may render our country wholly independent of the north of Europe, for its supply, or at any rate liberate it from the apprehension of ever being put to serious inconvenience by any change of political sentiments in sovereigns. The welfare of my native province and its parent state, has ever been with me the strongest incentive to exertion; and a ray of hope that I may be an humble instrument towards promoting a pursuit which would redound to the advantage of both, hath occasioned me to enter more largely into this subject than I at first intended. If my expectations are too sanguine to be borne out by the opinions of persons more enlightened thereon than I can pretend to be, I would much rather they would be attributed to an erroneous judgment, than a willingness to commit myself to the chance of misleading a single individual, by hazarding any unguarded or unfounded representations.

"To ascertain, in the scale of importance, to what degree the North American colonies rise, their present value, and how much that value is capable of being increased, it is necessary to take a view of their commercial concerns, in order to bring their resources fairly before us. In attempting to introduce this subject, I feel no small degree of diffidence, from the reflection that it is one much out of the line of my professional pursuits, in the discussion of which erroneous opinions are very liable to intrude, and that by meddling with it I may be blamed by many for the imperfect performance. My object is to attract to this point the attention of men well informed on the intricate questions of mercantile policy,* in the hope that some much abler pen than mine,

---

* In discussing this very important subject, Mr. Bouchette, with all his modesty, is infinitely more competent than me. Our professional pursuits were indeed similar, and as far as those pursuits tend to disqualify us for examining the arcana of trade, our intellectual impediments are equal: but in an intimate knowledge of Canada, and of course with the adjacent regions, Mr. Bouchette has no rival; therefore his opinions where not warped by political or national feelings, are entitled to great credit.

may, at no remote period, place it in a more clear and palpable state, rather than to promote decision by any observations of my own. The extent of my endeavors will be limited to conveying some general ideas of the capabilities possessed by these provinces, of rising into commercial greatness, if their interests be attended to and protected. The situation of both Upper and Lower Canada, are replete with conveniences for trade. The great extent and many ports of the St. Lawrence accessible to ships of considerable burthen; its inland navigation even to the extremity of the lakes; the numerous rivers and streams which fall into it, by which produce of all kinds may be conveyed from the most distant settlements to Quebec,* or other places of shipment, open

have minutely transcribed this gentleman's speculations on Canadian commerce, because I am aware that his observations concern the inhabitants of the contiguous states and territories of the United States, if possible even more than the persons to whom his words are addressed. With the single exception of its freezing in winter, the St. Lawrence does certainly possess, in climate, soil, productions natural and artificial, and in present culture, resources far beyond what the people of the United States have any adequate conception. In the revolutions of power, first impressions are terrible weapons; in the changes of commerce, previous establishments are rocks of *adamant*. If the rich and hourly increasing products of the St. Lawrence valley once flow to Montreal, to that city will they flow, maugre all that legal prohibition, or even the suggestions of private convenience can oppose to the current. Though our independence politically, is secured beyond the reach of British rivalry, it is the only instance where we are independent of that active and insidious government. Unfortunately we have citizens so morally dependant, as to induce them to expend the fruits of their talents to prevent our entire emancipation.

* This is only correct in its full extent below the Falls of Niagara; that cataract forming a formidable interruption to the navigation of the waters of the St Lawrence. Indeed the ship conveyance in that river and its connecting lakes are naturally divided into four sections, separated by irremovable impediments; first section, from Montreal downwards to the gulf; second, from Niagara to Ogdensburg; ships might descend below the latter village about five miles, to the head of the Grand Gallop Island and Rapids, but no incentive does now, or probably ever will exist, to induce owners of vessels to fall below the mouth of the Oswegatchie. The third section includes lakes Erie, Huron Michigan, and the mouths of their confluents, between the Falls of

greater facilities to mercantile speculations than perhaps any other country can offer. This river is the only channel by which the commodities of these two provinces find their way to distant countries, and is also by far the most natural, as well as most easily available egress for such productions of the districts of the United States that lie contiguous to its southern bank, as they are able to furnish beyond their own consumption. Prohibitory laws of the American Senate, have, indeed, of late been passed to bar its subjects from exportation by this route, but they have not obtained so much attention as it was imagined they would.[*] A very large tract of fertile country on their side of the border, is thickly settled and in high cultivation; the industry of its inhabitants always insures a large disposable stock of the fruits of their labors, which the vigilance and invention of a speculative disposition will not fail to discover means of transferring to the readiest market, in despite of enactments that are no less disagreeable than disadvantageous. By fostering this intercourse, Canada would always secure a vast addition of articles of the first necessity, in aid of its own surplus produce, to meet a great increase of its export trade, were that trade relieved by the British government from some of the impediments thrown in its way by existing regulations, that are highly favorable to American commerce.

"The principal exports from the Canadas, consist of new ships, oak and pine timber, deals, masts and bowsprits, spars of all denominations, staves, pot and pearl ashes, peltry, wheat, flour, biscuit, Indian corn, pulse, salt provisions, fish, and some other mis-

Niagara and the Saut St. Mary. The fourth section is composed of lake Superior and its confluent rivers. The commerce of the first two divisions, will naturally pass to Montreal and Quebec: that of the latter two, will, if the New-York canal was finished, in great part pass through that conveyence into the Hudson.

[*] The most efficacious prohibition would be a water route, open longer, leading to a better market, and included within our own country. Laws that contravene, to any great degree, the passions or avidity of mankind, have been, and always will be, nugatory. The universality of severe penal statutes against duelling, and the almost equal ubiquity of that practice, is a loud speaking commentary on what I have advanced above.

cellaneous articles, employing generally about 150,000 tons of shipping. In this enumeration, the articles of primary consequence to England, are the growth of the forests, whether considered as the source of employment to British ships and native sailors in the carriage of it, if they were able to contend for the freights against the indulgences granted to their opponents; or as to their being of great and continued consumption, therefore of indispensible necessity. Since the year 1806, the timber trade of the colonies, but of the Canadas in particular, increased in an extraordinary degree, until the state of the country at the commencement of hostilities with America not only checked its further progress, but from very obvious causes, reduced it below the standard of former years. This diminution, however, must be considered only accidental, and totally unconnected with the resources of the trade, which, according to the most discreet methods of calculation, is not only adequate to supply abundantly the demand of the British West-India islands with square timber, planks, deals, staves, and whatever comes under the general name of lumber, but to furnish a large proportion of the same for the use of Great Britain. This ability it was, and perhaps with many may be still the fashion to consider problematical; but let the return of exports from 1806 to 1810 be examined, and it will be readily seen, that in these four years they advanced from about 100,000 to 375,000 tons from all the provinces, of which nearly one half was from Quebec alone. To meet this demand, no difficulties were encountered in procuring the necessary quantities, either with respect to the number of hands to be employed in collecting it, or any thing like a failure in the forests; and had it been as large again, it might have been answered with proportionate facility. Within the period cited, the increase of this trade in the Canadas only was much more than equivalent to the total consumption of the West-India islands, estimated at 142,000 tons, which is but little less than half the quantity annually required for the use of the royal navy. The export of timber in this year, is, perhaps, the greatest of any that has taken place, yet the ease with which it was procured is certainly an argument that weighs strongly against the assertion, that the North American colonies are unable to supply the necessities of the West-Indies.

" With respect to the exportation of flour and grain, the proness is not certainly so satisfactory as that of timber;* yet this circumstance is far from being conclusive of inability to furnish such quantities as are required for the use of the West-India islands, whose annual demand for flour, grain, and biscuit, is computed at something more than 1,200,000 bushels. Of this quantity, Canada has hitherto seldom exported, upon an average, but little more than a third part. So great a disparity of numbers, is not a sufficient reason to abandon, without some further reflection, the supposition, that the supply may be made to equal the demand. Immediately, indeed, it could not; but after the lapse of a very few years, may not so desirable an object be obtained, when the good effects of an improved system of agricultural management, and to the encouragement of which the most rigid attention ought to be paid, begin to show themselves, combined with such measures as would make it the interest of the people of the well cultivated countries of the United States that he contiguous to our frontier, to bring their disposable produce to the ports of the St. Lawrence? The foundation of these advantages would certainly be laid, were the colonial merchants placed in a situation to contend against those of America, in supplying the islands. Until the commencement of hostilities with us, the latter enjoyed the profits of supplying our West-Indian possessions, both with provisions and lumber, and which were, in fact, secured to them by an act that passed the British parliament, in 1807, whereby the privy council was authorised to suspend the operation of the Act 12th Charles the Second, excluding foreign ships from trading with the English colonies. Under favor of this suspension, they employed an immense number of ships in this trade, every ton of which was a manifest detriment both to our provinces and

* When in Canada, several judicious persons resident in that country, expressed to me their opinion, that the lumber trade was the greatest existing impediment to the prosperity and improvement of the people, as it employed their active able bodied laboring men in that part of the year that ought to be appropriated to agriculture. There is little doubt, but that timber trade is a very unproductive branch of commerce, and that a country must remain at least in a dependant and precarious condition, where much attention is paid to an application of industry, where the profits are so small compared with the necessary exertion and consumption of time.

our commercial navy. The admission of American produce into the ports of Great Britain, upon paying the same duties only as are charged upon the importation of similar articles from our own colonies, is another very powerful check upon their prosperity, which from these various combinations against it, will experience much difficulty in rising to the eminence it would speedily attain, if that country, so recently ceased to be an inveterate enemy, be not again placed by the liberality of the British government in a situation to impede its progress, and be hereafter viewed in the same light, and put upon a par with other foreign nations, in respect to restrictions and countervailing duties; then the North American provinces will soon greatly improve their internal situation, and the mother country derive such benefit from them as will render her more independent of other nations for supplies of the first importance, than she has hitherto been."

[*Topographical Description of the Province of Lower Canada, with remarks upon Upper Canada.* By JOSEPH BOUCHETTE, Esq. London, 1815. Page 57—8.]

NO. 11.

GENERAL REMARKS

THE foregoing correspondence and extracts, contains the substance of my own personal observations, and such explanatory matter from others, as I could collect during my tour, and since its termination; I cannot, however, take leave of the reader, without claiming his patience during a recapitulation and an examination of some extraneous matter, which was not included in my original letters, though of some importance to elucidate the topography of the country over which I ranged. I am aware that such productions as mine, where few personal incidents are introduced, must draw their interest from the geographical information they may contain. It has been my endeavor to throw as much light as in my power, upon the natural structure, and present improvements of the tract over which I ranged; how far I have succeeded, is now before the reader. There is one object of general interest, upon which more is perhaps expected from me than I can fulfil; that is, the Grand Canal now in progress in the state of New-York. On the subject of this truly great work, I have been careful to collect all the information I could procure, and have now presented the result to the public. Not having visited Ballston or Saratoga Springs, I addressed a letter to the Rev. Reuben Sears, desiring that gentleman to give me such information as he possessed, respecting these places of public resort. Mr. Sears very politely and satisfactorily replied to my letter; his answer I have annexed to this Addenda, confident that it contains much valuable statistical matter.

In my letter to Mr. C. G. Haines, I have explained my views of the connexions that nature seems to have designed between New-York and Pennsylvania, and can add but little in this place to what I then stated. From the demonstrations I have given of the true respective levels, between the head waters of the branches of Ohio river and those which flow into lake Erie, the formation of water communication between these streams must be attended with great difficulty. We will now proceed to examine some of the various intended channels of intercommunication between the Mississippi and St. Lawrence valleys, and also the routes of the two New-York canals.

No doubt now remains, but that the Chicago and Illinois rivers, afford by far the most eligible natural connexion between the northern and southern waters of the United States. It appears that the great spine running from the Hudson to the Maumee river, terminates at, or is interrupted by the valley of the Illinois. The latter stream is formed towards its source by two branches, one of which rises south of lake Michigan, and the other (river Plein,) rises in the flat country west of the Chicago, and flowing south, unite to the south-west of the extreme south part of Michigan. The Chicago heads in the same plain with the river Plein, and winding for some distance parallel to the latter stream, thence turns east, falls into lake Michigan. The Chicago and Plein intermingle their sources, and afford one of those instances where rivers have their sources in plains, so nearly approaching the curve of a real sphere as to leave for the discharge of the waters scarce inclination sufficient to determine their courses. This is the case with the two rivers we are now reviewing. The precise descent of the Chicago, from its nearest approach to the Plein, to the level of lake Michigan has never been ascertained; but it is known to be without falls, or even rapids. The Plein also flows with a very slight current, and the two streams present almost a strait between the Mississippi river and lake Michigan.*

---

* The following interesting notice, decides the long contested problem of a natural water communication between the waters of the St. Lawrence and Mississippi rivers, and contains also some other items of valuable information.

FROM THE ST. LOUIS ENQUIRER.

"*Communication with the lakes.*—Messrs Graham and Phillips, commissioners on the part of the United States, and Mr. Sullivan, surveyor, have set out to lake Michigan, to mark the boundary lines of the lands ceded to the United States by the Ottawa, Chippewa, and Pottowattima Indians in the summer of the year 1816.

The land contiguous to this important pass, was ceded to the United States, by the savage tribes who formerly possessed the right of soil. The land thus ceded, is now about being surveyed, and in course will ere long be sold to individuals and set-

"They will run a line from the southern extremity of this lake, to the Mississippi.

"The Indians have ceded to the United States, what lies to the south of this line.

"The commissioners will run two other lines from the southwestern part of lake Michigan, to the Illinois river. The lines will be parallel to each other, and twenty miles apart. They will begin in the shore of the lake, at points ten miles north and south of Chicago, and will embrace the little rivers Chicago and Plein, and the carrying place between them, which form the channel of communication between lake Michigan and the Illinois river. The Indians have ceded to the United States, this important pass, with ten miles of country on each side of it, and it is the business of the commissioners to mark out the limits of the grant, that the American government may reduce it to possession.

"The communication between the lake and the Illinois, is a point which will fix the attention of the merchant and the statesman. They will see in it the gate which is to open the northern seas into the valley of the Mississippi, and which is to connect New-York and New-Orleans by a water line which the combined navies of the world cannot cut off. Never did the work of nature require so little from the hand of art, to complete so great a design!

"The lakes Superior, Huron, Erie, and Ontario, lie from west to east, in the direction of the St. Lawrence, manifestly seeking their outlet through the valley of that river. But the Michigan departs from that direction; she lays from north to south. United to the other lakes by a strait, she stretches the body of her water down towards the head of the Illinois river, as if intending to discharge herself through that channel into the Mississippi. And no hills or mountains intervene to prevent the conjunction; on the contrary, the ground between is flat, and covered with ponds in wet weather, which turn their waters partly to the lake and partly to the river. The Chicago and the Plein are the drains from these ponds; they have neither falls nor shoals: they have not the character of streams, but of canals; the water hardly moves in their deep and narrow channels. The Illinois itself is more a canal than a river, having hardly current enough to bend the lofty grass which grows in its bed. The French of Canada and of the valley of the Mississippi have communicated through this channel since the settlement of the countries. In high water, boats of ten or a dozen tons, pass without obstruc-

ded. The developement of the natural resources of this region, will be disclosed with the ordinary celerity, that marks the newly established settlements in our western *world*.

The course of lake Michigan contributes in some measure to diminish the natural advantages of its connexion with the Illinois. The mouth of the Calumet river, or southern part of lake Michigan, is near N. lat. 42; whilst the straits of Michilimakinac is about 45°, 40′, making a difference of latitude of 3°, 40′. This difference of geographical position exposes the two extremes of lake Michigan to great variety of climate; the navigation of the northern part being annually, and of the southern frequently impeded by ice. I have annexed to this Addenda, tables which will exhibit the relative distance from the city of New-York to St. Louis by the Canadian lakes and by the Ohio river. These routes, however, are so different from each other, in climate, facilities, and impediment, that very little accurate induction can be drawn from their respective length to determine a preference.

It can scarce be doubted, but that beyond Buffalo, when the contiguous countries are equally inhabited, the Illinois river and Canadian lakes will form the channel of communication with the upper waters of the Mississippi, in preference to the route by the Ohio. The navigation of the latter river is subject to great embarrassment from frost, and long dry weather in the fall season. So much of the northern channel of commerce permits the use of vessels of considerable tonnage, that transportation from Buffalo to Chicago, will be less expensive than that of any equal distance by the Ohio route. If the people of the United States ought to ever unite, in opening any channel of communi-

tion. In the dry season, they are unloaded, placed on vehicles, and drawn by oxen over a portage of a few miles, and launched into the river or lake, as the course of the voyage may require. Hundreds, nay thousands of boats have been seen at St Louis, which had made a similar passage.

"It may be hoped that the government will not limit itself to the barren work of marking the lines about this portage. While the state of New-York opens a canal of three hundred miles, the federal government should not be appalled at undertaking one of three hundred rods. It might be dug in the time that a long-winded member of Congress would make a speech against its constitutionality."

cation, it is that by the Illinois river and lake Michigan. If the various points, from St. Louis to Buffalo, were united by commercial facility, a numerous population would be the immediate consequence, a population that would spread a shield before the interior parts of our country, and would give a preponderance upon the St. Lawrence waters, to the people of the United States, which in future wars would prevent a repitition of some of the disastrous events of the late contest with Great Britain.

With the particular features of the country around lake Michigan, I am unacquainted, but from all the scattered information I have been able to procure, I am induced to believe that the shores of lakes Erie and Michigan are in a great part similar, and if such is the fact, the latter is environed with shores possessing all the attributes necessary to permit a dense and flourishing settlement. That part of the Michigan peninsula, projecting along the south-west side of lake Huron, is equal in soil to any other territory of so great extent in the St. Lawrence valley, or perhaps in any country. From Buffalo to Chicago, is a distance, following the inflections of the shores, of 850 miles, and including the western and northern banks of lake Michigan, of 1,200 miles. If we allow only the extension of 20 miles from the margin of the lakes for settlement, we have a fine border containing 24,000 square miles; to which if we add an equal width along the Chicago, Illinois, and Mississippi rivers, to St. Louis, 400 miles in length, the aggregate will produce an entire surface of 32,000 square miles, or 19,480,000 acres; and at the very thin population of 50 persons to the square mile, would contain 1,600,000 people. That the soil of this tract is capable of supporting more than four times the supposed number I have no doubt, and that in the lapse of less than thirty years from this time, it will contain more than one million and a half of persons I have as little doubt. Before the middle of the current century, if no catastrophe occurs to disturb the present course of events, there will exist, between the city of New-York and St. Louis, within less than fifty miles of the line we are now examining, more than five millions of people, or about one half as many as are now in the whole United States. This may perhaps excite a suspicion of visionary views in the writer, but some statistical facts may render the anticipation at least probable. It may be doubted, whether there is now under cultivation in the United States, as much productive soil as is contained upon the surface under review. If a pair of compasses is supposed to be set down in the city of Philadelphia, and extended to 100 miles radius, the sweep will include a surface of about 20,000 square miles of solid land, and more than one million and a half of people, or nearly a sixth part of the entire population of the United States. If 20,000 square miles is assumed as the land included in the radii of 100 miles from Philadelphia, and 1,500,000 as the population, then this surface must have an average population of 75 to the square mile, out of which 300,000 may be supposed to inhabit the cities of New-York, Philadelphia, Baltimore, and other towns. No person acquainted with the comparative regions, would hazard the assertion, that 20,000 square miles around Philadelphia, is equal in respect to soil, to an equal surface along the Mohawk, in west New-York, along the south side of lake Erie, in the Michigan peninsula, and upon the Illinois river; the fact is, that compared to each other, a decided preference is due to the latter over the former section, in the quality of the soil, and in general commercial advantages; all things considered, they are nearly equal. Many counties in the western states have already a population of more than 50 to the square mile, upon soil much less adapted to agriculture, manufactures, or commerce, than the north-western range from the city of New-York to St. Louis.

The route by lake Erie, Maumee, and Wabash, is in point of course, the most direct line of communication from the Canadian sea, to the Ohio and Mississippi rivers; but subject to some inconveniences not found by the Illinois and Michigan passage. Though not impeded by either falls or cataracts, the Wabash is a rapid stream, and for ascending navigation difficult; this stream is however navigable to very near its source, and waters a body of very excellent land. Maumee river has its sources on the same table land with those of the Wabash, and flowing to the north-east falls into lake Erie. The navigation of the latter river is obstructed by falls near its discharge into Maumee bay, or the extreme south-western curve of lake Erie. The country watered by the Maumee river is generally fertile and well adapted to the production of small grain. The Indian title being now extinct to considerable tracts on that river, settlement by a white population will speedily ensue. The route by the Maumeé and Wabash may be made useful to a large community on the banks of those streams, though as a channel of active intercourse between the Atlantic coast and the Mississippi valley, the northern route will be preferred.

Another route presents itself, which has been hitherto in great part overlooked; that is, by the Huron of lake Erie, or river Raisin, with streams falling into the south-east extremity of lake Michigan. From the narrowness of the table land of the Michigan peninsula, and from the great saving of distance by Michilimackinac, no doubt but that this former route will, at some future period, be found of great national utility, particularly in winter.

A projected union of Sandusky with the Sciota river, has been long conceived; of either the facility of execution, or benefits if completed, of this design I am unable to speak with certainty.

Viewing a map of the respective places, the most obvious connexion between the western parts of lake Erie, and the Ohio valley is by the Muskingum and Cayahoga rivers. If a canal or good turnpike road united these latter streams, the benefits would be immediate and certain. I find this subject has met the attention of the people of the state of Ohio, and if the statistical part of the following extract is correct, can be effected with great ease.

" CLEAVELAND, Nov, 17

" *Contemplated canal.*—We have conversed with gentlemen residing on the river Tuscarawas, (a branch of Muskingum river) who informs us, that boats could be constructed so as to carry 300 barrels of flour up and down the river to a portage of eight miles to the Cayahoga river—a navigable stream for boats of all sizes during the summer months, and as branches from both streams head in a large pond, it would be an easy matter to cut a canal, so as to unite those streams, and thereby secure to ourselves the trade of the Ohio river, and the vast and fertile country on the banks of the Muskingum. We would invite the attention of the state legislature to this important object, inasmuch as it would be a source of inexhaustible wealth to the state, and unite the interest of the south, with that of the more northern sections of our country.

" As the great western canal, uniting lake Erie with the Hudson river, is in a state of forwardness, and will in two or three years be completed, at once opening an uninterrupted communication between lake Erie and the city of New-York. The merchant can have his goods brought on for a trifle, and in return can transmit the surplus products of our country to a sure market This single circumstance, is amply sufficient to induce the legislature of Ohio to follow the example of their brethren in the east, and cut a canal of only eight miles, to bring the products from the fertile banks of the Ohio, through lake Erie to the city of New-York. If the state legislature, and heads of department are not blind to the interest of the state, they will not let the present session pass, without at least preparing to put this important work into execution."

This well written article deserves a more permanent record than the columns of a newspaper, I have embodied it into my addenda, as it may tend at least to stimulate enquiry into an important point of our geography and national policy.

From Cleveland to Buffalo, except by good roads, the intercourse will be difficult between the people who inhabit the shores of the Canadian sea, and those of the Ohio valley

We now approach the most important part of our enquiry, the *Primum Mobile*, of nearly all the exertion that will be made to give effect to any of the preceding improvements. The Grand Canal of the state of New-York; a work that has arrested less attention than the creation of new, or the delinquency of old banks; and yet a work that is destined to produce more lasting impressions upon our external and internal policy, than any undertaking since the formation of the federal constitution. Nothing can be more narrow, more selfish, more puerile, or more unfounded, than the supposition that the state of New-York, as she is only to be benefitted, ought to bear the expense of this great project. In fact, when completed, the state of New-York, in proportion to her extent and population, will gain less from the usufruct of the Canal, than a part of Pennsylvania, the northern part of the state of Ohio, all the Territory of Michigan, all the vast region beoynd, to the sources of lakes Superior and Michigan and all Upper Canada above the chute of Niagara. Without such a channel to the Atlantic coast, remote and detached masses of population will be either forced to form their commercial counexions with Montreal, or remain in a state of inactivity. This is exactly the case at the present moment. The man who confounds the subject of the Canal with local or personal politics, has very little sense of or respect for his own future fame; and such a mistake will be of more injury to those who commit it, than to the execution of the design. It will leave the imprint of its patrons on the face of the globe, an imprint that will remain centuries after the names of those who are now only rendered remarkable by office, will have passed to the deep silence of oblivion.

If a river flowed from Buffalo to Albany, with a slow and gentle current, unobstructed by rapids or shoals, with four feet water, nature would then have done for interior North America, only what the Canal is calculated to perform. To oppose or thwart such a work, from motives of rival politics, is, to say the least, unwise, inexcusable in an individual however obscure; but in those whose decisions have a higher authority, pernicious. Every road, bridge, or canal that is formed, of however small extent, contributes to unite society, to promote social and moral intercourse, and to render men more liberal and more happy. The man who gives his mite to accelerate the formation of such works, does a lasting good to his species. To obtain a high rank amongst mankind; to become at once the envy of rivals, and admiration of friends, is the lot of few men; but to contribute to national prosperity by aiding designs of public utility, is within the reach of all men. And it is now a time to pause, and reflect whether the resources of the United States can not be more advantageously employed in internal improvement than in foreign commerce. If this hour of reflection is neglected, posterity, whilst suffering the evils, may execrate the folly of the present generation.

We will now take a cursory survey of the intended route of the canal, and without waiting for petty details, rapidly glance over the facilities offered by nature, or impediments opposed to its execution.

The Canal leaves Buffalo, thence follows the shore of Niagara strait to the mouth of Tonnewanta creek, turns up the bed of that stream to where the level of lake Erie terminates, then leaves the Tonnewanta upon lake Erie level, which it follows to the brow of Ontario heights. The Canal then assumes its great eastern direction towards Rome; follows the Ontario heights through the sources of Eighteen Mile creek, Oak Orchard creek, Sandy creek, and some smaller streams to Genesee, which latter river the canal will pass by a dam, or on an aqueduct bridge, and winding thence over the heads of Irondequot creek, enters the sources of Seneca river by Mud creek. The Canal then follows the channel of Mud creek to the outlet of Canandaigua lake, and also down the united stream to its junction with the outlets of Seneca and Cayuga lakes. The latter point is the extreme depression of land between Rome and Buffalo, and thus far may the waters of lake Erie be made subservient to the Canal, if necessary. So many feeders flow across the Canal route, that a superabundance of water is to be found in all its length. I have here noticed the northern route, which, from lake Erie at the mouth of Buffalo creek, to the intersection of the Canal with Seneca river, is 99 miles. The commissioners who framed the report, under the law of the state of New-York, of the 17th of April, 1816, seem to have preferred the southern route, but for reasons not sufficiently explained in their report. The two routes diverge from each other at the point, 11 miles up the Tonnewanta, and again unite at the west bank of Genesee river. The northern route, as I have mentioned, never rises above the lake Erie level, but the southern route rises above lake Erie, to gain the summit level near Batavia, nearly 75 feet; a descent it must fall in approaching Genesee river, together with the difference of level of that stream and lake Erie, 194 feet; or in all, from the Batavia level to Genesee, 269 feet. The northern route avoids any descent between lake Erie and Genesee river, except the simple difference of level between these waters, and is exempt from any ascent whatever, above the lake Erie level. The northern route must also possess the insuperable advantage of a much greater, and more certain supply of water.

Neither route as far as Seneca river, meets any very serious impediments from natural obstacles, and can be no doubt executed within the estimates made by the commissioners.

The level near Rome is 48.5 feet higher than low water in Seneca river; the intermediate space generally a rich alluvion Here are presented some of the most curious phenomena of

North America. The singular adaptation of the space between Rome and Seneca river for a Canal, is described in the following very striking manner by the commissioners.

"The exuberant supply of water for the canal, in this section, must be at once perceived from an inspection of the topographical map. At its commencement, the waters of the Mohawk river will be used, and they can be increased to any extent, by introducing a feeder from Fish creek. Independently of numerous small brooks, the canal can derive as much water as can be desired from the Oneida, the Cowaslon, the Canasaraga, the Chitteningo, the Black, the Limestone, the Butternut, the Onondaga, the Nine-mile, the Skeneateles, the Bread, the Cold-spring, the Owasco, and the Crane creeks; some of which are the outlets of lakes, and others originate from perennial springs in high lands, and will never be affected by the clearing of the country.

"The adaptation of the grounds of this section, for a canal, is peculiar and extraordinary. After proceeding two miles and fourteen chains, it will be necessary to descend 6 feet; after which, the line of the canal proceeds 41 1-2 miles on one level. A descent of 19 feet then takes place, from the foot of which another level extends 30 miles. For the remainder of the distance to the Seneca river, there are three departures from the level—one of 8, one of 9, and one of 6 1-2 feet. Thus the whole extent of this section, occupying 77 miles, will require but six locks.

"In many places inexhaustible beds of gypsum exist, which can, by means of this canal, be conveyed cheaper to the great agricultural counties of the state, than it can be procured by importation. And nothing is more easy than, by a short lateral canal of 1 1-2 miles in length, to form a communication between Salina and the great canal, thus furnishing fuel to the works, and salt to the whole country. A level has been carried from that of the canal, at the foot of the two locks near Onondaga creek, which would require no greater depth of excavation than four feet, in any place, and no embankment, culvert, or lock."

Vide Commissioner's Report, page 39

It may be said with justice, that the country west of Utica, is peculiarly adapted to the formation of a canal; and if no farther progress should ever be made than uniting together by a water communication, the Mohawk and Seneca rivers, such a work ought to immortalize its projectors, and enrich those who carry it into execution. I have shown that the Mohawk river near Rome, at high water divides its stream and discharges water towards the Hudson and St. Lawrence rivers; of course this circumstance renders the volume of the Mohawk subservient as a feeder to the canal, both to the westward and eastward.

When writing on this subject, the idea first presented itself to my mind, that through either the Mohawk, or some valley to the south-west of that village, once flowed the St. Lawrence river. Rome is only 188 feet above lake Ontario; and the vallies of the Chittenengo, perhaps not so high even near the sources of that river.

Every step I advance in the inquiry respecting the Grand Canal, I am the more impressed with the belief that much valuable information would be gained by an accurate survey of the interlocking sources of the Susquehanna river and the streams flowing towards Oneida lake. The points chosen, Newton creek, and Seneca lake, to unite the Susquehanna river to the confluent waters of the Grand Canal, are the most obvious,* but I *now* very much doubt their being the only points of contact, where very useful improvements could be made. If ever lake Ontario was 188 feet above its present level, then was its waters discharged, either towards the Hudson or Susquehanna, or both. The ancient features of this continent, must have been very different from the present. It will be recollected, that the difference of level between lakes Erie and Ontario, is 334 feet; therefore, if the surface of the latter was again elevated 188 feet, its level would still be depressed below that of the former 146 feet.

No person of ordinary observation, who examines the shores of lake Ontario or the banks of St. Lawrence river, but will grant that abundant evidences remain to attest an elevation of lake Ontario of more than two hundred feet above its present surface. Evidences also exist, to prove that the recession of that lake was periodical. The chain of smaller lakes lying west of Rome, north of the dividing ridge, and east of Genesee river, were once bays of Ontario. It is very certain, that the space between the hills north of Utica, to those south of Skeneateles lake, is still far

* See page 135.

the lowest gorge in the separating ridge that exists between the Illinois river and lake Champlain; and admitting the ancient elevation of lake Ontario to the level of the Mohawk river near Rome, then through this pass once flowed the St. Lawrence waters. If such a disposition of things was ever the case, the ancient channel remains, and will, it is probable, be found the most eligible channel of communication that nature admits, between the waters of St. Lawrence and Susquehanna rivers.

Happily the Grand Canal in leaving that of the Mohawk, passes into the St. Lawrence valley, by this apparently ancient channel, and has received from nature a facility in effecting its execution, that no where else exists in all the line of connexion between the waters flowing towards the Atlantic coast, and those which enter the Ohio valley. The Susquehanna river is rendered remarkable, from rising north-west of the Allegany mountains, and from passing that entire chain in its course to the Atlantic ocean. The foregoing is however a characteristic which the Hudson participates with the Susquehanna; the Mohawk rises north-west of the spine of the Allegany, and also passes over a part of that chain, in its way to the Hudson, which latter pierces the residue.

After joining the Mohawk river near Rome, it is intended to follow the margin of that river with the canal, keeping the south bank. Except at the Little* and Cohoes Falls, no impediment of

"NEW-YORK, OCT. 28, 1818.

* "*Internal Trade.*—The following is an extract of a letter, addressed to the Editor, from a gentleman at the westward, whose intelligence and opportunities are such as to give confidence to his statements.

'From the Company's books at the Little Falls, I find that the number of *tons* of merchandise and produce, transported in boats through the *locks* at that place, during the year 1817, is *three thousand seven hundred and thirty-five.* From our limited trade, for the want of an uninterrupted water communication with the western part of the state, &c. I estimate the price of transportation per ton at $60—which will make an aggregate of $224,100 per annum.

'The receipts at those locks only, for the last year, were about $1,000—and this year they will amount to about $12,000.

'There may be a distinct branch of commerce between Utica and lake Ontario, &c. through Wood creek—but of this I have no account.

any consequence exists in the distance between Rome and Albany. Locks already exist at the Little Falls, which enable the farmers and merchants to transport their produce and merchandise, by water from the upper Mohawk to Schenectady. The note at the bottom of this page, will give some idea of the present.

'From an account taken for the purpose, at a turnpike gate above the Little Falls, (where it will be recollected an important road diverges to the north,) I calculate the number of two and three-horse waggons employed in transportation, (exclusive of the occasional trips of farmers' waggons, and of those removing families and furniture,) to be 290—making on an average twelve trips a year, and carrying both ways two and a half tons each. As the loads of such waggons do not generally go so far west as those of the larger waggons, the transportation is calculated at but $30 per ton—amounting to $180,000 per annum.

'Of five, six, and seven-horse waggons, there appears to be forty employed, carrying on an average six tons, both ways, and making at least six trips (I might say seven) per annum—their freight at $40 per ton, amounts to $57,600.

'For transportation by boats, - - - - $224,100
 do. small waggons, - - - 180,000
 do. large - - - - - 57,000

Total, $461,100

'I have submitted these statements to men who are competent to decide, and they pronounce them rather low than otherwise. The price of freight is lower than the estimate of *Sidney*; but I have reason to believe it is nearly correct, as a very large proportion is started and landed short of Buffalo; and produce is brought to, much cheaper than merchandise is carried from Albany.

'It will be observed, that nearly *half a million* is *now* paid for transportation annually, from above the Little Falls, and the Black river roads, of course on *one side only of the Mohawk, and upon the river itself*—and that the transportation has increased at least one sixth, since last winter, upon the river. What would the people say to a saving of but half of the above expense? What would they say if that saving was doubled, by adding to the account the thousands of loads yearly transported by the farmers themselves? And what would they not say, could they foresee the immense quantities of produce and merchandise which must necessarily pass this great thoroughfare to and from the western *world*, whenever the canal is opened?

'But I must not indulge fancy, when I am restricted by a want of both time and capacity to do any thing like justice to my subject. I have collected a few facts, which are at your disposal, if they are worth preserving."'—*Columbian*.

quantity and value of produce, which is transported through the locks at the Little Falls. It will be recollected, however, that if agriculture and commerce make roads and canals, roads and canals re-act, and in their turn augment agriculture and commerce. Therefore, no estimate made as things are now situated, can give an adequate conception of the trade of the Mohawk, if that stream was connected with Seneca river and lake Erie.

The middle section of the canal, is the only part which is yet in progress, and is now so far advanced, as to render it probable, that in the ensuing year, the communication with the Seneca will be completed, and the middle and eastern parts of the state united, which alone would be of incalculable gain to the state.

"The middle section of this canal," says the Utica Gazette, "is in nearly as great forwardness as that of the northern, and it is expected that it will be completed before the close of another season. This section extends from Utica to Seneca river, a distance of nearly 90 miles, and in its whole course has but one set of locks, and those at Salina, 60 miles west of Utica."

Writing upon the subject of the canal, I proceeded rather as a statist than an engineer; without attending to the minor details, my endeavor has been to develope the general features of the country through which this work is intended to pass, and rather to show its practicability and usefulness, than the ordinary means to effect its execution.

For further information respecting this project, I must refer to the following documents.

"Memorial to the New-York Legislature, when the Western Canal was first projected." Written by DE WITT CLINTON.

"Reports of Canal Commissioners."

"Memorial to the Congress of the United States, to solicit aid in making the Grand Canal."

"Considerations on the Great Western and Northern Canals, including a view of the *expense, progress,* and *advantages.*" Written under the direction of the New-York Corresponding Association for Promotion of Internal Improvements. By CHARLES G. HAINES.

This latter work, perhaps more than any other that has appeared, gives a luminous *expose* of the canal and its certain benefits to the nation, as well as state of New-York; and ought to be read impartially by every man who desires to think, speak, or judge correctly on the important subject upon which it treats. I did not visit the region in which runs the Northern Canal between the Hudson river and lake Champlain, therefore cannot include any details respecting that undertaking in this treatise.

Among the many benefits that the people of the interior of the state of New-York, will derive from a water communication with the Canadian sea, one of the greatest has hardly been noticed.—the lake fisheries, which may be extended to any possible demand. These fisheries have been hitherto in some measure checked by the dearness and difficulty of procuring salt. This inconvenience will be remedied by the canal, and the natural streams with which it will be connected.

"*Lake Fisheries.*—We cannot sufficiently appreciate the goodness of Providence, for the peculiar bestowment of his favors on the people of this state. The sources of New-York yet only dawn upon us.—Heaven has placed an exclusive supply of salt in the heart of the state, and this necessary article is dispensed for one shilling a bushel, where the transportation alone, if imported, would cost twelve. Not only are the inhabitants of the whole interior of the state provided at a low rate, but a large surplus is yearly exported. The current season, more than sixteen thousand barrels have gone through lake Ontario, for Pennsylvania and Ohio.—Gypsum too, in quantity equal to every purpose and beyond consumption, is found in vast beds where the distance must, but for the bounty of the great author of nature have denied the farmer this great aid in agriculture. These sources of wealth and convenience have been frequently described, while the no less liberal hand of Providence in furnishing the wants of many and the luxury of others, by means of the fish found in the lakes, is hardly known or acknowledged. The season for taking fish is just closing—I have not the data for an estimate of the yearly product of this lake, but have ascertained from the most correct sources the following to be the quantity and species of fish taken and salted this season, in this and Chaumont bays.

"Siscoes or lake Herring, 4,000 barrels,
    selling price $7 per barrel, is $28,000
"White fish,   1,200 bbls. price $9 is   10,800
"Salmon Trout,   400 bbls.   "   14 is   5,600
                                                 ———————
" Total,   5,600 bbls.   amount, $44,100

"The distance comprised is less than twenty miles, and the quantity is exclusive of the abundance distributed fresh in the country, contiguous to the fishing grounds. From this statement some opinion may be formed of the value, importance, and extent of our inland fisheries. Industry and labour are alone wanting to share this bounty, and the poor are enabled to provide a resource for winter with but little expense. To some they furnish the means of subsistence, while others at a distance seek them as a luxury. We are glad to have it in our power to state, that a law was passed by the late assembly to regulate the packing of lake fish, and provides for the appointment of inspectors, who have branded all those put up under their direction."

It was not the season for fishing when I was upon the Canadian lakes, I am therefore the less enabled to give either accurate or extensive information upon the subject. The inhabitants of the contiguous shores consider the fish of the lakes as a very serious part of their nourishment. The lower extremity of lake Ontario, the Bass islands in lake Erie, and the Manatoulin islands in lake Huron, are generally represented as affording the best fisheries in these respective lakes. The mouths of most of the rivers also abound with fish of various kinds, of excellent quality.

This article might indeed be extended to any length. The resources of the St Lawrence valley are so numerous, so widely spread, and, I might add until lately, so little appreciated, that a volume might be written to exhibit the neglected objects with which it abounds, and that may, and no doubt will ere long be brought into use.

I shall close this article by some observations upon travelling through the St Lawrence valley. Viewed in the light of a tour of pleasurable amusement, I cannot conceive of a country where more could be enjoyed, as far as the richest objects in nature are gratifying to our taste. From the city of New-York to that of Albany, and from the latter along the Mohawk and Seneca rivers, the traveller finds renewed gratification at every step. From Canandaigua to Buffalo, is the least interesting tract over which I myself passed; but even here, many circumstances in the improvement of the farms, villages, and roads, will afford ample gratification to minds who derive delight from seeing a wilderness changed to a cultivated country.

When arrived at Buffalo, a tract opens, that the coldest heart can scarce view with indifference. Here opens the expanse of lake Erie, the richly spreading landscapes along Niagara river, and above all, that cataract, that to have seen may be considered a privilege. The steam-boat will in a few days waft the traveller along the surface of lake Erie to Detroit; and whilst on this voyage, the swelling shores of that lake, the numerous islands in its south-west extremity, above all, the well cultivated shores and beautiful strait of Erie, with its towns, farms, and other objects, will combine to present a continually renewed feast to the mind. Returned to Buffalo, the Niagara strait can once more be passed with unabated pleasure. The steam-boats are again in readiness at Lewiston or Queenston, to waft the traveller along Ontario to Sacket's Harbor. The scenery upon the shores of Ontario is more varied, and of a bolder aspect than upon Erie, and though the least in extent of the five great lakes of Canada, Ontario is the most interesting of the whole group. With Niagara at the one extremity, and the St. Lawrence at the other, and receiving from its southern shores the Genesee, Oswego, and Black rivers, this noble sheet of water may claim the first rank, when viewed as the great connecting link, between the vast interior sea of North America, and the unequalled stream flowing from its eastern point. And as if to render its superiority over its more expansive rivals decisive, it possesses the two fine harbors of Kingston and Sacket's, where ships of the line of the first rate, now lie in silent majesty, awaiting the period of war, to waft the thunder of their hundred cannon over its deep and ocean-like bosom.

Beside the features of Black river, which as high as Watertown well deserve a visit from the curious traveller, many other objects near Sacket's Harbor, will amply reward the trouble and expense of a review. The spot is indeed classic ground. It was here that first budded the now majestic laurels of our living General Brown; and it is here, where rests the remains of the brave, the generous, humane, and chivalrous Pike. Upon the point of land overlooking the harbor, rests the ashes of this American hero; and few Americans will ever visit the spot without dropping a tear to the too early, but glorious exit of this gallant soldier. But Pike rests not alone;—other heroes sleep beside him. Many of the best and bravest men of the nation, fell upon the Canadian border. Their names have only in part survived the battle field: their dying sigh mingled with the last roar of the cannon, and left their memory to be cherished by a few relatives and friends, and forgotten by that country they so greatly served. The traveller in seeking their graves, will often seek in vain: no hand is found to point to the spot where the soldier sleeps. Fame lavishes her plaudits upon a few, and leaves the many to perish without a name; and often the man whose sword saved his country, has not even the poor memorial of a heap of earth, to render sacred the spot where his remains have been laid; and alas! too often his little orphans, mingle the bitterness of want, with tears for a father who can neither "hear them sigh, nor see them weep."

It would be nothing more than strictly correct to add, that from Sacket's Harbor to the city of Quebec, is a distance of about 380 miles that concentrates more to charm the eye, than can be found upon any equal extent in North America, if not upon the earth. The St. Lawrence river and islands, the shores and rapids, the distant mountains, the contrast of cultivated and forest land, villages, cities, vessels of great variety of size and form, and the majestic and pellucid river, all form a *tout ensemble*, that can with difficulty find a parallel.

Returning by the Richelieu river, lake Champlain, and Hudson river to Albany and New-York, will complete this truly delightful tour. The following list of stages and distances, will give more precise ideas of the time necessary to perform the foregoing tour.

		MILES	
New-York to Albany,*	- - - - - -	160	160
Utica,	- - - - - - - -	101	261
Auburn,	- - - - - - -	74	335
Geneva,	- - - - - - -	22	357
Canandaigua,	- - - - - -	16	373
Genesee river,	- - - - - -	26	399
Batavia,	- - - - - - -	26	425
Buffalo,	- - - - - - -	40	465
Dunkirk,	- - - - - - -	45	510
Erie,	- - - - - - - -	45	555

* I have given the above, because that number of miles is generally understood to exist between the two cities. The estimate is, however, erroneous; it is, within a small fraction of a mile, 145 miles from New-York to Albany.

		MILES.
Cleveland,	90	645
Sandusky Bay,	50	695
Bass Islands,	16	711
Mouth of Detroit river,	23	734
Amherstburg,	5	739
DETROIT CITY,	16	755
Return to Buffalo,	290	1,045
Thence to the falls of Niagara,	21	1,066
Queenstown and Lewiston,	7	1,073
Fort Niagara and Fort George, enter lake Ontario,	7	1,080
Genesee river,	74	1,154
Great Sodus Bay,	35	1,189
Oswego river,	28	1,217
Sacket's Harbor,	40	1,257
Cape Vincent, enter St. Lawrence river,	20	1,277
Brockville, Canada, and Morristown in U. S.	50	1,327
Ogdensburgh U. S. and Prescott in Canada,	12	1,339
Upper end of Grand Gallop Islands,	5	1,344
Lower end of ditto,	9	1,353
Hamilton, U. S.	10	1,363
Cornwall in Canada, St. Regis U. S. 45° N. lat.	35	1,398
Montreal,	60	1,458
Three Rivers,	105	1,563
Quebec,	65	1,628
Return to Montreal,	65	1,793
Plattsburg,	73	1,866
Albany,	178	2,044
New-York,	60	2,204

In the above table, the distances are given rather from public estimates than from real measurement, and are consequently too high, by perhaps nine or ten per cent, as is the case between New-York and Albany, the relative distances I believe to be nearly correct.

This fine tour can be made within the period of forty days, with ample time to see the most remarkable objects to be found upon the route. The necessary expense cannot be so easily estimated, but would certainly fall, for one person, below three hundred dollars. The best season of the year would be July and August; though to enjoy the luxury of a Canadian summer, the traveller must be on the St. Lawrence in July and the early part of August.

The address of Governor Clinton, to the legislature of the state of New-York reached the city of New-York, on the evening of the 7th January, 1819. The foregoing part of this Addenda was then in type, but I considered some part of the Governor's address of so much import, and so relevant to the subject on which the Addenda itself was founded, that I have taken the liberty to superadd the following extracts from that luminous production. I am the more emboldened to this procedure, from considering the sentiments expressed, and the facts conveyed by that excellent statesman, as national property.

" The progress of our internal improvements has equalled our most sanguine expectations In the course of the next session, the Northern Canal, extending from Whitehall at the head of lake Champlain, to Fort Edward, on the Hudson river, a distance of 23 miles, and the whole of the middle section of the Western Canal comprising ninety-four miles, and reaching from the Seneca river to the Mohawk river at Utica, will be completed and in a navigable state. Thus, in less than two and a half years, Canals to the extent of one hundred and seventeen miles will be perfected. And, as the eastern and western sections of the Canal from lake Erie to Hudson river will be about 260 miles, it is evident that, by the application of similar means and the exertion of similar powers, the whole of this internal navigation can be finished in six years from the present period. including also the improvements essential on Hudson river, from Fort Edward to the head of sloop navigation It is satisfactory also to know that, so far as we can judge from the lights of experience, the actual expenses have not exceeded the estimates of the commissioners. And, with all the advantages arising from encreased knowledge, from improved skill and from circumspect experience, we are firmly persuaded, that the aggregate expense will fall short of the total estimate. It is also a most gratifying consideration to find, that from the progressive and flourishing state of the fund appropriated to this object, the whole undertaking can be completed without providing any auxiliary resources, and without imposing any taxes on the community. From the commencement of the next year, the finished portions of the Canals will be in a state productive of considerable revenue.

" By the act respecting navigable communications between the great western and northern lakes and the Atlantic ocean, passed the 15th April, 1817, the commissioners are only empowered to make Canals between the Mohawk and Seneca rivers, and between lake Champlain and the Hudson river. Possessing, however, under that act, and the act to provide for the improvement of the internal navigation of the state, passed the 17th April, 1816, authority to make the necessary surveys, and to lay out the proper routes for the whole of the Western and Northern Canals, they have not overlooked the latter, although their attention has been principally devoted to the former object. By that initiatory arrangement, it was obviously the intention of the Legislature to bring the calculations of the commissioners to the touchstone of experiment, and to determine whether the resources of the state are adequate to the whole operation.

"This trial has taken place in the most satisfactory manner, and there cannot exist a doubt of the feasibility of the work, or of the ability of the state. It is therefore highly expedient that a law should be passed, during the present session, authorising the completion of the whole work as soon as possible. In the course of this year the routes can be then so far definitively settled, as to enable the formation of contracts to take effect in the spring of 1820, by which means a whole year will be saved to the operation, and the state will have the benefit of experienced contractors, who might, under a different state of things, be employed in other undertakings. And, when we contemplate the immense benefits which will be derived from the consequent promotion of agriculture, manufactures, and commerce—from the acquisition of revenue—from the establishment of character, and from the consolidation of the federal union, we must feel ourselves impelled by the most commanding motives, to proceed in our honorable career, by perfecting with all possible expedition this inland navigation.

"At the present period a ton of commodities can be conveyed from Buffalo to Albany by land for $100, and to Montreal, principally by water, for 25. Hence it is obvious that the whole of the vast region to the west of that flourishing village, and the greater part of the extensive and fertile country east of it, are prevented from sending their productions to our commercial emporium, and that they must either resort to the precarious markets of Canada, or, to places more distant, less accessible, or less advantageous. When the great western canal is finished, the expense of transportation from Buffalo to Albany, will not exceed $10 a ton. Almost the whole of the ascending trade ot the west will be derived from the city of New-York, and a great portion of the descending products will accumulate in that important depot. If half a million of tons are, at the present period, transported on the waters of the Hudson river, it is reasonable to suppose that the time is not distant, when the commodities conveyed on the Canals will be equal in amount. A small transit duty will consequently produce an immense income, applicable to the speedy extinguishment of the debt contracted for the Canals, and to the prosecution of other important improvements.

"In these works, then, we behold the operation of a powerful engine of finance, and of a prolific source of revenue.

"It is certainly more important, that the productive classes of society should have good markets, out of the state, than that they should be exclusively confined to indifferent or fluctuating markets in it. In the former case, wealth is diffused over the whole country, while in the latter, it is limited to a very few towns. A wise government ought to encourage communications with those places, where the farmer and manufacturer can sell at the highest, and buy at the lowest prices. And, as the acquisition of many markets encreases the chance of good ones, and diminishes, in many instances, the expences of transportation, and guards against the pernicious fluctuations of price, I look forward with pleasure to the speedy arrival of the time, when the state will be able to improve the navigation of the Susquehanna, the Allegany, the Genesee, and St. Lawrence—to assist in connecting the waters of the great lakes and of the Mississippi—to form a junction between the western Canal and lake Ontario by the Oswego river, and to promote the laudable intention of Pennsylvania, to unite the Seneca lake with the head waters of the Susquehanna."

The calculation contained in these extracts, of the time necessary to complete the Grand Canal between Albany and Buffalo, and the canal from the Hudson river to lake Champlain, are founded upon data, that are too well based to admit either refutation or cavil. If the state of New-York is left by the nation at large to carry into effect this mighty project, unaided, and in some measure opposed; and should a single state, thus placed, actually effect such an undertaking, the result will exhibit the most extraordinary instance of the energy of a small part, and the apathy of the residue of the people of the United States, that has yet met the eye of mankind. Such an issue, will be glorious indeed to New-York, but shameful to the nation; it will be a triumph of active reason, over inert prejudice. But in such modes and manner; in the struggle of science against prescriptive opinion, has the progress of mankind hitherto advanced. The Grand Canal will be an eternal monument erected to the memory of its projectors and executors; and the most solacing reflection, that presses upon the mind when contemplating this unequalled change made upon the physiognomy of nature, is, that not one drop of this artificial flood will be drained from the tears of suffering humanity. When the present generations have passed away, and when the future voyager is wafted along the picturesque vale of the Mohawk, amid all that can decorate the earth and delight the senses, he will recall with unmixed admiration the names of those whose genius procured such beneficence to the men of every passing age

NO. III.

BALLSTON SPRINGS.

It was with much regret that on my return to Albany, I could not spare time to visit Ballston. Curiosity to see one of the most noted places of public resort in the United States, would have led me to that village, and over its environs, but calls of a more imperative nature, deprived me of such a pleasure. The following letter contains very satisfactory information respecting those celebrated waters, and from its source is entitled to full confidence.

"*Ballston-Spa, November* 27, 1818.

"Sir,

"The name of Ballston, though frequently applied to the village at the mineral springs, belongs in strictness to a township about five miles square, the north boundary of which falls within, and embraces a part of the village; the principal portion of which lies within the adjacent township of Milton.

"This village was incorporated in 1807, by the name of Ballston-Spa, is under the government of three Trustees, annually chosen, and invested with certain privileges, for the better regulation of its own peculiar concerns, though for civil purposes generally, a part thereof acts with the town of Ballston, and a part with the town of Milton.

"The distinction between Ballston and Ballston-Spa, ought to be carefully observed by all who have occasion to correspond with visitants at these celebrated waters; a post-office being established, not only at this place but also in the town of Ballston, at some distance from the village. A similar observation might be made with respect to Saratoga, and Saratoga Springs.

"The village of Ballston-Spa is in the county of Saratoga, 26 miles north of the city of Albany, in a beautiful and romantic situation. It lies within and along side of a valley, through which flows a stream of water, emptying itself immediately below the village, into the Kayadarosseras creek. This valley commences at the south-west, where the stream, which had previously flowed towards the south, fetches a short compass round a point of land towards the north-east, runs some distance in that direction, then turns and passes off towards the east. The valley follows the course of the creek, is narrow at first; but after it has taken an eastern direction, its north bank suddenly recedes, and forms a beautiful plain, opening to view the Kayadarosseras and its buildings. The north-west side of the valley is bordered by sand hills, high and very steep. At the south-west end commences a smooth and gentle ridge of land, which runs east, sloping towards the north, until making a gradual circuit, it turns its inclining surface towards the west. The termination of this slope is the curving bank of the valley along its south-eastern side, on which bank the greater part of the village is built. The high sand hills on the north-west, the ridge of land on the south and east, with the open plain on the north-east, form the natural boundaries of the village.

"This village contains 112 houses, exclusive of out-houses, some of which being attached to taverns and large hotels, are extensive, and add considerably to the village. The number of inhabitants is 614. It is a place of considerable business throughout the year; the lands in the neighborhood, with the exception of the pine plains towards the north, being generally fertile, and the trade of the inhabitants centering here. There are at present six large stores for the sale of dry goods and groceries, an extensive hardware and two druggist stores; two printing offices, and a bookstore, with which is connected, for the accommodation of strangers, a circulating library and a reading room. On the Kayadarosseras, a large and never failing stream, mills for various purposes, with a cupola furnace have been erected, at a little distance from, and within sight of the village. The court-house for the county of Saratoga is located here, and is a large brick edifice, newly erected and well built. We have also two houses for public worship, an Episcopal and a Baptist church, in which respectable congregations statedly assemble; likewise an Academy, in which a numerous and reputable school is constantly taught. The inhabitants are intelligent, industrious, frugal, and remarkably temperate. A moderate degree of refinement and fashion prevails. Regularity and good order exist to a considerable degree, though as to religion and morality, it must be confessed, we fall much below the christian standard.

This place is famous for its mineral waters, which with those of Saratoga near by, have attracted uncommon attention, and annually draw great numbers from all parts to visit them, in the summer season. Hence in addition to several inns, there are three large boarding houses* expressly designed for the accommodation of strangers, at the season of general resort. The largest of these, the Sans Souci Hotel, will vie with any establishment of a similar nature, for the style in which it is kept, and as a spacious, airy, and commodious building. It presents a front three stories high, and 160 feet in length, extends back in a wing at each end 153 feet, is surrounded by a spacious and beautiful yard, which, with its extensive piazzas, large hall, and spacious assembly-room, render it a delightful place. Here the rich, gay, and fashionable, resort in crowds, during the months of July and August. It is calculated for the reception of 130 boarders, and frequently exceeds that number. Next to the San Souci, Aldridge's boarding-house is the most noted. It stands in the valley, at the foot of a high sand hill, nearly opposite the public, and formerly the principal spring, and is handsomely bordered on the east and south by a court-yard and garden, by the side of which flows the rivulet of the valley. The building itself is not elegant, yet the reputation of the house is deservedly high, and draws to it its full share of public patronage.

* *Ballston-Spa.*—By the Register kept at the Reading Room at Ballston Springs, (says the Commercial Advertiser) it appears that the number of persons who have visited those Springs, during the past season, 1818, amounts to two thousand five hundred. Of this number more than twelve hundred, it is stated, live south of New-York. It is also stated, that the whole number were accommodated with board and lodging as follows:

At J. B. Aldridge's	950
At Sans Souci Hotel	800
At David Cory's	500
At other houses	250
Total	2,500

[It is fair to calculate that the average expenditure at the above place, was 50 dollars a piece—In this case the sum total is 125,000 dollars.]—*Gaz.*

The third large boarding-house is Corey's, formerly Mrs. White's. It stands at the head of the valley, on the ridge of land, which runs along the south side of the village. The building and its accommodations rank with Aldridge's, yet being in a situation more retired and remote from the springs, though highly pleasant and agreeable, it is less known and less frequented.

The existence of this village, is owing entirely to the mineral springs, which in this favored spot, rise up from the bowels of the earth. These, exclusive of a sulphur spring which has attracted little or no attention, were but lately two in number, one on the private property of Nicholas Low, Esq. over which he has erected a handsome bathing-house, and the other in the public highway, nearly opposite Alldridge's boarding-house. According to Mead's Analysis, which sustains a high reputation, the public well contains in one quart of water:

	Grains.
Muriat of Soda	42
Muriat of Magnesia	1 3-4
Muriat of Lime	3 1-4
Carbonate of Magnesia	11 3-4
Carbonate of Lime	9 1-4
Oxide of Iron,	1
Total,	69

Of aeriform fluids:

	Cubic Inches.
Carbonic acid gas	61
Azotic gas	2 1-2
Total,	63 1-2

And Low's well contains exactly the same ingredients, in nearly the same quantities.

"The natural appearance of these springs is curious and pleasing; their waters are in continual agitation, are perfectly transparent, and have a saline, pungent, and to those accustomed to them, a most agreeable taste. They possess a stimulating and refreshing quality. Under the exhaustion of heat and fatigue, nothing can be more agreeable and reviving to the system. As powerful remedies also, in many cases of disease, they are well known and highly celebrated.

"These springs, however curious and excellent as they really are, have been recently eclipsed by a new spring, which little more than a year since burst from the earth. In the month of August, 1817, continual rains had swollen the creek, which passes through this place, to a very great height, and produced a destructive flood. In the centre of the village, the furious stream cut for itself a new course, and a few rods lower down, it again diverted a little from its former channel, which upon the subsiding of the water was left dry. In this deserted channel, which a few years ago had been artificially made for the purpose of turning the creek from its natural course, veins of mineral water were soon discovered issuing up through the sand, and forming on the surface a large fountain. As the water rose through a deep bed of loose gravel, blue clay, and quicksand, was foul, discoloured, and mingled with large quantities of fresh water; great difficulties were apprehended in getting it into a state proper for use. This object, however, has been happily accomplished, and in a simple and easy manner. Two tubes have been forced down to different depths, through which rise waters differing considerably in their qualities, and constituting in fact two new springs. The first tube was sunk to the depth of fourteen feet, is on a level with the surrounding earth, and being not perfectly tight at the top, never overflows with water. The depth of the second tube below the surface of the earth, is twenty-three feet, and into it an additional tube five feet long has been inserted, through the whole of which length, that is, twenty-eight feet, the water rises to the surface, boiling and sparkling in the most curious and beautiful manner, and falling down in every direction over the sides of the tube. These springs, especially the latter, it has been proposed to call the Washington fountain; and they are commonly distinguished from each other by the descriptive appellations of the low and the high tube.

"With regard to the qualities of these waters, I cannot do better than to make a few extracts from a letter, published in the New-York Evening Post, of the 26th of September last, written by Dr. Mead, to the Editor of that paper.

'I have found,' saith he, 'that the Washington fountain (meaning thereby the high tube,) contains more carbonic acid gas, than any other mineral spring which has ever been examined in this country, and certainly much more than any in Europe of which we have any correct account:—one quart of this water, or 55,750 cubic inches of it, contains nearly 76 cubic inches of this gas. The adjoining well does not contain any thing like the same quantity of gas.

'The next valuable qualities which these springs possess, arise from the quantity of iron which they contain, held in solution by the carbonic acid. According to my former analysis of the Ballston and Saratoga waters, I never found any of them to contain more than one grain of iron in a quart, but I think I may venture to state, from actual experiments, that the Washington fountain contains nearly double that quantity; but the adjoining spring not quite so much.

'With respect to the saline contents of these springs, they do not differ materially in quality from those waters at Ballston, the analysis of which I have given to the public. None of them contain sulphats; in this they differ from most mineral waters; their cathartic properties, therefore, are derived principally from the muriat of soda, or common salt, with which they are impregnated. The Washington fountain, however, contains less of this salt than any of the springs either at Ballston or Saratoga, while the adjoining spring contains much more than any of them, except the Congress spring.

'The Washington Fountain is so highly charged with carbonic acid gas, and contains also so much iron, that it may be ranked in the first class of tonic remedies; but at the same time, it is one the use of which requires much caution. It possesses all the good qualities which are attributed either to the waters of the Seltzer or Pyrmont, and some of them in a superior degree. It is superior to the Seltzer or Spa. in containing iron, in which they are both deficient; and it differs materially from the Pyrmont, in containing a sufficient quantity of muriate of Soda, to act as a cooling febrifuge, and to counteract, in some degree, the heating and stimulating qualities of the other ingredients, which, in some constitutions, would totally forbid the use of them. I have never as yet met with, nor have I heard of any water that so nearly resembles the waters of Germany, as the Washington fountain. It may be drank with great advantage in all cases of general debility, where there is great relaxation and loss of tone; and particularly in diseases of the stomach.'

"Of the adjoining spring, that is the low tube, Doctor Mead remarks, that it 'has been found to possess very powerful purgative qualities, and may be considered as a sort of intermediate between the waters of Ballston and Saratoga. It is evidently, even to the taste, more saline than any of the springs at Ballston, or than any, excepting one, at Saratoga; and I have found by analysis, that it contains nearly one-fifth more of muriate of soda or common salt, than any other, except that one; and besides, possesses in the same proportion, all the other ingredients, such as carbonate of magnesia, carbonate of lime, and iron. It cannot therefore be doubted, that it becomes a very active purgative, sufficiently effectual to answer almost all useful purposes, particularly if drank under proper management, and with due precaution; the neglect of which will not only prevent the Congress water from having the desired effect, but render too free a use of it highly injurious to the system.'

"Of a place abounding with such invaluable waters, the geology must be interesting. As that, however, is a science to which I make no pretensions, I beg leave again to refer to Doctor Mead, whose observations upon this subject, may be found in the introductory part of his chemical analysis of the waters of Ballston and Saratoga, from which the following extracts are made.

'In the center of the village of Ballston, an excellent opportunity is offered of examining the situation of the strata. A small rivulet runs through it, which has laid bare an entire range of flœtz or horizontal rocks, consisting of what may be called a calcario argillaceous schist or shale. This schist is nearly of a black colour, and from its staining the fingers, would appear to contain a portion of carbon; it effervesces slightly with acids, which shews that it also contains carbonate of lime; it breaks easily into laminæ of any thickness, and impressions of vegetables, chiefly of a species of grass, can be observed between the laminæ; but when large masses are exposed for any length of time to the atmosphere, it rapidly shivers, or decomposes.'

'Alternating with this schist, and near the same place, wherever the beds of sand will admit an inspection of the rock, solid masses of calcareous rocks are observed. This limestone is nearly of a black colour, its fracture is slaty, it abounds with shells of various forms, some of which are so very apparent in their structure and form, as not to be mistaken.

'Besides these rocks which I have attempted to describe, and which characterise a secondary country, it is necessary to state that those undulating hills which surround the village of Ballston, and which continue to prevail in the village of Saratoga, are formed principally of immense beds of fine siliceous sand, as may be particularly observed in the rear of Aldridge's boarding-house, where the height of one of these hills, which is very precipitous, cannot be less than 150 feet; under this sand lies immense beds of stiff blue clay, which hardens when left for any time exposed to the atmosphere; it effervesces slightly, but does not dissolve in acids, from which I should rather call it an argillaceous marle; it appears with some probability to have been formed by the decomposition of the schist in the neighborhood; it is to be found by digging in the valleys in any direction, and it can be well observed on the side of a declivity near Lowe's well, where a considerable saline efflorescence can be seen on its surface, particularly after rain, owing to the chrystallization of the salt, which is produced by the sun's rays. This is a very interesting fact, and as exactly such a peculiar species of clay is found to prevail in the soil from which the waters of Cheltenham arise, it may tend in some degree to explain from whence waters of this description receive their saline impregnation.

'No metallic veins of ore have been discovered in this neighborhood in any direction; and except iron, which is found in all the low grounds, in the state of an argillaceous or bog iron ore, I know of no other metalic deposit.'

"This village, though now considerable, will probably still increase, and receive additional improvements. The waters, with those of Saratoga, are unrivalled, and may be confidently expected to draw increasing crowds of visitants. The new springs are a most valuable acquisition, and contiguous to them is an extensive brick edifice, originally intended as a factory, but now unemployed, which, with capital and enterprise, might be converted into a superb boarding-house, which doubtless would be filled with guests, and prove not only an ornament to the village, but a profitable establishment.

With sentiments of respect,
Yours.
REUBEN SEARS

WILLIAM DARBY.

ROUTE FROM THE CITY OF NEW-YORK TO ST. LOUIS,

BY HAMILTON, PITTSBURG, CINCINNATI, LOUISVILLE, AND THE OHIO AND MISSISSIPPI RIVERS.

		MILES
Newburg,		60
Cochecton,	60	120
Hamilton,	294	351
PITTSBURG,	261	615
Steubenville,	59	674
Cincinnati,	363	1037
Louisville,	131	1167
Mouth of Ohio,	393	1560
ST. LOUIS,	198	1758

ROUTE FROM THE CITY OF NEW-YORK TO ST. LOUIS,

BY ALBANY, BUFFALO, DETROIT, MICHILIMAKINAC, LAKE MICHIGAN, ILLINOIS, AND MISSISSIPPI RIVERS.

		MILES
Albany,		160
Canandaigua,	213	373
Buffalo,	92	465
Erie,	90	555
Cleveland,	90	645
DETROIT,	110	755
Fort Gratiot,	67	822
Michilimakinac,	190	1012
Mouth of Chicago river,	280	1292
Head of Illinois do.	40	1332
Mouth of do.	400	1732
ST LOUIS,	30	1762

It will be at once seen by an inspection of this table, that the difference in distance, by the two routes, is trifling; and, all things considered, no great diversity exists naturally in the facility offered, or impediments opposed to mercantile transportation; but with the Grand Canal from Albany to Buffalo, the advantages are obviously in favor of the northern route.

NO. V.

The following very valuable letter came to hand this morning, (Wednesday, January 20th.) I rejoice to have it in my power to include its contents in my Addenda. Those persons who are acquainted with Mr. Briggs, will appreciate the information thus conveyed on the interesting subject of internal improvements, the more, as little doubt can be harbored as to the judgment, and no suspicion can be fostered against the veracity of the author.

W. D.

"*Albany*, 1st mo. 1819.

" MY ESTEEMED FRIEND,

" I duly received, at the village of Herkimer, thy favor of 22d ult. requesting information of the actual state and progress of the work on the Canals of the state of New-York, and that I would promptly answer the following queries:

' 1st. How much of the Canals is actually completed?

' 2d. What places are connected by the parts which are finished?

' 3d. The names of the Engineers employed, and where?

' 4th. Any other circumstances that you may deem of importance respecting the Canals?'

" At the time I received thy letter I was engaged, almost night and day, in making laborious calculations for a detailed report to the Board of Canal Commissioners; and, fearing that the short space of time until this report ought to be presented would scarcely admit of my doing justice to the subject, I requested my friend David Holt to make to thee my apology, for the delay of my answer, which I found to be unavoidable. I now embrace with pleasure the first opportunity, which my arduous duties have permitted, to answer thy queries.

"1mo. Portions of the Canals amounting to 65 miles are *actually completed*—46 1-2 miles of the Western, and 18 1-2 miles of the Northern; 15 miles more are *half done*, and there is as much work performed on the remaining parts, as is quite equal to the finishing of those 15 miles, making an aggregate equal to 80 miles of finished Canal.

"2do. No important places are yet connected by the parts finished, on account of some works not completed crossing streams in the Western, and locks in the Northern Canal. But, in the course of next season, Whitehall on lake Champlain, will be connected with Fort Edward on Hudson's river, by 23 miles of Canal; and the salt-works at Onondaga with Utica on the Mohawk, by 60 miles. Between Utica and Onondaga, the Canal passes inexhaustible beds of the finest gypsum; so that, unless the weather should be beyond probability unfavorable, or some other improbable occurrence, 83 miles of Canal will, before the close of next season, begin to yield revenue.

"3tio. The Engineers are Benjamin Wright, James Geddes, and Isaac Briggs; Canvass White, James Ferguson, Valentine Gill, and Asa Moore, have also been employed. I believe Canvass White has been placed in the rank of Engineer, and James Ferguson still remains an assistant. Valentine Gill has been employed as a Draftsman, and Asa Moore as Surveyor. During the late season Wright and White have been employed on the middle section of the Western Canal; Geddes and Ferguson on the Northern; and Briggs, Gill, and Moore, in exploring and locating the Canal and its locks, on the Eastern section, from Utica down the valley of the Mohawk.

"4to. In my answer to the 2d query, I have said, that 83 miles of Canal will, before the close of next season, begin to yield revenue. I will here add, that, in fair probability, the season after next, (1820,) may *commence* with an active navigation on 117 miles of Canal; and, if the legislature should, at their present session, authorise *the whole* of the Western Canal to be made *as speedily as it can be economically done*, there may be, at the close of 1820, many miles more in great forwardness, and the whole Canal may be finished, before the close of 1825, as easily as, and at a smaller expense, than in any longer period.

"By a sound and prudent fiscal management, no burdens on the people, beyond the present taxes, and these only for one year more, will be necessary to accomplish this noble work.

"When the expense of a great project is *previously* estimated, it usually happens that, after the thing is finished, the actual expense greatly exceeds the estimate. In the whole work hitherto done, the contrary is found to be the fact, and an animating fact it is, the actual expense falls considerably short of the general estimate made in 1817, when the subject was proposed to the legislature. Although experience afforded such encouragement in the middle section, yet there remained doubts respecting the Eastern section, where probably the greatest difficulties exist. I have, during the late season, carefully and minutely examined 40 miles of this section, which portion includes some of the principal difficulties, and it is my decided opinion, that this portion of the Canal can be made for an expense averaging 16 per cent, or 2,700 dollars per mile, *less than the estimate of the Commissioners.*

" I have said that, after one year more of the present taxes, *no* burdens on the people will be necessary for the Canal. Suppose no more than 120,000 tons to be transported in one year, a distance of 117 miles, at a toll of 1 cent per ton per mile, this would yield 140,400 dollars, the interest of 2,340,000, at 6 per cent. Every succeeding year would add more freight, and bring into use an additional portion of Canal. The consequences are so obvious, that I am persuaded it is unnecessary to pursue further the calculation. A stimulus to useful industry and an increase of individual happiness—the extension and enlargement of all the resources of the state—an accelerated augmentation of its population, wealth, and power—and, instead of burdens, an abundant revenue; these would be the consequences of a liberal and enlightened policy.

" Respectfully, thy friend,
"ISAAC BRIGGS.
"WILLIAM DARBY."

INDEX.

Note, ad. signifies Addenda.

A.

Abino, point 171, note 172.
Albany, author arrives there, p 9; aspect of the country between and Kinderhook, p. 34, 35; fine view of, *ib.*
Allouettes, Point des, 97, note.
Amherstburg, p. 101, note; described, 193.
Amsterdam, village of, p. 45.
Andre, Major, p. 14.
Arnold, General, p. 14.
Ashtabula river, 209.
Athens, village of, p. 27.
Auburn, village of, 212, 218; census of, *ib.* note; state prison at, 218.
Audrain, Peter, Register of the land office at Detroit, supplies the author with a manuscript map of part of the Michigan territory, 191.

B.

Batavia, village of, 154.
Ballston, road to, 44.
——— Spa, li. ad.
Bay de Nivernois, now Sacket's Harbor, 70.
——— Chaumont, 71.
Barclay, Commodore, defeated by Commodore Perry, 211.
Bass Islands, 184, 185.
Black river, at Watertown, 68; at Brownville, 69; its rapidity, *ib.*
Black Rock, 138.
Bloomfield, village of, 152; country near, its features, 153.
Bois Blanch Island, 193.

Booth's Factory, 21.
Bouchette, Mr. Joseph, quoted, 86, 87, 92, 116, 203, 205.
Boundary line, between the United States, and Upper Canada, proceedings on, 87.
Breck, Mr. Samuel, 138.
Bridge, over Wappinger's creek, 20.
——— over Kinderhook creek, 30.
——— over the Mohawk river, at Schenectady, 43.
——— over west Canada, 54.
——— over Deer river, 66.
——— over Black river at Watertown, 68; at Brownville, 69.
——— at the Falls of Niagara, 166
——— over Cayuga lake, 215.
Briggs, Mr. Isaac, information obtained from, respecting the Little Falls, 49; gives the author the latitude of Utica, and the variation of the magnetic needle at that village, 55; letter from him respecting the Grand Canal, lxi. ad.
Brock, General, his death, 169.
Brockville, town of, 7, 105 note, 107 note.
Brown, General Jacob, his residence, 69; wounded, 169; his military career, where commenced, xliv. ad.
Brown, Samuel R., quoted 203.
Byron, Lord, quoted, 164 note.
Buffalo, village of, 137, 155.

creek near, 156; harbor of, *ib.* 157; destroyed, 170; road from Fort George to, 170; farther reflections upon its harbor, 171.

Burgoyne, General, his march towards Albany, 24; surrenders his army, 25.

C.

Canada creek, east, 47.
——— creek, west, 53.
——— Upper, province of, 74; observations and reflections on 76, 87; its climate misunderstood, 121.

Canal, between Seneca lake and Tioga river, 136 note.
——— grand, in the state of New-York, 160, xxxiv. ad.
——— by Chatauque lake, 175.

Canadaway, 174.

Canandaigua, village of, 131; described, 135; population, *ib* note; road from to Buffalo, 212, 215; revisited by the author, 212; observations upon, 213.
——— lake of, 131, 133, 134.

Canards, riviere aux, 193.

Cape Rosier, 112.

Cass, Governor, 196; concludes a treaty with several Indian tribes, *ib.* note

Carthage, curiosity near, 128.

Cataract, of Caterskill, 33.
——— of the Cohoes, 38.
——— Little Falls, 48.
——— Niagara, 101, 161, 169.
——— of Velino, description of, by Lord Byron, quoted, 164 note.
——— of Seneca outlet, 214.
——— near Ithaca, 215 note.

Cattaraugus creek, 156.

Catskill, village of, 27, 32.
——— mountains, (Catsbergs) 17; fine view of, from Rhinebeck, 24; their elevation by Capt. Alden Partridge, 26, note; where seen to most advantage, 26; covered with snow, May 3d, 1818, 27 note; seen from Columbiaville, 31; from Albany, 35; from Troy, 36; their peculiar range, 226.

Caterskill Falls, 33.

Cayuga creek, 156.
——— village, 214.
——— lake, 215.
——— bridge, *ib*

Cayahoga river, 178.

Cazenovia creek, 156.
——— village, 212, 223.

Chatauque lake, 175.

Chaumont, Mr. Ray de, quoted, 64 note.
——— bay, 71.

Chenal Ecarte, 202, 205.

Chenango river, 220, 221.

Cherry Valley, village of, 212, 222.

Chippewa river, 160; battle of, 169; river described, 203.

Claverack creek, 29, 30.

Cleveland, village, 178, 179.

Clinton, Governor, his inaugural discourse, 42; description of the Little Falls, 48; extracts from his address, xlviii. ad.

Columbiaville, 30; scenery near, 31.

Cunningham's Island, 179.

D.

Danbury, township or peninsula, 181.

Deer river, 66.

Detroit, river of, 99.
——— city of, 100 note, 137, 187, 200.

Dunkirk, bay and harbor described, 173; prospects of future prosperity, 176.

Dutchess county, N. Y. its aspect, 17; timber in imprudently destroyed, 18, 19; its extent and population, 19.

E.

Eddy's map of the state of New-York, 134.
Erie, town of, 210; harbor, ib.
——— lake of, 100 note; storms on, ib.; extent and quantity of water in, 117; destructive storm on, 171 note; dangers of its navigation, 172; distance from lake Huron, 191.
——— fort, 168, 170.
Essex county, Upper Canada, 194, 195.
Esopus, see Kingston.

F.

Fall creek, 215.
Falls of St. Mary, 94.
——— of Niagara, 101, 160.
——— of Montmorency, 112.
——— in Fall creek, 215 note.
Fairport, village of, at the mouth of Grand river, 177.
Fire lands, tenure of from what derived, 181; now forms part of Huron county, ib.
Flax, its culture in Canada, ad. xvi. xix.
Fishkill landing, 12.
——— mountains, passage of the Hudson river through, 9, 10; their component parts, 11 note; their height measured by Capt. Alden Partridge, 11 note, 12; scenery, 14.
Fredonia, formerly Canadaway, 174.
French of Canada, their character, 86.

G.

Gelder, Dr. Van, his poem upon Fort Putnam, 13 note.
Genesee river, 153; flats of, ib.
Geneva, village of, 129; described, 130; revisited by the author, 212, 213.
Goat Island, 166 note.
Gourlay, Mr. Robert, reflections upon his operations in Upper Canada, 76; proceedings respecting, in the provincial legislature, 77; observations on, ib.
Grand, or Ouse river in U. C. described 100 note, 177, 203.
Grand Island, in Niagara river, 158, 159 note.
Grand Gallop Islands, 106 note; described, 124.
Granger, Mr. Gideon, 213.
Gratiot, Fort, 200.
Greene, General, 14.
Greene county, 32, 33.
Gros Isle, in Detroit river, described, 192, 193.

H.

Hamilton, village of, on St. Lawrence river, 87.
——— village of, on Allegany river, 7, 140.
Harrison, General, reconquers Michigan territory, 187; defeats General Proctor, ib.; again, 211.
Hawkins, Colonel Samuel, his *fete champetre,* on one of the St. Lawrence islands, 106 note.
Haines, C. G. esq. correspondence with the author, 135, 150.
Hen and Chickens, islands, 186.
Herkimer village, 54.
Highlands, a term used for the passage of the Hudson river through the Fishkill mountains, 20.
History, reading of neglected in the United States, 22; lessons drawn from, 80, 81.
Hudson river, its aspect in winter 9; its passage through the Fishkill mountains, 9, 10, 11; did not always flow into New-York bay, 11; creeks of, 20; peculiar features of its banks, 28, 29.

INDEX.

Hudson, town of, 27, 28, 29.
Hull, General, reflections upon his operations in the Michigan territory, 188.
Huron river, in the state of Ohio, 182.
―――― of lake Erie, 201.
―――― of lake St. Clair, 202.
―――― lake, 95; communication between and lake Ontario, 98, 99 note; extent and quantity of water, 117; distance from lake Erie, 191.

I.

Ithaca, village of, 216 note.

K.

Kinderhook creek, 29, 33
―――― village of, 33, 34.
Kingston, town of, in Upper Canada, 97 note; 104.
―――― village of, 24; taken and burnt by the British, ib., present state of, 25; situation, ib.
Kirk & Mercein, Booksellers of the city of New-York, their edition of Cuvier's theory of the Earth, 11 note; 42.

L.

Lakes and rivers compared, 108 note.
Lay's map of the state of New-York, 134.
Little Falls, 48; description of, by Gov. Clinton, ib. note; scenery near, 49, 52; changes that this cataract has undergone, 52
Louisville, town of, 137.
Lyons village, 129, 131.

M.

Maitland, Sir Peregrine, Governor of Upper Canada, proceedings of, respecting Mr. Robert Gourlay, 77.
Malden, 193.
Manufactures, American, disadvantages opposed to, 16, 21, 22.
Matteawan, factory at, 16; Indian name for Fishkill, 16 note; scenery on, ib.; Schenck's factory on, 16.
Maumee bay, 208, 209; country near compared to that upon the gulf of Mexico, 209.
Mexican gulf, 209.
Michigan lake, 95, 108, 117.
―――― peninsula, 96 note.
―――― territory, 96 note; population of, 197, 200; geological structure, 198, 199; settlements in, 200; climate, ib.
Mingan settlement, 112.
Mississippi river, contrasted with the St. Lawrence, 88, 90, 91, 92.
Mohawk river, 42, 48, and sequel; valley of near Utica, 57; its features, 225.
Montreal, city of, elegance of its site, 109 note; population of, ib.; noticed, 137.
Mountains, Fishkill, 11, and sequel.
―――― Catskill, (Catsbergs) 17; seen from Hudson, 29; from Columbiaville, 31; from Albany, 35; from Troy, 36.
Murder creek, 134.

N.

Natchitoches, 137; compared with Detroit, 190; noticed. 137.
Newburg, its site, 10, 12.
New-Orleans, ship of the line on the stocks at Sacket's Harbor, observations on, 71, 72.
―――― city of, 145, 189.
New-York, seasons at compared to those at Albany, 9.
Niagara, cataract of, described by Mr. Bouchette, 101.
―――― by the author of this treatise, 160, 169
―――― river, 102.
―――― fort, 170.
Normans Kill, 227.

INDEX.

O.

Ogdensburgh, village of described, 7, 73, 74, 87, 106.
Ogden's Island, 87, 124.
Ogilvie, Colonel, his observations respecting the St. Lawrence and Ottawa rivers, 93 note, 96 note.
Ohio river, contrasted with the St. Lawrence, 74, 145.
—— state of, boundary between and Pennsylvania, 177; range of the Erie ridge through, 182.
Olean, or *Hamilton*, on the Allegany river, 145; transit of merchandise between and the city of New-York. *ib.* note.
Ontario, lake, 102; its depth, 103, 104, 108 notes; noticed 109 note, 127; recession of, 128 note; noticed, 129; interesting features of, xliv. ad.
Oppenheim, village of, 47.
Orleans, island of, 113.
—— New, city, 145, 189.
Oswego river, 104, 217.
Ottawa river, 93, 97, note.
Otisco lake, 220, 221.
Owasco lake, 218.
Ouse or Grand river, 177, 203.

P.

Palatine, village of, 46.
Painesville, village of, 178.
Partridge, Capt. Alden, measures the height of Fishkill mountains, 11 note; those of the Catsbergs, 26 note; some others, *ib.*
Peninsula, between Sandusky and Portage rivers, and extending between Sandusky bay and the Bass Islands, 179; described 180, 181.
Perry, Commodore, 171 note; captures a British squadron on lake Erie, 185; the vessels of both fleets now in Erie harbor

Pike, General, his grave, xliv, ad.
Pine lands upon the Hudson, 33, 34; compared with those of Louisiana, Alabama, and Mississippi, *ib.*; their sterile aspect, 38.
Poughkeepsie, town of, 21; Booth's factory at, *ib.*
Prescott, town of, 7, 107 note.
Proctor, General, defeated by General Harrison, 211.
Putnam county, 14; taken from Dutchess, 19.
—— General, 15.
—— fort, its situation, 13; Dr. Van Gelder's poem upon, 13 note; its scenery, 14, 15.
Put-in-bay, 100 note, 185, 186.

Q.

Quebec, city of, 102, 112, 127.
Queenstown, 102.
—— heights of, 203.

R.

Raisin, or Grape river, 201.
Rhinebeck, village, 23.
Ridge, between lake Erie, and Ohio waters, 173; its elevation, 173; visible near the mouth of Grand river from the entrance into Sandusky bay, 179; its range through the state of Ohio, 182; through the state of New-York, 217, 224.
Rivers, Ottawa, Musquinonge, St. Maurice, St. Anne, Jacques Cartier, Saguenay, Betsiamites, Manacouagan, 93.
Rivers and lakes, their features, 108 note.
Rouge, riviere, 201.
Route from New-York to St. Louis by Pittsburg, &c. lx. ad.
—— by Detroit, &c. lx. ad.
—— from New-York to Detroit, and down the St. Lawrence, to Quebec, and return to New-York, xlv ad
Rutland, village 67.

S.

Sacket's Harbor, 56; country between and Utica, 57, 70; review at, 72; country between and the Thousand islands, 73; military works at, 104 note; grave of General Pike, xliv. ad; views near, *ib.*

Saguenay river, 93; described, 97 note.

Sandwich, Upper Canada, 194, 195.

Sandusky bay, 180; described, 181.

——— village of, 185.

Schenck's factory on the Mateowan, (Fishkill) 16.

Schenectady, village of, its distance from Albany, 39, intermediate country, *ib*; situation of, 40; surprised by the savages, *ib*; Union College at, 41.

Schoharie creek, enters the Mohawk river, 45; described, 227.

Schlosser, fort, 160

Scott, General Winfield, visits Sacket's Harbor, 72; wounded, 169.

Seneca, lake, 213; outlet of, 214.
——— river, 217.

Shawangunk, mountain, 20.

Simcoe, lake, 97.

Sisters Islands, 186.

Skeneateles, lake, 219.

Smith's Gazetteer of Upper Canada, quoted, 203.

Sodus bay, described, 126.

Spafford's Gazetteer, quoted, 32, 33.

Steam-boats, their arrangement defective, 9; Walk-in-the-Water, 173 note.

St. Clair, river, 99.
——— lake, 191.

St. Francis, lake, 107, 108, 124

St. Lawrence, river of, 73; contrasted with the Mississippi, *ib.* its real commencement, *ib.*; commerce upon, 76; compared to the Hudson, 38, 89; table of the surface drained by, 89; contrasted with the Mississippi, 88; noticed, 90, 91, 92, 106 note, 107 note; excellent ship navigation in, 108 note; compared with the Oronoco and Plate rivers, *ib.*; contrasted with the Amazon and Mississippi, 109 note; beauty of its islands, *ib.* note; effect of frost on, 115, 116; compared with the Hudson, Delaware, Susquehanna, Rio de la Plate, and Elbe, 116; quantity of water in enormous, 117; timber on its shores, 120; features of its banks where visited by the author, 119; islands in contrasted with those in the Mississippi, 123; navigation of between Montreal and Ogdensburgh, 125; between Ogdensburgh and Kingston, 125.

——— valley of, its natural advantages, 205; climate, 206.

St. Regis, Indians claim the right of soil to the St. Lawrence islands, 125.

Sugar river, 66.

Superior, lake, 93; extent and quantity of water, 117.

Susquehanna river, 223.

T.

Table of the area drained by the St. Lawrence, 89; by the Mississippi, 90.

——— of the extent and quantity of water in the Canadian sea, 117.

——— of the stationary distances from lake Erie to lake Huron, 191.

Table Rock, near the Falls of Niagara, 166 note, 212.

Thames river, U. C. 100 note; described, 202

INDEX.

Thousand Islands, described, 74; their termination, 74; noticed, 105 note.
Tonnewanta creek, its character, 154, ib.; described, 159.
Toronto cliffs, 103.
Treaty with several nations of savages, 196 note.
Trenton, village of, 63; adjacent country, ib.
Tripes Hill, 45.
Troup, Colonel Robert, 130.
Troy, village of, 36; situation of, ib.; in what manner built, 37; its environs, 38.
Turkey Island, in Detroit river, 193.

U.

Utica, village of, 42; country between and Albany, ib. and sequel; occupies the site of Fort Schuyler, 55; latitude, ib.: population of, 56; roads from, ib.
Union College at Schenectady, 41.

V.

Valleys of the St. Lawrence and Mississippi, 136 note; compared, 139.
Venice village, 184.
View near Utica, 57.
—— from Newburg, 11.
—— from West Point, 12.
—— from Fort Putnam, 14.
—— along the Hudson, 20.
—— of the Catsbergs, from Rhinebeck, 24.
View from Kingston, 26.
—— from Hudson village, 29.
—— from Columbiaville, 31.
—— near Albany, 35.
—— near Troy, 36.
—— of the country adjacent to Schenectady, 39.
—— near Utica, 57.
—— near Geneva, 130.
—— near Canandaigua, 131
—— of the Falls of Niagara, 164
—— from Queenstown heights, 168.
—— from the mountains near the village of Cherry Valley, 223.
—— of Sacket's Harbor, xliv. ad.
—— of the grave of Gen Pike, ib.

W.

Wappinger's creek, 19
Washington, General, 14
Watertown, 67; adjacent country, ib.
Walk-in-the-Water, steam boat, 173, ib. note; her first trip from Buffalo to Detroit, 173 note; return to Buffalo, 207.
Waterloo, village of, 212.
West Point, 12; its local, 13; its scenery, 14, 15; students at, their seclusion, 15.

Y.

Yates, Mr. his interesting history of Canandaigua, 132.
York, city of, in Upper Canada, seat of government there, 98

THE END

CPSIA information can be obtained
at www.ICGtesting.com
Printed in the USA
LVHW111941230122
709154LV00008B/807